Tax Policy Lessons from the 2000s

Editor
Alan D. Viard

The AEI Press

Publisher for the American Enterprise Institute

WASHINGTON, D.C.

Distributed to the Trade by National Book Network, 15200 NBN Way, Blue Ridge Summit, PA 17214. To order call toll free 1-800-462-6420 or 1-717-794-3800. For all other inquiries please contact the AEI Press, 1150 Seventeenth Street, N.W., Washington, D.C. 20036 or call 1-800-862-5801.

Library of Congress Cataloging-in-Publication Data

Tax policy lessons from the 2000s / Alan D. Viard, editor.
    p.cm.
    Includes bibliographical references.
    ISBN-13: 978-0-8447-4278-6 (alk. paper)
    ISBN-10: 0-8447-4278-3
    1. Taxation—United States. 2. Income tax—United States. 3. United States—Economic policy—2001- I. Viard, Alan D.

    HJ2381.T378 2009
    336.200973—dc22

                                                            2008053970

13 12 11 10 09   1 2 3 4 5

Gift 10|09

Printed in the United States of America

Contents

List of Illustrations

Tables

Introduction

Alan D. Viard

The U.S. tax system stands at a crossroads, with a number of important policy choices on the horizon. Notably, the 2001 and 2003 tax cuts are scheduled to expire at the end of 2010. President Obama proposes that the tax cuts be permanently extended for households with incomes below $200,000 ($250,000 for married couples) and that a package of new middle-class tax cuts be adopted. At the same time, he calls for letting most of the Bush tax cuts expire for households with the highest incomes. These policies will have significant implications for the marginal tax rates on both labor and capital income. President Obama also supports a cap-and-trade program to combat global warming; and he and Congress are moving to adopt tax (and spending) measures to provide fiscal stimulus during the ongoing recession. Finally, the nation continues to face a long-run budget imbalance.

As Congress and President Obama confront these issues, they will need to answer a number of questions. What role can taxes play in setting environmental policy? How do increases in tax rates affect the amount of work people do and the amount of taxable income they report? How are the economic effects of tax cuts altered when they are financed by deficits? How does the tax system affect businesses' financial and investment decisions?

During the last decade, economists have learned a great deal about these issues, even though much remains uncertain. On May 30, 2008, the American Enterprise Institute gathered a number of scholars to describe what the economics profession has learned during the 2000s about the key tax policy issues now confronting the nation. This volume contains six of those papers, each followed by a discussant's response.

In the first chapter, Gilbert E. Metcalf explores what we learned during the 2000s about environmental taxation. He begins by noting that the United States makes less use of environmental taxation than other advanced nations. He discusses concerns about the regressivity of environmental taxes, noting that such taxes may be less regressive than they seem and that measures can be adopted to offset their impact on low-income groups.

Metcalf examines the argument that environmental taxes not only improve the environment, but also raise revenue, thus making it possible to lower taxes that discourage work and other economic activity, thereby yielding further economic gains. Metcalf points out that this story is incomplete, because environmental taxes themselves impair work incentives. While it is possible to have an environmental reform that also lowers disincentives, such an outcome depends on which taxes are reduced. Metcalf notes that the presence of disincentives has very subtle effects on the proper role of environmental taxes.

Metcalf also compares cap-and-trade and carbon taxes as ways to address global warming. He notes that both approaches are superior to a regulatory approach and that the differences between them largely rest upon how they respond to uncertainty. Acknowledging the political preference for cap-and-trade programs, he discusses ways to reduce price volatility in such programs to make them more like a carbon tax. He criticizes proposals to allocate free permits to firms in cap-and-trade programs, noting that doing so confers a windfall gain on firms' stockholders and undermines both the equity and the efficiency of the program. President Obama avoids this problem in his cap-and-trade plan because he proposes that all of the permits be auctioned rather than given away free of charge. Nevertheless, the question of whether to auction the permits or give them away may be a topic of contentious debate in Congress.

Nada Eissa's chapter discusses the lessons learned in the 2000s about the impact of taxation on labor supply. After discussing the econometric complications in this area, Eissa reviews and summarizes the numerous studies estimating the labor supply effects of taxation. She notes that studies have generally found that taxes have little impact on the number of hours worked by those in the labor force, but may have a significant impact on decisions to enter or leave the labor force, particularly by women. Eissa concludes that the labor supply effects of tax reforms therefore largely depend on how the reforms alter incentives to participate in the labor force. In particular, she finds that the 2001 tax cut likely yielded economic efficiency gains by increasing labor force participation. Some of President Obama's proposed middle-class tax cuts are intended to encourage labor force participation; Eissa's work suggests that the presence and size of such an effect should be an important part of an efficiency evaluation of these proposals.

Eissa describes a number of other factors that may alter how taxes influence labor supply. She notes some evidence indicating that taxes may affect the occupations people choose and the extent to which they invest in human capital, but she observes that more research is needed in these areas. She also points out that the complexity of current tax policies may make it difficult for workers to understand how additional work would affect their tax liability. Although workers' misperceptions may affect how they respond to tax policies, Eissa cautions against any assumption that workers ignore taxes in making their labor supply decisions.

A chapter by Seth H. Giertz addresses the general issue of how tax rates influence the amount of taxable income taxpayers report. To some extent, this topic incorporates the issues examined by Eissa; changing their labor supply is one way taxpayers may change the amount of taxable income they report. But taxpayers may also change their taxable income through many other types of behavioral responses, including shifting their income into tax-exempt forms or spending their income on tax-deductible items. Giertz notes that the overall responsiveness of taxable income to tax rate changes can offer a good measure of the revenue and efficiency effects of a tax rate change under certain assumptions.

Giertz canvasses a lengthy literature that has provided econometric estimates of the responsiveness of taxable income to marginal tax rates. He discusses several econometric complications that arise in making such estimates, including the need to account for changes in income inequality, to recognize that the tax rate is itself a function of the taxpayer's behavioral changes, and to distinguish between permanent and temporary responses. He notes that the literature has yielded a wide range of estimates for the elasticity of taxable income with respect to tax rates.

Giertz applies these estimates to some provisions of the 2001 and 2003 tax cuts. He finds that reductions in the top brackets yield large reductions in deadweight loss per dollar of revenue given up. Reductions in the lower brackets produce less of an efficiency gain per dollar of revenue given up. (For all brackets, of course, the ratio of deadweight loss to revenue is highly dependent on the estimated responsiveness of reported taxable income to marginal tax rates.) Giertz's work suggests that President Obama's proposal to permanently extend the 2001 and 2003 marginal tax rate reductions in the lower, but not the higher, brackets has unattractive efficiency implications, although the proposal's distributional effects may be appealing.

John W. Diamond and I contribute a chapter that examines the impact of deficit-financed tax cuts as seen through the prism of computable general equilibrium (CGE) models. We focus on economies with overlapping generations, those in which agents do not fully offset the effects of fiscal changes on the well-being of their descendants. We review previous studies, most of which focused on how deficit-financed tax cuts change the path of output and other macroeconomic variables over time. The studies generally found that the impact of deficit-financed tax cuts depends upon what types of taxes are cut, how long the resulting deficits continue before measures are adopted to service the debt, and what types of tax increases or spending cuts are ultimately used to service the debt. Increases in steady-state output tend to occur if reductions in transfer payments or government purchases are used to finance tax cuts that reduce marginal rates, provided that the spending reductions take effect reasonably soon after the tax cuts are adopted.

We confirm these findings in a new round of CGE results. Our results reveal that reductions in dividend and capital gains taxes are more likely to increase output than are reductions in other taxes. We also discuss the impact of deficit-financed tax cuts on the well-being of the various generations, finding that such tax cuts typically improve the well-being of current generations and reduce the well-being of future generations. Future generations tend to be worse off even when the policy increases the steady-state level of output. Our work suggests that, to avoid harm to future generations, tax cuts should be accompanied by spending cuts.

The subject of Dhammika Dharmapala's chapter is what we have learned in the 2000s about the effects of taxes on corporate dividends and financial policy. His analysis largely focuses on the provision of the 2003 law that lowered the top tax rate on dividends from 35 to 15 percent. The reduction was originally scheduled to expire at the end of 2008, but was subsequently extended to the end of 2010. President Obama has called for a permanent 20 percent top tax rate on dividends.

Dharmapala finds that the tax cut triggered a large and immediate increase in dividend payments by firms, with the biggest increases occurring in firms whose stockholders were most affected by the tax cut. He draws on this recent experience to judge the validity of the two major views of dividend taxation. Under the new view, dividends are a residual determined by the difference between the payoffs from the firm's existing investments and the firm's spending on new investments. Under the old view, dividends are a fixed fraction of investment payoffs. Dharmapala finds that the pattern of stock price increases across firms lends support to the new view.

Dharmapala carefully considers how financial market globalization alters the impact of the dividend tax cut. Because the tax cut applied to Americans who hold stock in U.S. firms and in a restricted set of qualifying foreign firms, economic theory suggests that the cut should prompt U.S. taxpayers to shift their investments toward U.S. firms and qualifying foreign firms and away from other foreign firms. Dharmapala finds statistical confirmation for the shift toward qualifying foreign firms. In a world in which foreign stockholders can buy shares in U.S. companies, he notes, a tax cut for U.S. stockholders is an imperfect way to offset the corporate tax burden on U.S. businesses.

In the last of the main chapters, Alan J. Auerbach and Kevin A. Hassett discuss the lessons learned in the 2000s about the impact of taxes on business investment. They focus on two recent policy changes: partial expensing and the 2003 dividend tax reduction studied by Dharmapala. The partial expensing policy allowed firms to immediately expense—rather than depreciate over time—part of the costs of equipment investment made from late 2001 through the end of 2004. Congress and President Bush also provided partial expensing for 2008 investment as part of the February 2008 stimulus package and the provision may be extended in 2009 as Congress and President Obama seek further economic stimulus.

Auerbach and Hassett note that the impact of partial expensing depended upon whether firms thought that the practice would be extended beyond

2004 (it ultimately was not extended). They also observe that an increase in investment demand due to the policy might show up in increased prices for investment goods as well as in increased quantity of investment. After reviewing the evidence, they conclude that partial expensing yielded a modest increase in equipment investment, but suggest that additional research on this question would be useful.

Auerbach and Hassett also note that the impact of the dividend tax cut on investment is greater under the old view of dividend taxation than under the new view. Drawing upon an extensive set of studies in order to assess the two views, they find that the best model may be one in which some firms are described by the old view and some by the new view. They find strong evidence that the tax cut boosted dividend payouts (consistent with Dharmapala's analysis), but weaker evidence that the tax cut boosted business investment.

Taken together, these studies reveal that much has been learned in the 2000s about how taxes affect economic behavior, although many questions remain unanswered. This collection provides a map of both the progress that has been made and the work yet to be done. It offers valuable guidance for the policy decisions likely to be made on environmental taxation, marginal tax rates, dividend taxation, and the taxation of business investment during the next few years.

1

Environmental Taxation: What Have We Learned in This Decade?

Gilbert E. Metcalf

Environmental taxes in the United States are like virtue: much discussed but little practiced. This chapter surveys the use of environmental taxes in the United States. I note that our reliance on these taxes is much below the standards of other developed countries. Moreover, I note that the taxes Americans consider "environmental" are quite imperfect as instruments for protecting the environment, as they typically tax attributes correlated with but not coterminous with pollution.

In contrast, our theoretical understanding of environmental taxes in a second-best world made major advances in the past fifteen years. I review this recent literature and make some assessment of the most important policy lessons gleaned from this new knowledge. First, the use of revenues from an environmental tax has efficiency as well as distributional implications in a world with preexisting distortionary taxes (i.e., the real world). Using green tax revenues to lower particularly distortionary taxes can have important efficiency gains. Despite this fact, it is not necessarily the case that the optimal environmental tax should exceed the social marginal damages from pollution, as the double-dividend hypothesis suggests. In fact the relation between the optimal environmental tax increment and social marginal damages is sensitive to the particular reform under-taken and the consequent redistributions that are effected by that reform.

The author wishes to acknowledge support from the American Enterprise Institute and helpful comments from Rob Williams.

The literature also provides a better understanding of the relation between environmental quality and the degree of distortions in the pre-existing tax system. A reading of the second-best literature on public good provision suggests that the optimal level of environmental quality would go down in a second-best world relative to a first-best world. In fact the opposite is likely to occur. While an increase in the supply of a public good requires additional public revenue (at potentially high social cost), an increase in the supply of environmental quality can generate additional public revenue through the tax on pollution that may finance a reduction in other distortionary taxes.

The literature also helps us better understand the distributional implications of environmental taxes. It shows that while environmental taxes might be distortionary, environmental tax reforms can be distributionally neutral or take on any degree of progressivity one desires. The point here is that any regressivity in environmental taxes can be undone with carefully designed tax reductions in a revenue-neutral reform. The literature offers further evidence that a lifetime distributional analysis blunts the regressivity of environmental taxes significantly. The regressivity of many environmental taxes appears to be blunted a bit in the long run in a general equilibrium setting.

Finally, I discuss the momentum that appears to be building in this country to institute some form of carbon pricing in order to reduce U.S. greenhouse gas emissions. Here the message is more optimistic. I argue that the advances that economists have made in their understanding of important efficiency and distributional issues have translated into significant policy advances in proposals wending their way through Congress.

The U.S. Experience with Environmental Taxes

I begin with a brief overview of environmental taxes in the United States and a comparison with other countries. The major environmental tax at the federal level is the motor fuels excise tax equal to 18.4¢ per gallon of gasoline. Of that, 0.1¢ is dedicated to the Leaking Underground Storage Tank Trust Fund and the remaining 18.3¢ to the Highway Trust Fund.[1] Of that 18.3¢ per gallon, 2.86¢ is dedicated to the Mass Transit Account and the remaining 15.44¢ to the Highway Account.[2]

The gas guzzler tax was enacted as part of the Energy Tax Act of 1978. It levies a tax on automobiles that obtain fuel mileage below 22.5 miles per gallon. Tax rates range from $1,000 to $7,700 per vehicle. In 2004 the tax collected $141 million (Guenther 2006). The gas guzzler tax explicitly excludes sport utility vehicles, minivans, and pickup trucks, which represented 51 percent of the new vehicle sales in 2006 (U.S. Census Bureau 2008, table 1027). Until recently, the light truck category (comprising SUVs, minivans, and pickup trucks) was the fastest-growing segment of the new vehicle market, with an annual growth rate of 2.5 percent between 1990 and 2006. In contrast, new car sales fell at an annual rate of 0.7 percent over that period. Recent high gas prices led to a sharp falloff in sales of these vehicles. Whether this trend will persist depends on the future direction of oil prices. As of November 2008, oil prices had fallen by over one-third from their peak.

The Energy Policy Act of 2005 (EPACT) resurrected the Oil Spill Liability Trust Fund tax at the original rate of 5¢ per barrel. This tax had previously been in effect from 1990 through 1994. The Joint Committee on Taxation estimates that this tax will raise $1.25 billion between 2005 and 2010 (U.S. Congress 2005). The tax is imposed on crude oil received at U.S. refineries as well as imported petroleum products. Domestic crude oil for export is also subject to the tax if the tax has not been previously paid.

The coal excise tax funds the Black Lung Disability Fund. It is levied on coal mined in the United States at a rate of 4.4 percent of the sales price up to a limit of $1.10 per ton of underground coal and $.55 per ton of surface-mined coal. According to the federal budget for fiscal year 2008, this tax raised $639 million in 2007.

Gasoline sold for sport motorboats is taxed at the same rate as highway gasoline and diesel fuel, and the funds are allocated to the Aquatic Resources Trust Fund (subject to an annual cap on transfers that effectively reduces the share of tax on motorboat fuels shifted to this trust fund). Finally, commercial vessels using the Inland Waterway System (barges for the most part) pay a fuel tax of 22.4¢ per gallon of fuel sold.

States levy a variety of environmental taxes, starting with a tax on motor fuels. Rates vary across states but averaged 18.2¢ per gallon as of the beginning of this year (American Petroleum Institute 2008). In addition to excise taxes, states levied on average an additional 10.4¢ per gallon,

typically through a general sales tax on gasoline purchases. State governments also levy a variety of pollution fees, hazardous waste charges, tire-
disposal fees, and other assorted charges. U.S. Environmental Protection
Agency (2001) describes these in considerable detail.

The Organisation for Economic Co-operation and Development
(OECD) and European Environment Agency (EEA) maintain a database on
instruments used for environmental policy. They report for the United
States aggregate revenues of $74.9 billion from environmental taxes and
charges in 2005. Of this, 94 percent is federal and state taxes on motor fuels
(OECD/ EEA 2008).

Comparing the use of environmental taxes across countries, we see that
the United States ranks low in its reliance on these taxes. Figure 1-1 shows
environmental tax collections as a percentage of GDP. The United States
collects 0.9 percent of GDP in these taxes at the federal and state level. Only
Mexico is lower, with a share of 0.8 percent. In contrast, the Czech
Republic, Denmark, Finland, Italy, Luxembourg, the Netherlands, Portugal,
and Turkey all collect more than 3 percent of GDP from environmental
taxes and charges. The pattern does not change if taxes are reported as
a percentage of total tax revenues (figure 1-2). The United States is still at
the bottom of the pack, with environmental taxes equal to 3.5 percent of
total tax collections. If the United States had relied on environmental taxes
to the same extent as other OECD countries in 2005 (2.23 percent of GDP),
it would have collected over $100 billion more in 2005 than it actually did,
an increase of over 150 percent.

Since motor fuel taxes are such a dominant source of environmental
tax revenues in all OECD countries, it is instructive to compare gasoline
tax rates across these countries. Figure 1-3 shows the tax rate (in dollars
per gallon) for various OECD countries as of the beginning of 2007. The
total excise tax rate for the United States is over 40¢ per gallon.[3] In
contrast, the average unweighted tax on gasoline in the other countries
exceeds $2.00 per gallon. The rate is particularly high in the UK, Germany,
Turkey, and the Netherlands, where it exceeds $3.00 per gallon.

Below I discuss the treatment of carbon emissions in the European
Union (EU) and the United States. A carbon pricing policy change under
the next administration could change the relative importance of environmental taxes and charges (including the value of auctioned permits in a

FIGURE 1-1

ENVIRONMENTAL TAXES AS A PERCENTAGE OF GDP, 2005

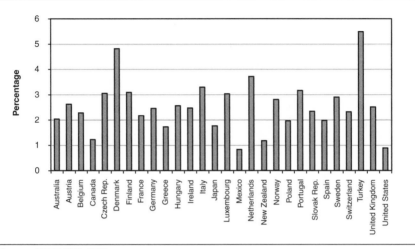

SOURCE: OECD/EEA 2008.

FIGURE 1-2

ENVIRONMENTAL TAXES AS A PERCENTAGE OF TOTAL TAXES, 2004

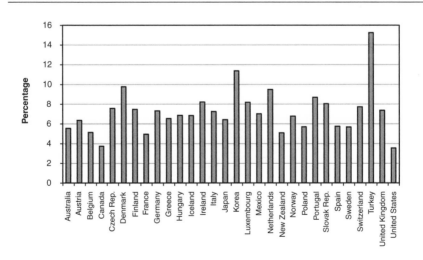

SOURCE: OECD/EEA 2008.

FIGURE 1-3

TAX RATE ON UNLEADED GASOLINE, 2007

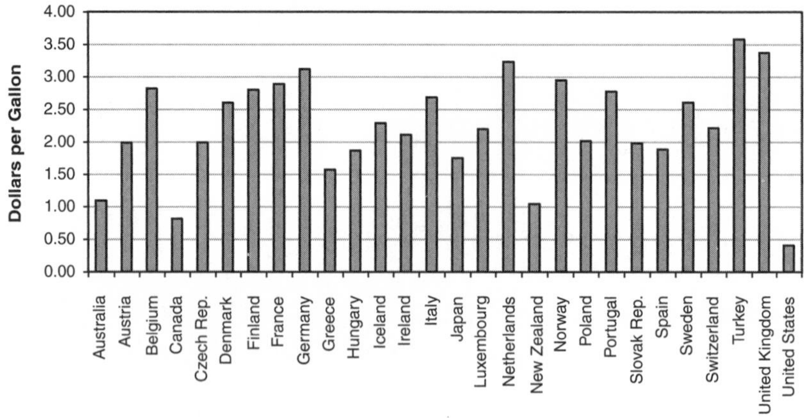

SOURCE: OECD/EEA 2008.

cap-and-trade system) in government budgets. But as of now, the summary data show that the United States is an outlier in its reliance on environmental revenues. In fact, one could make a case that taxes on motor fuels do not really count as an environmental tax, since they are for the most part earmarked in the United States for the Highway Trust Fund. That earmarking suggests they might better be characterized as a benefit tax.

Is the United States taxing pollution at the right level? Clearly not for those pollutants that are not currently taxed.[4] Parry and Small (2005) consider the range of externalities associated with driving (congestion, tailpipe pollution, health problems, etc.) and conclude that the U.S. tax on gasoline is roughly half its optimal level. The tax in the United Kingdom, in contrast, is roughly twice as large as its optimal level.

Little work has been done on pollution taxes other than those on gasoline. A small literature exists on states' use of fees for hazardous waste. Levinson (1999a, 1999b) considers how state-level taxes affect the interstate transport of hazardous waste and finds that in-state disposal is highly sensitive to taxes. Sigman (2003) reviews the literature on state-level hazardous waste taxes and argues that the taxes influence behavior, but—given the extant regulations and liability facing waste-generating firms—may not be welfare-enhancing. The research suggests the benefits of both coordinated national legislation (as opposed to state-level legislation) and coordination among the various policy instruments used to discourage improper hazardous waste disposal.[5]

In sum, the contrast between the United States and other OECD countries suggests considerable scope for increasing American reliance on environmental taxes.

Advances in the Theory

In this section I review recent advances in our understanding of efficiency and distributional issues associated with environmental taxes.

Efficiency Considerations of Environmental Taxation. A flurry of intellectual activity in the late 1990s led to some important advances in our understanding of the efficiency implications of environmental taxation and optimal design of environmental tax rates. These theoretical developments took as their point of departure the Pigouvian principle that the optimal tax rate on a pollutant is equal to its social marginal damages. Beginning in the mid-1980s, the concept of the environmental double-dividend hypothesis began to gain currency. The concept is straightforward: an environmental tax pays a dividend by discouraging polluting activities. It then pays a second dividend by raising revenue that can be used to lower other distorting taxes. So far so good. Therefore, policy activists concluded, it must be the case that the optimal tax on pollution should exceed the social marginal damages of the pollutant, since there is this extra dividend (or benefit) arising from the use of this tax.[6]

This conclusion, while intuitively appealing, is incorrect. It ignores the fact that the environmental tax, though beneficial in discouraging pollution, adds to distortions in production or consumption and has a first-order excess burden in the presence of other distortionary taxes.[7] The theory is rigorously laid out by Bovenberg and de Mooij (1994) and by Parry (1995).[8]

Bovenberg and de Mooij's model assumes a "clean" good, a "dirty" good, and endogenous labor supply. Taxes were levied on the dirty good and labor.

Fullerton (1997) points out that in a general equilibrium setting, identical tax outcomes can be achieved with different sets of instruments. Thus, Bovenberg and de Mooij could have obtained the same equilibrium with differential commodity tax rates and no tax on labor supply. While the equilibrium finding is unaffected, Fullerton notes, the finding that the optimal tax on pollution falls short of social marginal damages is affected. As Bovenberg notes in correspondence with Fullerton quoted in Fullerton's paper, the precise result is that the Pigouvian tax *increment* falls short of social marginal damages in the optimum. In other words, if Bovenberg and de Mooij's model considered commodity taxes rather than a tax on the dirty good and labor supply, the result would be that the difference in tax rates of the dirty good less that of the clean good was less than social marginal damages.

This result has been formalized in a number of papers as the finding that the second-best Pigouvian tax increment equals social marginal damages divided by the marginal cost of public funds (e.g., Bovenberg and van der Ploeg 1994). Since the marginal cost of public funds tends to exceed 1 in the presence of distortionary taxation, this gives the desired result.[9] This result is found in a model with an income tax and no non-environmental commodity taxes. Williams (2001) generalizes the result to allow for a fully general linear system of income and commodity taxes. Changing the tax normalization changes the value (measured in dollars) of marginal social damages. But this is just a units issue. Williams shows that the ratio of the optimal tax differential to social marginal damages is constant across normalizations and less than 1 for a system of linear commodity and income taxes. This is reassuring, since the tax normalizations used in the literature are a far cry from the actual tax normalization in the actual tax code, with its complex combination of income and commodity taxes. It would be discomfiting if one needed to assess the environmental tax differential relative to social marginal damages using the actual U.S. tax code normalization.

An extra set of assumptions drives these results. Bovenberg and de Mooij (1994) as well as Fullerton (1997) assume homothetic subutility function for commodities that is weakly separable from leisure. With this assumption, it would be optimal to employ a uniform commodity tax in the absence of the externality. Therefore the point of departure in adding externalities is to compare the difference between the rates on the dirty and clean goods. Parry (1995) considers a more general model in which the polluting consumption good is a relatively strong or weak substitute with leisure. The distortionary impact of the environmental tax is strengthened (weakened) to the extent that the dirty good is a relatively strong (weak) substitute with leisure.[10] This is a straightforward application of the Corlett and Hague (1953) result—that where leisure cannot be taxed separately from the time endowment, it is desirable to tax goods that are complements of leisure.[11]

While Parry focuses on consumption externalities, the Bovenberg and de Mooij result can be easily modified to allow for production-side externalities. Williams (2002) considers potential health impacts of pollution in a more expansive framework and notes that pollution's effect on health can have significant implications for the optimal tax rate. If the health impacts of pollution, for example, diminish labor productivity, then an additional benefit arises from reducing pollution. This suggests a higher tax rate on pollution than in the absence of the health impact. If, on the other hand, reducing pollution lowers medical expenses, consumers receive a positive income effect from the environmental tax that discourages labor supply (assuming leisure is a normal good). This leads to a lower optimal environmental tax than occurs in the absence of the health interaction. Williams terms this a benefit-side tax-interaction effect that has broader implications than health and pollution. It illustrates the important point that modeling the entire impact of pollution is important for determining the optimal second-best tax on pollution and its relation to the social marginal damages of pollution.

Kaplow (2006) notes that the various environmental tax reforms discussed in the literature above limit themselves to linear income taxes, and he suggests that an environmental tax reform should be thought of as a two-step process. In the first step, the income tax is adjusted so that the environmental tax reform cum income tax adjustment is distributionally neutral (taking into account the distribution of environmental benefits). In this first step, the first-best Pigouvian rule holds that the environmental tax rate should be set equal to social marginal damages. In the second step, the income tax is adjusted to obtain whatever income tax outcome actually occurs under the proposed environmental tax reform. Kaplow's conclusion is that the deviation of the environmental tax rate from the first-best

Pigouvian prescription stems from the increased redistribution arising from the reform, rather than from any preexisting tax distortions.[12] Kaplow's point is essentially one of interpretation. One can analyze environmental taxes in a distribution-free environment. Or one can recognize that general environmental tax reforms will induce redistribution and that this will affect the relationship between the Pigouvian tax increment and social marginal damages. The message from the Kaplow analysis is this: the specific environmental tax reforms suggested by policymakers will induce different amounts of redistribution, and as a result the relation between the optimal environmental tax rate and social marginal damages will be reform-specific.

This is an unsatisfying result at one level. Part of the difficulty is that this discussion focuses on a variable of secondary interest. Knowing the optimal tax rate and its relation to social marginal damages is important. But what we really care about is the optimal level of pollution. All the results above focus on the relation between the tax rate on pollution and its social marginal damages. A different question is how the government's need for revenue and its reliance on distortionary taxes affect the optimal level of environmental pollution. Metcalf (2003) uses a simple general equilibrium model to show that an increase in the need for tax revenues to finance government spending can lead to a fall in the optimal Pigouvian tax increment even while environmental quality improves. The falling Pigouvian tax increment gives rise to a commodity substitution effect as consumers shift toward more consumption of the pollution-generating commodity. The increased level of overall taxes lowers the real wage, giving rise to a leisure substitution effect as labor supply falls. Since leisure has no effect on pollution in this model, the ultimate impact of the higher overall tax rates on environmental quality is ambiguous. Metcalf demonstrates that for reasonable parameter assumptions, pollution falls as government revenue needs rise. The point here is not that Metcalf has correctly captured the complexity of the economy in his simple model, but rather that one cannot draw any inferences about the amount of pollution by noting that the Pigouvian tax increment is falling in response to a rise in required government revenue.

Metcalf's analysis, which takes as its point of departure an optimal tax system, is marginal in nature. Gaube (2005) considers a related experiment: this experiment compares the optimal provision of environmental services in a second-best world, in which distortionary taxes must be used, to optimal provision in a first-best world, where lump-sum taxes are available. Assuming that we are not in a Laffer world, where increasing environmental tax rates reduce environmental revenue, Gaube shows that the provision of environmental services in this second-best world is higher than in the first-best world. In other words, we have a more pristine environment. This is in striking contrast to the result in Atkinson and Stern (1974), which is that the second-best provision of public goods will be lower than the first-best provision.[13] Gaube's example assumes quasi-linear preferences with a homothetic subutility function over consumption. The intuition, however, is quite general for understanding the contrasting results for public goods and pollution control in a second-best world. While an increase in the supply of a public good requires additional public revenue (at potentially high social cost), an increase in the supply of environmental quality can generate additional public revenue through the tax on pollution.

Distributional Considerations with Environmental Taxation. One concern with increasing reliance on environmental taxes is the perceived or real regressivity of these taxes. Measuring the distributional impact requires determining 1) which environmental tax is to be changed (or implemented); 2) what will be done with the revenue; 3) on what basis the welfare of households is to be determined; and 4) over what time period the burdens will be measured. Environmental damages tend to be associated with the production or consumption of commodities. This means that an environmental tax acts to a large extent as a commodity tax. Commodity taxes in general tend to be regressive when viewed in an annual income framework. Metcalf (1999), for example, finds that a carbon tax, a gasoline tax, air pollution taxes, and taxes on the use of virgin materials are all to a greater or lesser degree regressive. He makes the point that while an environmental tax may be regressive, an environmental tax reform can have any desired distributional outcome. The key is to focus on how the revenue from an environmental levy is used. If it is recycled through reductions in regressive taxes, the overall reform can be distributionally neutral or even progressive. This insight has been brought to bear in a proposal to implement a revenue-neutral and distributionally neutral carbon tax reform (Metcalf 2007c, 2007d).

Distributional analyses require that households be ranked by some measure of economic well-being. Typically, annual income is used for this ranking.

As the literature on tax incidence now recognizes, however, annual income measures of well-being tend to bias distributional analyses of consumption taxes in a regressive direction. (See Fullerton and Metcalf 2002 for a general discussion of this point.) This occurs for two reasons. First, young and old households with annual income at great variance from their lifetime expected (or realized) income tend to show up in the lowest income deciles. These groups will have consumption-to-income ratios that are not sustainable in the long run. The young may be borrowing against future possible earnings, while the elderly may be drawing on a lifetime of savings. In either case, using annual income for these groups will bias consumption taxes toward regressivity. Second, households engaging in consumption smoothing in the presence of temporary income fluctuations will also generate a regressive bias. A consumption-smoothing household with a negative (positive) income shock will have a temporarily high (low) consumption-to-income ratio and in this way contribute to a regressive bias.

To overcome this bias, some measure of lifetime income is required. Thus in an analysis of federal excise taxes, Poterba (1989) uses current consumption as a proxy for lifetime income, under the assumption that households make consumption decisions on the basis of lifetime income. The consumption proxy reduces the regressivity of the taxes considerably. Seeking to assess the Clinton administration's British thermal unit (BTU) tax proposal, Bull, Hassett, and Metcalf (1994) use this approach, along with a variant on the current consumption approach, to better control for transitory consumption fluctuations. Hassett, Mathur, and Metcalf (2007) apply that approach to a U.S. carbon tax and find that a lifetime incidence approach mitigates much of the regressivity of the tax that appears in the annual income analysis.

Hassett, Mathur, and Metcalf's approach assumes the tax is fully shifted forward to consumers. This is consistent with short-run results from computable general equilibrium (CGE) modeling of carbon taxes. See, for example, the study by Metcalf et al. (2008). It also finds that roughly half the burden of the tax comes from the indirect portion of the tax. This is the increase in the prices of non-energy commodities (food, clothing, entertainment, etc.) brought about by the higher cost of energy consumed in the production of those commodities. While the percentage price increase for any of these commodities is quite small, the vast majority of consumer expenditures, on average, are on these commodities. This is important

FIGURE 1-4

CARBON TAX: ANNUAL INCOME

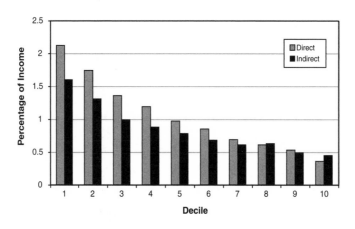

SOURCE: Hassett, Mathur, and Metcalf 2007.
NOTES: Carbon tax is shown as a percentage of annual income; income deciles are shown along the x axis.

because the burden of the direct portion of the tax (price rises in energy purchases) is more regressive than the indirect burden whether one uses an annual or lifetime income approach. See figures 1-4 and 1-5 for results from this analysis.

Finally, these analyses have assessed environmental taxes at a point in time using a measure of lifetime income. An alternative approach would be to assess lifetime environmental tax burdens relative to lifetime income. This approach is used to evaluate the lifetime progressivity of the U.S. tax system by Fullerton and Rogers (1993) but has not been applied to environmental taxes. Such an approach requires making assumptions about the tax code over the long term, since this is a prospective analysis. Nevertheless, it would be a useful contribution to the literature.

The analyses discussed above are partial equilibrium analyses (although informed by results from general equilibrium analysis) and focus on the uses side of income. Fullerton and Heutel (2007) undertake a sources-side general equilibrium analysis of pollution taxes and explore a number of special cases. One would expect that the burden of pollution taxes would fall disproportionately on the factor which is a closer complement to

FIGURE 1-5
CARBON TAX: LIFETIME INCOME

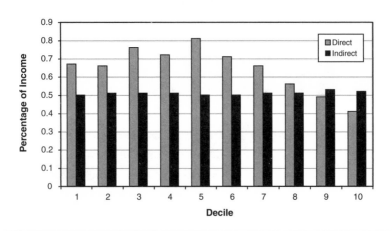

SOURCE: Hassett, Mathur, and Metcalf 2007.
NOTES: Carbon tax is shown as a percentage of lifetime income; income deciles are shown along the x axis.

pollution. While that tends to be the case, they show examples where that pattern does not occur.[14] The experiment makes clear how important it is to measure the degree of substitutability or complementarity between pollution and other factors, and it identifies key parameters required for carrying out a general equilibrium incidence analysis.

As noted in the first section, the predominant environmental tax in the United States is the gasoline tax. Using data from the Consumer Expenditure Survey, West (2004) models the choice of vehicle as well as driving patterns and argues that, given the lower probability of car owner-ship among lower-income households, the regressivity of gasoline taxes is limited to the upper half of the income distribution. She also notes that policymakers have been more inclined to adopt indirect taxes on gasoline consumption such as a gas guzzler tax, essentially a tax on engine size, or to provide subsidies to new vehicle purchase, than to tax gasoline directly. She notes that these indirect taxes may be more regressive than a gasoline tax. Similarly West (2005) finds that a tax on emissions is more regressive than a tax on gasoline consumption because lower-income households are more likely to drive older, less efficient vehicles.

In summary, considerable progress has been made in understanding optimal environmental tax rates in a second-best world.[15] Two points bear emphasizing. First, the literature makes the important point that the revenue use from environmental levies has potentially important efficiency consequences as well as distributional consequences in a second-best world.[16] Second, the literature advances our understanding of the relationship between the Pigouvian tax increment and social marginal damages in a second-best world. While of theoretical importance, this result is of second-order importance for U.S. policymakers, who have not yet embraced the use of taxes to address environmental concerns. That this result has limited practical importance is especially clear when one recognizes the difficulties in precisely measuring the social marginal damages of important pollutants. Getting a price in the right neighborhood of social marginal damages is probably about as much as we can hope for.

The New Frontier: Carbon Pricing

On January 1, 2005, twenty-five countries in Europe embarked on a major policy experiment in the use of market-based instruments to control greenhouse gas emissions. That date marked the beginning of the first phase of the European Union's Emissions Trading Scheme (ETS). The ETS is a cap-and-trade program which sets country-by-country caps on carbon emissions in energy-intensive industries and the utility sector, and which issues permits to be surrendered upon emissions. The permits could be traded among, within, and across countries in the EU, thereby putting a price on carbon emissions.[17] This is the second large cap-and-trade program set up to address environmental concerns following the successful implementation of a cap-and-trade program for sulfur dioxide emissions from large power plants under the Acid Rain Program of the Environmental Protection Agency (EPA). (See Ellerman et al. 2000 for a description and assessment of this program.)

Cap-and-trade programs have emerged as a popular alternative to environmental taxes and offer instead a market-based incentive to reduce pollution. Since both of the major presidential candidates in the United States committed to significant reductions in U.S. greenhouse gas emissions, it is instructive to assess the benefits and drawbacks of a tax-based versus permit-based approach to reducing emissions.

Cap-and-trade (CaT) programs and taxes (Tx) are in many ways duals of each other. A pure CaT program fixes the amount of emissions over some time frame and lets the interplay between demand for and supply of permits determine their price. A pure Tx program fixes the price of emissions but lets the amount of emissions fluctuate depending on supply and demand. Under both systems, firms will operate at the point where the marginal cost of abatement equals the price of emissions (either the permit price or the tax rate). Since the marginal cost of abatement is equalized across firms, emissions are reduced in a cost-effective manner.[18]

It is now well understood that in the absence of uncertainty over the marginal cost of abatement, CaT and Tx systems have the same economic effect. If the permits are fully auctioned then the systems are entirely identical except in appearance. The two market-based approaches differ 1) under uncertainty over marginal abatement costs, and 2) in their administrative and implementation details.

Once one allows for uncertainty in marginal abatement costs, the two policy approaches differ in an expected net benefit sense. Weitzman (1974) looks at conditions under which a Tx system provides higher or lower expected social benefits than a CaT system in a world with uncertainty.[19] His analysis demonstrates the importance of the relative slopes of marginal damages and abatement costs in choosing the optimal instrument.

Weitzman's analysis needs some modification in the case of greenhouse gases, since marginal abatement costs are a function of the *flow* of emissions, while marginal damages are a function of the *stock* of gases in the atmosphere. Hoel and Karp (2002) analyze the problem with stock effects in which governments may employ either an *open-loop* or a *feedback* policy. In an open-loop setting, policymakers choose a set of policies *for all time* in the current period to maximize expected net benefits. In the more realistic (but more complicated) feedback setting, policymakers choose a set of policies but are allowed to adjust the policy as uncertainty is revealed over time. Hoel and Karp set out conditions that allow one to rank Tx versus CaT policies and find that Tx dominates CaT for a set of parameters consistent with scientific understanding of the global warming problem. Their analysis assumes that cost shocks are uncorrelated across time. This is a significant limitation, as many of the sorts of cost shocks that might occur (e.g., technology shocks) are likely to have high levels of persistence over time. Newell and Pizer (2003) generalize Hoel and Karp's open-loop analysis to allow for serial correlation of cost shocks and find that—across a broad range of parameter assumptions about abatement costs and marginal damages—carbon taxes are more efficient than CaT systems in the face of uncertainty. A study by Karp and Zhang (2005), which analyzes the more realistic setting in which cost shocks are correlated over time and policymakers use feedback policies, continues to find that taxes dominate tradable permit systems.

The one caveat to the finding that Tx dominates CaT is the presence of "tipping points," abrupt or discontinuous increases in marginal damages at some level of greenhouse gas concentrations in the atmosphere. Such a tipping point might occur if concentrations above some amount lead to sufficiently high temperatures that the West Antarctic ice shield breaks off and raises sea levels by perhaps five meters (Schneider et al. 2007, table 19-1). What concentrations would make such an event likely are unknown. In light of this fact, a commitment to reduce emissions to fixed levels regardless of cost cannot be justified by any model of social welfare maximization. To give primacy to specific emission reductions, regardless of the cost, implausibly makes controlling emissions the top policy priority, trumping all others.

From an administrative perspective, a Tx system can be more quickly implemented than a CaT system. Coal producers already pay an excise tax to fund the Black Lung Trust Fund, and oil producers pay a tax to fund the Oil Spill Trust Fund. (See Metcalf 2007b for a description of these funds.) We also have precedents—federal fuels tax credits—for refundable credits for sequestration activities. In contrast, we have no administrative structure in place for running a carbon CaT program.[20]

It is clear that either the CaT or Tx approach is preferable to a regulatory approach. Ellerman, Jacoby, and Zimmerman (2006) consider how Corporate Average Fuel Economy (CAFE) standards could be integrated into a CaT system and estimate that the cost of carbon emission reductions through CAFE is in the neighborhood of $350 per ton of CO_2 equivalent; this is considerably higher than estimates of permit prices under the Lieberman-Warner Climate Security Act (S.2191) (Paltsev et al. 2007, appendix D). This estimate helps make two points. First, sector-based regulatory policies that are not integrated more broadly into a carbon reduction scheme can be very expensive. Second, the early reductions in carbon emissions are likely to occur in the industrial and electric utility sectors rather than in the transport sector. Since the source of emissions has no bearing on damages associated with climate change, sector-based approaches are likely to be quite inefficient.[21]

While most economists view a carbon tax as a better way to control emissions than a CaT system, policymakers have shown a distinct preference for CaT. This preference for CaT systems over Tx systems can be explained by a number of factors. First, the Acid Rain Program in the United States and the introduction of emissions trading in the EU's ETS create some familiarity with trading systems, and their success inspires emulation. The EU's choice of a CaT approach over a Tx approach is cited as evidence of the political advantages of the former over the latter. But the European experience is not entirely applicable to the United States, and in any case the CaT was not the EU's first choice. In the early 1990s, the EU had attempted to institute EU-wide taxes on carbon and energy, but it was unable to reach the unanimous agreement among member countries required to enact EU fiscal policy. A CaT approach, in contrast, is deemed a regulatory policy requiring only a majority of countries to support the policy (see Convery and Redmond 2007).

Second, environmentalists have preferred the apparent certainty of emissions control under a CaT system. This certainty is illusory, however. Even if a law is passed that sets a fixed cap with no possible relief for high permit prices, then in the unhappy event that the marginal costs of abatement are unexpectedly high, Congress can always amend the law to loosen the caps. In effect, Congress serves as the ultimate safety valve.

Third, the United States has resisted adding new taxes since the Reagan revolution in 1980. This resistance reflects in large part an ongoing debate over the appropriate size of the federal government and its role in the U.S. economy. Metcalf (2007d) has proposed a revenue-neutral carbon tax swap to sidestep this debate. A carbon tax swap would require that the revenue raised through a carbon tax be used to reduce existing taxes so that the U.S. tax burden on average would remain unchanged.[22]

Fourth, policymakers have used the free allocation of permits to build political support for CaT programs. This practice comes at considerable efficiency and distributional costs. From an efficiency point of view, there always exists an environmental tax swap that is welfare-enhancing relative to a lump-sum return of the revenue.[23] From a distributional perspective, free permits provide windfall profits to permit recipients. These windfalls show up as increases in equity values of the firms receiving permits. Since equity holdings tend to be concentrated in the upper part of the income distribution, this windfall transfer is quite regressive.[24]

While permits under EPA's Acid Rain Program and the EU's ETS were given away to affected sectors, newer CaT proposals auction an increasing number of the permits. The Warner-Lieberman bill, for example, auctions just over one-quarter of the permits in 2012, and the share rises to nearly 70 percent by 2031. Stavins (2007) calls for initially auctioning half of the permits and increasing the percentage to 100 percent over twenty-five years.

While a carbon tax appears to be a more straightforward approach than cap-and-trade and to have greater efficiency benefits, the political obstacles remain large. What has emerged is a number of proposals to modify CaT systems to make them more like Tx systems. Recall that the major difference between a CaT and Tx system is the fixing of emissions or price. Certainty over price is useful for firms making long-term capital investments, for politicians who must answer to interest groups if carbon prices are unexpectedly high, and for the economy, which would be adversely affected by high carbon prices. If passed, S.2191 would implement a Carbon Market Efficiency Board that could adjust borrowing rules and other provisions to try to reduce the likelihood of high carbon prices. It is unclear how successful such an approach could be. One of the board's functions, for example, would be to shift emission allowances forward in time to release more permits in the short run. But with the total stock of permits between 2012 and 2050 fixed, such a shifting reduces permit prices in the short run at the expense of higher prices in the long run. Firms that see high prices in the near term as a signal of even higher prices in the longer term will have an incentive to bank any newly released permits and so undo the efforts of the board to reduce prices.

A more straightforward way to reduce price volatility is through a combined safety valve and price floor that creates a band within which prices will vary. The price cap can be achieved through the government's readiness to sell permits at a fixed price (the safety valve price). If this cap is reached, the CaT system in effect converts to a Tx system. The floor can be maintained by the government's setting a reserve price on permits that it auctions.[25]

With a tighter band within which prices can fluctuate, the CaT system has economic impacts that increasingly resemble those of a Tx system. Such a CaT system has been suggested by Orszag (2008), among others. The upper limit on the band protects the economy against the adverse effects of high carbon prices. The lower limit assures utilities and industries that they will receive a reasonable return on investments in carbon-free or emission-reducing capital.

This approach as well as other safety valve approaches serves to make the CaT system operate like a Tx system. The similarities go further. Thus the arguments for one system over another are harder to sustain. One argument that has been made on behalf of CaT is that if the federal government will have to buy off the energy industry to obtain its support for carbon pricing, then it is better to provide the industry with a lump-sum distribution in the form of an allocation of free permits rather than distortionary tax breaks in the form of exemptions under a carbon tax.[26] The argument suffers from a failure of creativity in tax design. One can replicate *any* lump-sum distribution of permits in a CaT system with tax breaks in a Tx system. One could replicate the free allocation of permits, for example, by taxing the energy sector's emissions above some floor.

The United States is likely to enact some sort of carbon pricing scheme in the Obama administration. While efficiency and administration considerations point to the carbon tax as a preferred pricing device, political obstacles to a tax remain. An interesting development in the past ten years has been the reshaping of a cap-and-trade system that preserves the political appeal of a permit-based system while adding many of the best attributes of a tax. This hybridization of systems may be what is required to get an effective policy enacted in Congress. We shall see.

Conclusion

When we review where the United States stands in its attitude toward and use of environmental taxes, several points emerge. First, the most obvious fact is that the United States relies very little on environmental taxes in comparison with other developed countries. Moreover, the environmental taxes in place are not textbook examples of environmental taxes, as they tend to be taxes on consumption or production attributes correlated with pollution but not on the pollution itself.[27]

Second, recent theoretical literature has made important advances in our understanding of environmental instrument design in a second-best world. It has shown that the revenue use from environmental levies has important efficiency as well as distributional consequences in a second-best world. It has also advanced our understanding of the relationship between the Pigouvian tax increment and social marginal damages in a second-best world. As I suggested above, however, this result, while of theoretical importance, is of second-order importance for U.S. policymakers, who still resist using taxes to address environmental concerns. Given the difficulties that exist in precisely measuring the social marginal damages of important pollutants, this result is more theoretically than practically important.

Finally, the current focus on climate change and the need to control greenhouse gas emissions suggest that the United States may soon significantly increase its reliance on environmental taxes, whether explicitly or implicitly. While the United States may not enact a direct carbon tax, any cap-and-trade system that emerges is likely to have many of the attributes of a tax. If such a cap-and-trade system is put in place, it will be in large part due to the advances made in our understanding of environmental policy design over the past ten to fifteen years.

Notes

1. The tax was most recently raised (to 18.3¢ per gallon for gasoline) on October 1, 1993. See Jackson (2006) for a history of changes to this tax.

2. The mileage rating is calculated as approximately 55 percent of the Environmental Protection Agency's city mileage rating and 45 percent of the highway rating.

3. The OECD/EEA rate for the United States is slightly below that of the American Petroleum Institute dataset. It may be that different weighting schemes are used to construct the averages in the two datasets.

4. Where firms are subject to regulations that restrict pollution, an important question is the relative cost of regulatory approaches to a tax-based approach. Some pollutants, most notably SO_2 emissions from electric utilities, are subject to caps with tradable permits. These act like taxes in setting a price on pollutions and letting firms use market mechanisms to drive pollution reduction. I discuss the relative merits of taxes versus cap-and-trade systems below.

5. A limited literature from this past decade exists on the use of taxes to control other externalities. One recent paper by Brueckner and Girvin (2008) considers optimal tax design to address noise pollution from aircraft.

6. Fullerton and Metcalf (1998) provide a detailed history of the double-dividend hypothesis and the debate over the optimal setting of environmental tax rates.

7. This distortionary impact is of second-order importance and can be ignored in the absence of other distortionary taxes. This is the case developed by Pigou (1938).

8. Goulder (1995) termed the positive welfare impact of using environmental revenue to lower other distorting taxes the *revenue-recycling* effect and the negative welfare impact of the tax's first-order distortionary impact the *tax-interaction* effect.

9. One must be careful in making the leap from the magnitude of the marginal cost of public funds and excess burden. The marginal cost of public funds depends critically on the tax normalization and captures only the distortion between a taxed good and the normalized commodity. See section 5 of Auerbach and Hines (2002) for an excellent discussion of this issue.

10. This assumes that labor is the only endogenous factor of production.

11. Pirttila (2000) develops this idea explicitly. West and Williams (2007) estimate the cross-price elasticity between labor supply and gasoline consumption and find that gasoline is a relative complement with leisure. Hence the optimal tax on emissions associated with gasoline use will tend to be higher, taking this complementarity into account.

12. The first-best result also requires that leisure be weakly separable from consumption and that consumers have homogeneous preferences.

13. Atkinson and Stern's result is more general. But the specification of preferences in Gaube's example ensures that the result holds as stated in the text.

14. In their numerical analysis, they do not actually model existing taxes on pollution but rather the shadow price of pollution arising from various regulatory restrictions on pollution. They then consider an experiment where the pollution "tax" is increased by 10 percent and measure the resulting changes in factor prices.

15. Bovenberg and Goulder (2002) provide an exhaustive review of different ways in which environmental externalities affect consumption and production in perfect and imperfect markets.

16. Goulder, Parry, and Burtraw (1997) stress this point, and Fullerton and Metcalf (2001) make the more general point that there are efficiency benefits of government capturing the scarcity rents from environmental regulation.

17. Ellerman, Buchner, and Carraro (2007) describe the design and allocation process in the first phase of the ETS.

18. A CaT or Tx system should provide for the possibility of carbon sequestration, for example through carbon capture and storage. No carbon price should be levied on fossil fuels where sequestration takes place. In practice this means that no permits would be required for sequestered carbon in a CaT system, and a tax credit would be allowed under a Tx system.

19. The relative advantage of price versus quantity instruments depends on uncertainty in the marginal abatement cost curve only. Uncertainty over the marginal damages of emissions affects the net benefits of an emissions control policy but does not affect the relative superiority of one policy instrument over another.

20. The Acid Rain Program is a helpful precedent, but the value of permits is an order of magnitude smaller than the potential value of carbon emission permits. It also is highly concentrated among a small set of electric utilities.

21. Other pollutants or market failures may provide a rationale for reducing oil consumption or tailpipe emissions. This simply reflects the fact that multiple instruments are generally needed to address multiple market failures.

22. Revenue could also be used to achieve efficiency gains. Orszag (2008) claims that the cost of a 15 percent reduction in carbon emissions from a CaT program could be cut in half if the revenue were used to cut taxes on capital income. See also Metcalf (2007a).

23. This is a statement of the weak double dividend (see Goulder 1995) for a taxonomy of double dividends. Not every tax swap is welfare preferred to a lump-sum distribution. Babiker, Metcalf, and Reilly (2003) provide an example of an apparently reasonable tax swap in Europe that is inferior to lump-sum distribution.

24. See Dinan and Rogers (2002), Parry (2004), and Metcalf (2007d) for further discussion of this point.

25. This approach works only if most, if not all, of the permits are auctioned. Alternatively, the government could charge a permit acquisition fee for permits it gives away or auctions. This approach has the advantage that it need not be modified as the mix of free and auctioned permits changes over time.

26. Bovenberg and Goulder (2001) have calculated that only a small portion of permits would need to be freely allocated to the energy sector to avoid a loss in equity values. This follows from the ability to pass the tax forward to consumers.

27. Fullerton, Hong, and Metcalf (2001) assess the welfare losses arising from employing taxes on imperfect proxies for pollution.

References

American Petroleum Institute. 2008. State motor fuel excise tax rates. http://www.api.org/policy/tax/stateexcise/index.cfm (accessed May 9, 2008).

Atkinson, Anthony B., and Nicholas H. Stern. 1974. Pigou, taxation and public goods. *Review of Economic Studies* 41 (1): 119–128.

Auerbach, Alan J., and James R. Hines Jr. 2002. Taxation and economic efficiency. In *Handbook of public economics*. Vol. 3, ed. A. J. Auerbach and M. Feldstein, 1347–1421. Amsterdam: Elsevier Science.

Babiker, Mustafa H., Gilbert E. Metcalf, and John Reilly. 2003. Tax distortions and global climate policy. *Journal of Environmental Economics and Management* 46: 269–87.

Bovenberg, A. Lans, and Ruud de Mooij. 1994. Environmental levies and distortionary taxation. *American Economic Review* 94: 1085–89.

Bovenberg, A. Lans, and Lawrence Goulder. 2001. Neutralizing the adverse industry impacts of CO_2 abatement policies: What does it cost? In *Distributional and behavioral effects of environmental policy*, ed. C. Carraro and G. E. Metcalf, 45–89. Chicago: University of Chicago Press.

———. 2002. Environmental taxation and regulation. In *Handbook of public economics*. Vol. 3, ed. A. J. Auerbach and M. Feldstein, 1471–1545. Amsterdam: Elsevier Science.

Bovenberg, A. Lans, and Frederick van der Ploeg. 1994. Environmental policy, public finance and the labour market in a second-best world. *Journal of Public Economics* 55 (3): 349–90.

Brueckner, Jan K., and Raquel Girvin. 2008. Airport noise regulation, airline service quality, and social welfare. *Transportation Research: Part B: Methodological* 42 (1): 19–37.

Bull, Nicholas, Kevin A. Hassett, and Gilbert E. Metcalf. 1994. Who pays broad-based energy taxes? Computing lifetime and regional incidence. *Energy Journal* 15 (3): 145–64.

Convery, Frank J., and Luke Redmond. 2007. Market and price developments in the European Union emissions trading scheme. *Review of Environmental Economics and Policy* 1 (1): 88–111.

Corlett, W. J., and D. C. Hague. 1953. Complementarity and the excess burden of taxation. *Review of Economic Studies* 10: 295–337.

Dinan, Terry, and Diane Lim Rogers. 2002. Distributional effects of carbon allowance trading: How government decisions determine winners and losers. *National Tax Journal* 55 (2): 199–221.

Ellerman, A. Denny, Barbara Buchner, and Carlo Carraro. 2007. *Allocation in the European emissions trading scheme*. Cambridge: Cambridge University Press.

Ellerman, A. Denny, Henry D. Jacoby, and Martin B. Zimmerman. 2006. *Bringing transportation into a cap-and-trade regime*. Cambridge, MA: MIT Joint Program on the Science and Policy of Global Change.

Ellerman, A. Denny, Paul L. Joskow, Juan-Pablo Montero, Richard Schmalensee, and Elizabeth M. Bailey. 2000. *Markets for clean air: The U.S. Acid Rain Program.* Cambridge: Cambridge University Press.

Fullerton, Don. 1997. Environmental levies and distortionary taxation: A comment. *American Economic Review* 87 (1): 245–51.

Fullerton, Don, and Garth Heutel. 2007. The general equilibrium incidence of environmental taxes. *Journal of Public Economics* 91 (3-4): 571–91.

Fullerton, Don, Inkee Hong, and Gilbert E. Metcalf. 2001. A tax on output of the polluting industry is not a tax on pollution: The importance of hitting the target. In *Distributional and behavioral effects of environmental policy*, ed. C. Carraro and G. E. Metcalf, 13–43. Chicago: University of Chicago Press.

Fullerton, Don, and Gilbert E. Metcalf. 1998. Environmental taxes and the double-dividend hypothesis: Did you really expect something for nothing? *Chicago-Kent Law Review* 73: 221–56.

———. 2001. Environmental controls, scarcity rents, and pre-existing distortions. *Journal of Public Economics* 80 (2): 249–67.

———. 2002. Tax incidence. In *Handbook of public economics.* Vol. 4, ed. A. Auerbach and M. Feldstein, 1787–1872. Amsterdam: Elsevier Science.

Fullerton, Don, and Diane Lim Rogers. 1993. *Who bears the lifetime tax burden?* Washington, D.C.: Brookings Institution.

Gaube, Thomas. 2005. Second-best pollution taxation and environmental quality. *B. E. Journal of Economic Analysis and Policy* 1 (1): 1–16.

Goulder, Lawrence H. 1995. Environmental taxation and the "double dividend": A reader's guide. *International Tax and Public Finance* 2: 157–83.

Goulder, Lawrence H., Ian W. H. Parry, and Dallas Burtraw. 1997. Revenue-raising versus other approaches to environmental protection: The critical significance of preexisting tax distortions. *RAND Journal of Economics* 28 (4): 708–31.

Guenther, Gary. 2006. Tax preferences for sport utility vehicles (SUVs): Current law and legislative initiatives in the 109th Congress. Washington, DC: Congressional Research Service.

Hassett, Kevin A., Aparna Mathur, and Gilbert E. Metcalf. 2007. The incidence of a U.S. carbon tax: A lifetime of regional analysis. NBER Working Paper No. W13554, Cambridge, MA.

Hoel, Michael, and Larry Karp. 2002. Taxes versus quotas for a stock pollutant. *Resource and Energy Economics* 24: 367–84.

Jackson, Pamela J. 2006. *The federal excise tax on gasoline and the Highway Trust Fund: A short history.* Washington, DC: Congressional Research Service.

Kaplow, Louis. 2006. Optimal control of externalities in the presence of income taxation. NBER Working Paper No. 12339, Cambridge, MA.

Karp, Larry, and Jiangfeng Zhang. 2005. Regulation of stock externalities with correlated abatement costs. *Environmental and Resource Economics* 32: 273–99.

Levinson, Arik. 1999a. NIMBY taxes matter: The case of state hazardous waste disposal taxes. *Journal of Public Economics* 74 (1): 31–51.

———. 1999b. State taxes and interstate hazardous waste shipments. *American Economic Review* 89 (3): 666–77.

Metcalf, Gilbert E. 1999. A distributional analysis of green tax reforms. *National Tax Journal* 52 (4): 655–81.

———. 2003. Environmental levies and distortionary taxation: Pigou, taxation and pollution. *Journal of Public Economics* 87 (2): 313–22.

———. 2007a. Corporate tax reform: Paying the bills with a carbon tax. *Public Finance Review* 35 (3): 440–59.

———. 2007b. Federal tax policy toward energy. *Tax Policy and the Economy* 21:145–84.

———. 2007c. A green employment tax swap: Using a carbon tax to finance payroll tax relief. *Tax Reform, Energy and the Environment Policy Brief.* Brookings Institution and World Resources Institute. Washington, DC.

———. 2007d. A proposal for a U.S. carbon tax swap: *An equitable tax reform to address global climate change.* Washington, DC: The Hamilton Project.

———, Sergey Paltsev, John Reilly, Henry Jacoby, and Jennifer F. Holak. 2008. Analysis of U.S. greenhouse gas tax proposals. NBER Working Paper No. 13980. Cambridge, MA.

Newell, Richard G., and William A. Pizer. 2003. Regulating stock externalities under uncertainty. *Journal of Environmental Economics and Management* 45: 416–32.

OECD/ EEA. 2008. Economic instruments database. http://www2.oecd.org/ecoinst/queries/ (accessed May 8, 2008).

Orszag, Peter R. 2008. Containing the cost of a cap-and-trade program for carbon dioxide emissions. Testimony before Senate Committee on Energy and Natural Resources. Washington, DC: Congressional Budget Office.

Paltsev, Sergey, John M. Reilly, Henry D. Jacoby, Angelo C. Gurgel, Gilbert E. Metcalf, Andrei P. Sokolov, and Jennifer F. Holak. 2007. *Assessment of U.S. cap-and-trade proposals.* Cambridge, MA: MIT Joint Program on the Science and Policy of Global Change.

Parry, Ian W. H. 1995. Pollution taxes and revenue recycling. *Journal of Environmental Economics and Management* 29 (3): S64–S77.

———. 2004. Are emissions permits regressive? *Journal of Environmental Economics and Management* 47: 364–87.

Parry, Ian W. H., and Kenneth A. Small. 2005. Does Britain or the United States have the right gasoline tax? *American Economic Review* 95 (4): 1276–89.

Pigou, Arthur C. 1938. *The economics of welfare.* London: Weidenfeld and Nicolson.

Pirttila, Jukka. 2000. A many-person Corlett-Hague tax rule with externalities. *Oxford Economic Papers* 52 (3): 595–605.

Poterba, James. 1989. Lifetime incidence and the distributional burden of excise taxes. *American Economic Review* 79 (2): 325–30.

Schneider, Stephen H., Serguei Semenov, Anand Patwardhan, Ian Burton, Chris H. D. Magadza, Michael Oppenheimer, A. Barrie Pittock, Atiq Rahman, Joel B. Smith, Avelino Suarez, and Farhana Yamin. 2007. Assessing key vulnerabilities and the risk from climate change. In *Contribution of group II to the fourth assessment report of the Intergovernmental Panel on Climate Change*, ed. M. Parry, O. Canziani, J. Palutikov, P. J. van der Linden, and C. E. Hanson, 779–810. Cambridge: Cambridge University Press.

Sigman, Hilary. 2003. Taxing hazardous waste: The U.S. experience. *Public Finance and Management* 3 (1): 12–33.

Stavins, Robert N. 2007. *Proposal for a U.S. cap-and-trade system to address global climate change: A sensible and practical approach to reduce greenhouse gas emissions.* Washington, DC: The Hamilton Project.

U.S. Census Bureau. 2008. *Statistical Abstract of the United States.* Washington, DC: Government Printing Office.

U.S. Congress. Joint Committee on Taxation. 2005. Estimated budget effects of the conference agreement for Title XIII. of H.R. 6, the "Energy Tax Incentives Act of 2005." JCX-59-05. July 27.

U.S. Environmental Protection Agency. 2001. *The United States experience with economic incentives for protecting the environment.* Washington, DC: Office of Policy, Economics and Innovation.

Weitzman, Martin. 1974. Prices vs. quantities. *Review of Economic Studies* 41 (4): 477–91.

West, Sarah E. 2004. Distributional effects of alternative vehicle pollution control policies. *Journal of Public Economics* 88 (3-4): 735–57.

———. 2005. Equity implications of vehicle emissions taxes. *Journal of Transport Economics and Policy* 39 (1): 1–24.

West, Sarah E., and Roberton C. Williams III. 2007. Optimal taxation and cross-price effects on labor supply: Estimates of the optimal gas tax. *Journal of Public Economics* 91 (3-4): 593–617.

Williams, Roberton C., III. 2001. Tax normalizations, the marginal cost of funds, and optimal environmental taxes. *Economics Letters* 71 (1): 137–42.

———. 2002. Environmental tax interactions when pollution affects health or productivity. *Journal of Environmental Economics and Management* 44 (2): 261–70.

2

A Response to Gilbert E. Metcalf

Roberton C. Williams III

Gilbert Metcalf has written an excellent chapter on recent developments in our understanding of environmental taxation. It provides a clear overview of the few environmental taxes that are currently in use, and an excellent survey of the most important advances in the academic literature on environmental taxes over the last decade.

I find very little to disagree with in it. My comments therefore will expand on Metcalf's analysis, highlight some key points that deserve more emphasis, and draw conclusions for future policy. My comments follow roughly the same order as Metcalf's chapter. I will begin by discussing practical experience with environmental taxes, then move on to look specifically at carbon emissions regulation, which represents the most important potential application of environmental taxes currently under debate. I will review what we can learn from experience and academic research on carbon policy, and draw on those lessons to make some suggestions about what form U.S. carbon policy should take.

Environmental Taxes in the United States

As Metcalf points out, environmental taxes play only a very small role in the tax system in the United States: total environmental tax revenue (including both state and federal taxes) amounts to less than 1 percent of gross domestic product (GDP). To provide some sense of context, a U.S. carbon tax of $20 per ton—roughly in line with economists' estimates of the marginal damage from carbon emissions—would raise more than $100 billion per year in revenue. That's more than all existing U.S. environmental taxes put together.

The experience of other countries also provides useful context. Metcalf notes that the average environmental tax revenue in countries in the Organisation for Economic Co-operation and Development (OECD) is substantially higher than in the United States: roughly 2.5 times as large, as a share of GDP, or approximately equal to what the U.S. share would be after implementing a carbon tax.

The vast majority of that environmental tax revenue comes from motor fuel taxes, both in the United States and in the average OECD country. But one might ask whether motor fuel taxes are truly environmental taxes. Metcalf's chapter points out that most motor fuel tax revenue in the United States is earmarked for spending on highways, and suggests that because of that earmarking, a motor fuel tax might be more accurately characterized as a benefit tax.

This raises the question of what makes a particular tax an "environmental" tax. Metcalf's argument here seems to imply that it depends on how the revenue is used. But such a definition has obvious problems: for example, a carbon tax certainly seems as if it should be considered an environmental tax, even if the revenues are used for a nonenvironmental purpose (such as funding cuts in other taxes).[1]

Alternatively, one could use a definition based on intent: if a tax is intended to reduce pollution emissions, then it's an environmental tax. This seems like a better definition. And it might well be a better way to interpret Metcalf's point: that the earmarking of motor fuel tax revenues suggests that these taxes were intended as a way to pay for road construction and maintenance, not as a way to reduce pollution emissions from vehicles. Of course, such a definition has its own problems—different policymakers may well have different intentions for a given policy, plus intentions are often hard to discern—but seems attractive nonetheless. And based on this definition, motor fuel taxes (at least in the United States) generally would not qualify as environmental taxes, thus leaving environmental taxes playing a truly minuscule role in the current tax system.

A third possible definition would depend on the tax base: an environmental tax is a tax on pollution emissions or on some good strongly correlated with emissions. While there's still a question of where to draw the line—how strong a correlation between the taxed good and emissions is required for a tax to be "environmental"—this definition avoids the problem of trying to discern intent. Based on this definition, fuel taxes are environmental taxes: fuel use is strongly (though certainly not perfectly) correlated with pollution emissions.[2]

Regardless of how one defines an environmental tax, though, it remains clear that most environmental regulation uses instruments other than taxes. Despite economists' efforts, much environmental regulation still relies on a command-and-control approach. And even where market-based regulation exists, recent policies have relied much more on tradable permit systems than on environmental taxes (for example, trading systems for sulfur dioxide and for nitrogen oxides in the United States, and for carbon emissions in the European Union [EU]).

Lessons for Carbon Policy

Metcalf provides an excellent survey of key recent research on environmental policy. Therefore, rather than critiquing that survey, I will focus more on what that literature suggests for how to design a policy to reduce carbon emissions. The literature has two important implications, each of which is also supported by preliminary results from the EU carbon trading system.

First, research on second-best optimal environmental policy shows the importance of choosing a policy instrument that raises revenue—such as an emissions tax or a system of tradable permits in which the permits are auctioned—and of putting that revenue to good use. Second, research on environmental regulation under uncertainty finds that for a long-lived stock pollutant such as carbon dioxide, a price-based instrument such as a carbon tax will tend to be more efficient than a quantity-based policy such as tradable permits, because it leads to a much less volatile carbon price. However, a tradable permit system can include features designed to reduce price volatility (for example, provisions allowing banking and borrowing of permits, or explicit price floors and ceilings), which would mitigate this disadvantage of tradable permits, and could even make a permit system more efficient than a tax.

The literature on second-best environmental policy makes a number of important points, perhaps the most important of which is that there is an efficiency cost of regulating via freely allocated permits rather than via taxes or auctioned permits. But even though Metcalf's chapter highlights this result and relates it to carbon policy, it still doesn't put enough emphasis on this crucial issue.

Revenue recycling is particularly important for carbon policy—even more so than in the regulation of other pollutants—for two main reasons. The first is simply the magnitude of the potential revenues. A $20 per ton carbon tax in the United States would raise approximately $100 billion per year in revenue.[3] That's roughly thirty times the total value of the permits issued each year under the current U.S. sulfur dioxide (SO_2) permit trading system.[4] Since the amount of money at stake is far greater, it is important to make sure that potential revenue is captured and used in an efficient manner. And a $20 per ton carbon tax is relatively modest: some proposals would impose a far higher price on carbon. Stern (2007), for example, calls for reductions in carbon emissions that would require a carbon tax rate of roughly $300 per ton.

Second, any politically viable carbon policy proposal would reduce carbon emissions by a smaller percentage than the reductions typical for other pollutants. For example, the SO_2 trading program has reduced SO_2 emissions by roughly 40 percent from 1980 levels (and the reduction would be substantially larger if measured relative to a no-regulation baseline), whereas a $20 per ton carbon tax would yield roughly a 15 percent reduction in carbon emissions (relative to a no-regulation baseline). The literature has shown that the more modest the reduction in emissions from a given policy, the more important revenue recycling will be in determining the cost of the policy.[5]

Figure 2-1 presents the ratio of the cost of carbon regulation via freely allocated permits to the cost of the same regulation using taxes or auctioned permits with revenues recycled to cut income tax rates, for a range of different reductions in carbon emissions.[6] It shows that for a 5 percent reduction in emissions, using a system of freely allocated permits will cost more than seven times as much as the same reduction using taxes with revenue recycling. That ratio falls as the reduction in emissions gets larger, though the system of freely allocated permits is still more than twice as expensive even for a 25 percent reduction in emissions.

All these calculations presume that the revenues from the carbon tax or permit auction are recycled to cut income tax rates. But this is not the only possible productive use for the revenue. Alternative uses, such as funding

FIGURE 2-1

EFFECT OF FREE PERMIT ALLOCATION
ON COST OF CARBON REGULATION

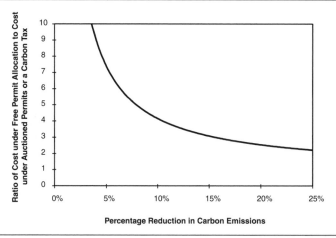

SOURCE: Policy simulations using the computable general equilibrium model from Parry, Williams, and Goulder (1999).

public good provision or reducing the budget deficit, could be more efficient.[7] The key is not to use the revenue in a wasteful manner: spending it on worthless government programs, for example, would be far more costly than regulating via freely allocated permits.

Another alternative use for carbon tax revenue would be to fund a lump-sum transfer to households. This would have the same efficiency cost as freely allocated permits. However, the distributional consequences would be very different. Depending on the value one places on income redistribution, such a policy could be either more or less attractive than using carbon tax revenue to fund income tax cuts.

Freely allocated permits are often justified on distributional grounds: that is, permits need to be given to firms free of charge in order to compensate them for the increased costs imposed by the regulation. However, Bovenberg, Goulder, and Gurney (2005) show that such compensation would require only a small share of the total number of permits (or a lump-sum transfer of a small share of the carbon tax revenue), and that freely allocating all the permits would dramatically overcompensate firms in carbon-intensive industries, leading to profits and equity values far above what they would be without any carbon regulation at all.[8]

Recent experience with the EU carbon trading program bears this out: electricity prices have gone up as a result of the program, while average costs have risen by much less, leaving electricity generators with tens of billions of euros of windfall profits, a politically unpopular result. British members of Parliament have proposed a windfall profits tax to address this, but the problem could more easily have been avoided by freely allocating far fewer permits to electricity generators, and auctioning the remainder.

The second key lesson for carbon policy from the literature is that for a long-lived stock pollutant such as carbon, regulating via a tax will typically be more efficient than using tradable permits, because the tax provides a stable price for carbon emissions, whereas the permit price can be quite volatile. For a flow pollutant—one that has only immediate effects—that price volatility may be a good thing. If marginal pollution damage increases sharply when pollution emissions increase, then having the price of pollution also increase sharply in that case (as under a permit system) means that the price of pollution would closely correspond to the marginal damage.

However, for carbon, the effect of a ton of emissions this year is nearly identical to the effect of a ton of emissions next year, because what matters is the total stock of carbon built up in the atmosphere over a long period of time. Because the marginal damage per ton is virtually identical across years, it's inefficient to have very different prices in different years, as can happen under a permit system.

Metcalf does an excellent job of reviewing much of the relevant literature on this issue. But there are a few points that I'd like to add.

First, this is another case where preliminary experience with the EU carbon trading system supports the theoretical arguments made in the literature. Carbon permit prices under the EU system have been quite volatile. That volatility was particularly evident in 2006, when permit prices went from over thirty euros per ton to less than ten euros per ton over a period of roughly one month. Price swings since then have been less dramatic, but permit prices are still far more volatile than is efficient.

Second, while Metcalf's chapter mentioned that price caps and price floors can reduce price volatility and thus boost efficiency under a permit trading system, it did not go on to point out that a permit system with a price floor and price ceiling can actually be more efficient than a tax. This is not a new result, but dates back to a study by Roberts and Spence (1976), which shows that a hybrid policy that includes both price and quantity regulation—such as a permit system with a price floor and a price ceiling—can always be designed such that it is at least as efficient as (and typically more efficient than) the optimal tax or optimal permit quantity alone. Of course, actually achieving that greater efficiency requires setting the price ceiling and price floor properly, which is quite a challenging problem. But it is still worth noting that such a hybrid policy could be more efficient than a tax alone.

Finally, allowing permit banking and borrowing is another way to reduce permit price volatility and thus boost the efficiency of a permit system. Banking and borrowing smooth out the price changes that result from changes in the demand for permits: a large drop in permit demand in a particular year would cause a large drop in the permit price if the permits can be used only in that year, whereas if permit banking is allowed, then such a drop in demand would lead to more permits being banked for the future, thus spreading out the effect on price over multiple years and reducing the effect in any given year.

Papers on taxes vs. permits for regulation of a stock pollutant generally compare taxes to nonbankable permits. Williams (2002) points out that allowing banking puts permits on a much more even footing with taxes. Nonbankable permits will be more efficient than taxes only if the marginal damage curve for emissions in a particular year is steeper than the marginal cost curve; this will almost never be the case for a stock pollutant, because even a large change in emissions in one year will have only a small effect on the total stock. However, bankable permits will be more efficient than taxes if the long-term marginal damage curve is steeper than the marginal cost curve; this is a much weaker condition (though nonetheless one that seems unlikely to be satisfied in the case of carbon, where the marginal cost curve appears to be steeper than even the long-term marginal damage curve).

A Brief Proposal for a U.S. Carbon Policy

Drawing on the important points in Metcalf's chapter and in my comments above, I conclude with a brief outline of the key features I would include in a carbon regulation system for the United States.

Most economists involved in the debate over carbon policy fall into one of two camps: they strongly prefer a carbon tax or they strongly prefer a system of tradable carbon permits. But I don't see that distinction as being particularly important in and of itself. A carbon tax is simpler and more transparent, which is an advantage, though not necessarily a big one. And a tax would certainly have major advantages over a permit system similar to the U.S. SO_2 trading program or the EU carbon trading system. But a permit system can be designed differently. If permits are auctioned rather than freely allocated, and if the system includes a price floor and price ceiling, then a permit system would do just as well as a tax on the two key issues of recycling revenue and handling uncertainty.

A small share of that revenue could be used to compensate carbon-intensive industries.[9] I would then use the remainder to finance cuts in other taxes, such as either the income or payroll tax, or to reduce the budget deficit. And I would make those tax cuts slightly progressive in order to offset the distributional effect of the carbon tax, which is slightly regressive. Such a policy would be roughly distributionally neutral, both across the income distribution and in terms of its effect on carbon-intensive industries.

Finally, a key aspect of any carbon policy is that it should be easy to adjust as we learn more about both the costs of reducing emissions and the potential damage such emissions will cause.

Notes

1. Indeed, using carbon tax revenues to fund cuts in other taxes would likely increase carbon emissions slightly (relative to what they would be if revenues were used to fund a lump-sum rebate, for example), by encouraging more economic activity.

2. However, even when a direct tax on emissions is impossible, fuel taxes alone are still not the most efficient policy for reducing emissions. Fullerton and West (2000) show that a combination of taxes on gasoline use, vehicle size, and vehicle age is substantially more efficient than a tax just on gasoline.

3. This figure comes from my own rough calculations based on results from Bovenberg, Goulder, and Gurney (2005). For more details on a similar calculation, see Green, Hayward, and Hassett (2007).

4. Because SO_2 permit prices have been quite volatile, the total value of permits issued has also been volatile. But based on the clearing price of $380 per ton in the Environmental Protection Agency's March 2008 permit auction, the annual value of SO_2 permits issued is approximately $3.4 billion.

5. For example, see Parry, Williams, and Goulder (1999).

6. The cost estimates used to generate this figure are the same as those used to generate figure 2 in Parry, Williams, and Goulder (1999), and come from simulations using a simple computational general equilibrium model of the U.S. economy. For more details on the model, see Parry, Williams, and Goulder (1999).

7. If the benefit-cost ratio for the public good is exactly the same as the cost of public funds (which is the case at the optimal level of public good provision), then using the revenue to fund public good provision will be just as efficient as using it to fund income tax cuts. If public good provision is initially below the optimal level, then funding public good provision would be more efficient than funding income tax cuts, whereas if it is initially above the optimal level, then funding public good provision would be less efficient. Similarly, if the budget deficit is initially greater than the optimal level, then using carbon tax revenue to reduce the deficit would be more efficient than using it to fund income tax cuts.

8. To see how such windfall profits can arise, consider the highly simplified case of a firm that can reduce emissions only by changing output, and that emits pollution exactly equal to the number of permits it receives. For this firm, the policy has no effect on average cost—the firm is neither buying nor selling permits—but still raises the firm's marginal cost because producing one more unit of output requires purchasing permits. That increase in marginal cost will lead to a higher equilibrium price for the firm's output, and with average costs the same, profits will also be higher.

9. Bovenberg, Goulder, and Gurney (2005) find that fully compensating carbon-intensive industries requires only about 15 percent of carbon policy revenues.

References

Bovenberg, A. Lans, Lawrence H. Goulder, and Derek J. Gurney. 2005. Efficiency costs of meeting industry-distributional constraints under environmental permits and taxes. *RAND Journal of Economics* 36 (4): 951–71.

Fullerton, Don, and Sarah West. 2000. Tax and subsidy combinations for the control of car pollution. NBER Working Paper No. 7774, Cambridge, MA.

Green, Kenneth P., Steven F. Hayward, and Kevin A. Hassett. 2007. Climate change: Caps vs. taxes, American Enterprise Institute. *Environmental Policy Outlook.* June 2007.

Parry, Ian W. H., Roberton C. Williams III, and Lawrence H. Goulder. 1999. When can carbon abatement policies increase welfare? The fundamental role of distorted factor markets. *Journal of Environmental Economics and Management* 37: 52–84.

Roberts, Marc, and Michael Spence. 1976. Effluent charges and licenses under uncertainty. *Journal of Public Economics* 5: 193–208.

Stern, Nicholas. 2007. *The economics of climate change: The Stern Review.* Cambridge: Cambridge University Press.

Williams, Roberton C., III. 2002. Prices vs. quantities vs. tradable quantities. NBER Working Paper No. 9283, Cambridge, MA.

3

Evidence on Labor Supply and Taxes, and Implications for Tax Policy

Nada Eissa

By any measure, the last decade represents an especially active period in the modern history of the United States tax system. A series of tax acts—signed into law by President Bush in 2001, 2002, and 2003—has dramatically changed the federal income tax code. These tax acts all had important effects on the tax liabilities and incentives faced by taxpayers. In fact, a central motivation of the tax cuts was to improve incentives and thereby encourage long-term economic growth: policymakers held that "high individual income tax rates reduce incentives for taxpayers to work, to save and to invest," and that they therefore "have a negative effect on the long-term health of the economy" (U.S. House of Representatives 2001).[1]

It is difficult to argue against improving incentives, since they do matter, both in fact and theory. The Economic Growth and Tax Relief Reconciliation Act of 2001 (EGTRRA) and the Jobs and Growth Tax Relief Reconciliation Act of 2003 (JGTRRA) improved work incentives through a combination of provisions, including a doubling of the child tax credit,[2] lower tax burdens for joint filers (marriage penalty relief), and a higher exemption for the Alternative Minimum Tax (AMT relief), but primarily through the reduction in statutory marginal income tax rates. These changes also matter for much more than "work" behavior (i.e., whether to participate in the labor market, and how many hours to work). They matter for choices about the form of compensation (as wages, fringe

The author would like to thank Steve Davis and Alan Viard for helpful comments, Dan Feenberg for help with TAXSIM, and Sam Easterly for research assistance.

benefits, or other income), for human capital accumulation (schooling and training), and occupational choice—all of which should be considered part of the labor supply response.

This chapter evaluates the effects of the Bush tax cuts on labor supply behavior. The impact of tax cuts on labor supply—broadly defined—can be gauged by evaluating the taxable income response, which has been the near-exclusive focus of recent evaluations of the behavioral response to tax reforms. Much about the full range of behavioral responses can be learned from the taxable income elasticity (see the chapter by Giertz in this volume); but it is also informative to separately evaluate different dimensions of labor supply, since they respond differently to taxes. This chapter will focus on the impact of tax cuts on labor force participation and hours worked. This is not entirely by choice, but rather forced by the relative lack of direct evidence on how tax cuts affect decisions such as compensation choice and human capital accumulation.

Several related literatures arguably provide indirect evidence on labor supply responsiveness, including analyses of cross-country differences in hours worked and marginal tax rates and of informal labor markets (see Steve Davis's response to this chapter below). Much of that evidence is quite intriguing: for example, long-term differences in hours worked between Americans and Europeans can be explained by differences in tax rates on labor income (Prescott 2004; Ohanian, Raffo, and Rogerson 2006). But, in the context of cross-country comparisons, it can be highly misleading to abstract from the institutional details of a specific tax transfer program (or provision of social assistance benefits). European countries provide a very different set of transfer and social insurance programs than does the United States, and analyses that focus only on taxes miss a potentially critical element of the budget set. As a result, much of that work remains somewhat speculative and should be viewed as raising issues for further research rather than providing hard evidence for our current understanding of behavioral responses to taxes.

No studies have directly evaluated the effects of recent tax reforms on labor supply; therefore I review the relevant empirical literature and discuss its implications for labor supply effects. Recent empirical evidence largely confirms that labor supply (even narrowly defined) does respond to taxes, especially for some demographic groups— casting doubt on claims that labor supply is inelastic with respect to taxes. Early empirical work (starting with Hall 1973) established that taxes have little effect on one dimension of labor supply, namely hours worked by males. What is interesting is that this small (intensive) elasticity of hours worked now characterizes the responsiveness of females as well, including married women. Yet evidence of responsiveness at the extensive margin of entry and exit from the labor market abounds, especially for less-skilled workers and for single and married mothers. In fact, this evidence is found consistently, using different estimation technique and over different time periods. The nature of this labor supply response—along the extensive but not the intensive margin—has important implications for the welfare evaluation of taxes (and of transfer programs).

The bulk of empirical work on taxes and labor supply has generally assumed a static model, but an important element of labor supply responses is dynamic. Over the life cycle, individuals choose when to enter the labor market (how much schooling to get) and when to retire. In addition, workers reallocate their work as wages fluctuate over time. A large parallel literature has attempted to estimate the intertemporal elasticity of labor supply, though only a few studies explicitly account for taxes and transfers. That work generally finds small to modest intertemporal responses, though substantial uncertainty about the magnitude of the response remains (Blundell and MaCurdy 1999; Ziliak and Kniesner 1999). Intertemporal responses are especially relevant for considering the effects of recent tax cuts, because so many of the changes were phased in and arguably anticipated. Perhaps the single most significant element is the legislated sunset of the entire set of tax cuts on December 31, 2010 (unless further legislation makes them permanent).

Below, I briefly review the main provisions in EGTRRA and JGTRRA, especially as they relate to work incentives, and I evaluate the size of the tax cuts for taxpayers in the March Current Population Survey (CPS).

I then address issues that arise in evaluating labor supply, focusing on the complexity of the budget set and basic identification concerns in the empirical literature. This section presents the budget set faced by most taxpayers before the tax cuts and argues that their complexity limits the potential responses.

The next section summarizes what is known about the impact of taxes on labor supply. This summary is structured to help place the extensive literature in context. It first reviews the evidence on male labor supply, arguing that hours worked by men are nearly universally estimated to be inelastic to taxes. An intriguing result with males, found by Moffitt and Wilhelm (2000), is the sizable response of wage and salary income to the Tax Reform Act of 1986 (TRA86). Next, I evaluate female labor supply, focusing first on married women and then on female household heads. With the latter group, the distinction between two measures of labor supply—employment (extensive margin) and hours worked by labor force participants (intensive margin) becomes critical. Recent evaluations of tax cuts for single mothers (through the Earned Income Tax Credit [EITC]) consistently find a large positive impact on their employment, and interestingly no impact at all on their hours of work. Married women are generally found to be responsive to taxes, though recent research suggests they respond more like men once they enter the labor market.

I then look at what the evidence on labor supply suggests about the impacts of the Bush tax cuts. Using reasonable elasticities, I evaluate the likely impacts of the Bush tax cuts on labor supply (measured by labor force participation and hours worked). I also present unadjusted labor supply data from the March CPS showing that any response is likely to be very moderate. This section also examines the implications of discrete choice for the welfare evaluation of tax reform.

Tax Policy Changes in the 2000s and Their Impact on Labor Supply Incentives

The Bush tax cuts—passed in 2001, 2002, and 2003—lowered all federal marginal rates, but they also contained several other provisions relevant for earned income. To maintain the tax cuts within budget guidelines, just about all provisions were phased in over several years, and the entire legislation was to sunset after 2010. Table 3-1 summarizes the relevant provisions of the tax cuts.

The first tax legislation, EGTRRA, was passed on June 7, 2001, and was the most sweeping of the three. It reduced federal marginal rates for all taxpayers, doubled the child tax credit, temporarily raised the alternative minimum tax exemption, and reduced taxes on married couples filing jointly.

TABLE 3-1

SUMMARY OF MAJOR TAX CUT PROVISIONS FOR LABOR SUPPLY

Provision	2000 Tax Code	EGTRRA/ JGTRRA (2004)
Tax Schedule		
10% tax bracket	N/A	Up to $7,000 (single filers); $14,000 (joint filers); $10,000 (heads of household)
Higher tax brackets (%)	15.0 28.0 31.0 36.0 39.6	15.0 25.0 28.0 33.0 35.0
Child Credit		
Child credit	$500, limited refundability	$1000, refundable to a maximum of 15% of earned income above $10,000
Relief from Marriage Penalties		
Standard deduction for joint filers	167% of that for single filers	200% of that for single filers
15% tax bracket for joint filers	Upper threshold is 167% of that for single filers	Upper threshold is 200% of that for single filers
Earned income tax credit for joint filers	Joint and head-of-household filers face the same credit schedule	Maximum credit region extended for joint filers; beginning of phaseout extended by $3,000 for joint filers
Itemized Deductions and Personal Exemptions		
Limits on itemized deductions	Deductions are reduced by 3% of amount of income above a threshold (to a maximum reduction of 80%)	No reduction in deductions
Personal exemption phaseout	Value of personal exemptions is reduced by 2% for each $2,500 of adjusted gross income above a threshold	No phaseout of exemptions
Alternative Minimum Tax		
Exemption for the alternative minimum tax	$33,750 for single filers, $45,000 for joint filers	Temporarily increased exemption

SOURCE: CBO 2007.

In 2000, the federal income tax schedule consisted of five brackets, ranging from 15 to 39.6 percent. The 2001 tax cut lowered the top federal marginal tax rate from 39.6 to 35 percent by 2006; and the 28, 31, and 36 percent rates by three percentage points, also by 2006. Rates were set to decline 0.5 percentage points in 2001 and 2002, and an additional percentage point at the beginning of 2004. For low-income filers, EGTRRA created a new 10 percent tax bracket; this applied to the first $12,000 of taxable income (for joint filers). All these legislated tax cuts were accelerated to the beginning of 2003 by JGTRRA.

In addition to reducing marginal rates, the 2001 bill increased gradually the maximum amount of the child credit, to $1,000 in 2010, and made it partly refundable. A household with no income tax liability could therefore receive a refund, though it would be subject to limits that depend on earnings. EGTRRA also eliminated the phaseout of deductions and exemptions for higher-income taxpayers, lowering their marginal tax rates and tax liabilities.

To alleviate the marriage penalty in the federal code, the 15 percent tax bracket for a married couple was increased from 167 percent to 200 percent of the single-filer bracket, as was the value of the standard deduction (phased in by 2008 and 2009, respectively). A marriage penalty, which occurs when a married couple faces a greater tax liability filing jointly than they would filing as unmarried individuals, is primarily the outcome of a progressive tax schedule on family (rather than individual) incomes. The legislated changes offset this penalty by ensuring that two single people keep their single-taxpayer standard deduction when they marry, and that their joint income continues to face the 15 percent tax rate. These provisions do not eliminate the marriage penalty for higher-income taxpayers or even for taxpayers with incomes in the 15 percent bracket—if they have children and are eligible for the EITC. The tax cuts did offset some of the marriage tax in the EITC by increasing the income at which the phaseout and loss of the credit begin for joint filers.

JGTRRA expanded on the 2001 tax cuts and accelerated the phase-in of many provisions that had been scheduled to take effect in 2003. It broadened the 10 percent bracket for 2003 and 2004, and lowered statutory rates for the top four brackets to levels that EGTRRA had set to begin in 2006. It widened the 15 percent bracket for joint filers so that the top income in this bracket was double the top income in the 2003 single bracket, and it increased the child credit from $600 to $1,000 for 2003. JGTRRA also accelerated earlier provisions phasing in the elimination of limits on itemized deductions and personal exemptions for higher-income taxpayers.

Impact on Labor Supply Incentives. The remainder of this section reviews the changes in marginal and average tax rates between 2000 and 2006 using survey data and gauges the direct impact of the Bush tax cuts. The tax cuts had no impact on marginal rates for taxpayers in the 15 percent bracket, for those subject to the AMT, and for people without positive income tax liability; but they did have a moderate impact on marginal tax rates. Auten, Carroll, and Gee (2008) show that EGTRRA and JGTRRA shifted the distribution of tax-payers across the federal tax schedule, with an increase (decrease) in the number of taxpayers with marginal tax rates below 10 percent (above 40 percent). At the top of the distribution, the number of taxpayers with marginal tax rates of 40 percent or more decreased from 1.8 million in 2000 to only 546,000 in 2005 (far below the projected 2.3 million taxpayers in 2005).

To further examine the impact of the tax cuts on work incentives, I use data from the 2001, 2003, 2005, and 2007 March CPS. The March CPS includes detailed information on demographic characteristics and income for the previous calendar year, though it lacks information on various tax deductions. I define tax units and calculate marginal and average tax rates using the National Bureau of Economic Research (NBER) TAXSIM model. To simplify, tax calculations assume all married couples file jointly. All filers take the standard deduction unless their imputed state income taxes exceed the value of the deduction, in which case they itemize.[3] Marginal tax rates are based on the tax owed on an additional ten cents of income earned by the tax-filing unit, and so are effective marginal tax rates. For this reason the range can extend well beyond the top statutory marginal rate in any year. In fact, the highest effective federal marginal rates for primary earners simulated by TAXSIM are well over 50 percent, though only 1 percent of tax-payers face marginal rates that exceed the statutory maximum in any year.

Figures 3-1a–3-1c show the distributions of effective federal marginal tax rates for primary earners, secondary earners, and female household heads in 2000, 2002, 2004, and 2006. The vertical lines are set at the 15 and 39.6 percent marginal tax rate. The data show very different

FIGURE 3-1a

MARGINAL TAX RATES, PRIME-AGE WORKERS

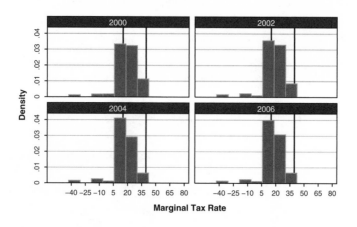

SOURCE: 2001–2007 March CPS.

FIGURE 3-1b

MARGINAL TAX RATES, WORKING MARRIED WOMEN

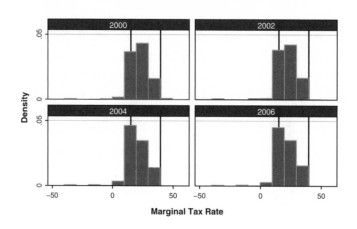

SOURCE: 2001–2007 March CPS.

FIGURE 3-1c

MARGINAL TAX RATES, FEMALE HOUSEHOLD HEADS

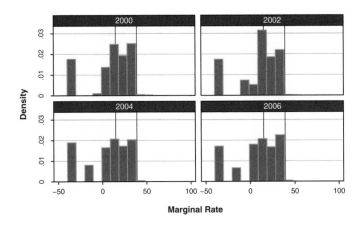

SOURCE: 2001–2007 March CPS, data for female household heads ages 23–59.

distributions for the three groups, with married women more concentrated further up the rate distribution, and household heads facing some of the lowest and highest marginal rates at the federal level. This large variation in the tax rates of female household heads reflects the influence of the EITC. The EITC provides a refundable credit, so that even a taxpayer with no tax liability could receive a refund from the federal government for the credit's full value. For the lowest-earning workers, the credit effectively creates a negative tax rate of up to 40 percent. Moreover, because the marginal rate declines substantially for taxpayers once they earn too much to qualify for the credit (from a high of 36 percent to 15 percent), it would be misleading to map the tax rate distribution to earnings. Nonetheless, the figures show a consistent decline in the share of taxpayers facing higher marginal rates and an increase in the share facing the 15 percent marginal rate. Notably, some taxpayers continue to face marginal tax rates in the 35–40 percent range, even after the tax cuts are fully phased in.

To measure more precisely the impact of the tax cuts, I simulate 2004 taxes for each individual in the 2000 sample. The impact of the tax cuts is the difference between the actual tax rate in 2000 and the tax rate in 2004

TABLE 3-2

EFFECT OF **EGTRRA** AND **JGTRRA** ON MARGINAL AND
AVERAGE FEDERAL INCOME TAX RATES

	Marginal Tax Rate (2000 law)	Δ Marginal Rate (2004 law)	Average Tax Rate (2000 law)	Δ Average Rate (2004 law)
All	17.3 (15.5)	–2.6 (4.6)	9.8 (12.0)	–2.8 (1.6)
Secondary earners	21.5 (12.4)	–3.3 (5.5)	10.9 (11.2)	–3.4 (1.5)
Household heads	3.8 (27.8)	–3.3 (7.0)	–5.5 (15.8)	–2.7 (2.1)
Top 1%	38.6 (0.9)	–4.9 (1.4)	41.0 (4.9)	–4.6 (0.8)

SOURCE: Author's calculations.

(for 2000 income). Table 3-2 presents the findings: EGTRRA and JGTRRA lowered average tax rates for all taxpayers as a group and for different groups (classified by marital status and income). On average, marginal tax rates fell by about 2.6 percentage points, from 17.3 to 14.7 percent. This cut is primarily the result of changes in statutory tax rates and the tax schedule, and of provisions related to marriage penalty relief (CBO 2007).

Table 3-2 also shows that taxpayers with children and those with higher incomes gained the most from the tax cuts. Marginal rates fell by about 3.3 percentage points for secondary earners and head-of-household filers; and nearly five percentage points for taxpayers at the very top (ninety-ninth percentile) of the CPS income distribution. These rates include neither state income nor payroll taxes. Including state and payroll taxes to calculate the effective rate raises the level, to 34.1 percent in 2000, but does not affect the size of the tax cut. Applying 2004 tax law leads to a 2.3 percentage point cut in the marginal tax rate. This occurs because state income taxes (and payroll taxes) remained largely unchanged over this period.

Figure 3-2 presents the average federal marginal tax rate by income decile, and shows there was some variation in the size of the tax cuts across the income distribution. The largest decline in the sample was 4.1 percentage points for individuals with income in the third decile and 1.7 percentage points for those in the fifth decile.

FIGURE 3-2

IMPACT OF **EGTRRA/JGTRRA** ON **MARGINAL FEDERAL TAX RATES**

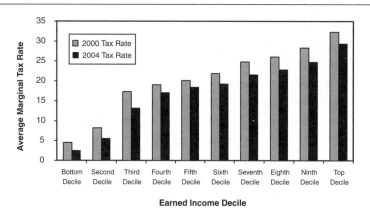

SOURCE: Author's calculations.
NOTES: All prime-aged (23–59) individuals. 2004 tax rate is calculated for 2000 incomes inflated using CPI.

Over this period, average tax rates (tax liability as a share of total income) also declined, by an average of 2.8 percentage points for all taxpayers, from 9.8 percent to just below 7 percent of income (column 4 of table 3-2). For both secondary earners and the top 1 percent of tax-filing units, the decline was larger: 3.4 and 4.6 percentage points.[4] As with marginal tax rates, the largest impacts are due to changes in statutory tax rates and brackets, with AMT and marriage penalty relief having a similar but smaller impact. The average tax rate is important for the distributional impact of the tax cuts, but also for the decision to enter the labor market.

The size of the tax cuts predicted in the 2001 CPS sample are consistent with findings in CBO's (2007) analysis of eliminating the legislated sunset at the end of 2010, though the two methods are very different. CBO examines a policy change in 2011 but uses a representative sample of income tax returns filed in 2002, and so "ages" the data based on projected demographic trends. The effects of the tax cuts are then calculated for this "aged" sample of returns. CBO finds the Bush tax cuts, on average, would reduce marginal and average tax rates by about three percentage points each. CBO also examines the implied labor supply (and earnings) effects of the tax cuts using elasticities from the literature. I use these elasticities in the next section to predict the labor supply effects for prime-age taxpayers in the CPS.

A Simple Framework for Evaluating the Impact of Tax Cuts in the 2000s?
In the standard model of labor supply, individuals value leisure and consumption of other goods. In the simplest static partial equilibrium model, the tax cuts influence hours of work through two effects that push in opposite directions. Lower marginal rates raise the price of leisure (relative to other goods) and encourage individuals to work more hours (substitution effect). The tax cuts also reduce overall tax burdens, however. The resulting increase in after-tax income leads individuals to consume more of all goods including leisure and so to work fewer hours (income effect). The net effect of the tax cuts on hours worked therefore depends on the relative size of these substitution and income effects, as well as on the magnitude of the reductions in marginal and average tax rates.

By expanding the budget set, the reduction in tax burdens also affects individuals' decisions about entering the labor market. This latter effect is unambiguous in the case of a single individual with no unearned income. For secondary earners, a lower tax burden discourages entry into the labor market through the income effect.

One caveat is worth noting at this point. These predictions are substantially complicated by nonlinearities in the budget set. (Below I discuss more fully the implications for behavioral responses and for the empirics of labor supply models.) With a nonlinear budget set, the overall impact on hours worked and labor force participation depends in addition on the distribution and composition of tax changes and of taxpayers across the tax schedule. To show this dependence, figure 3-3 presents a simple illustration of how reducing the marginal rate along the first segment (and on unearned income) influences hours worked by different workers. The budget set before the tax is given by ABC with two rates: 15 percent (AB) and 28 percent (BC). After the tax cut, the budget set shifts to ADEFG, reflecting a higher net unearned income[5] (AD) and the new 10 percent bracket (DE). All taxpayers beyond the 10 percent bracket benefit from the lower rate along the first bracket, even those whose marginal rate remains unchanged at 15 percent. This occurs because their disposable income

FIGURE 3-3
BUDGET SET FOR HYPOTHETICAL WORKER

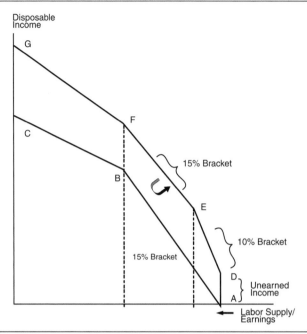

SOURCE: Author's diagram.

rises. As a result, they reduce their hours of work (if leisure is a normal good). Additionally, provisions that reduce taxes on unearned income cause some workers to drop out of the labor force.

I take a far simpler approach to predicting the labor supply response. I use the mean change in marginal and average tax rates and calculate the wage and income effects on annual hours worked (see table 3-3). These calculations miss the heterogeneity of the effects and responses at different points along the tax schedule, but they are meant to be purely illustrative.

The basic conclusion is that the effect of the tax cuts on labor supply (measured by annual hours worked) is likely to be very modest. At the average hourly wage of $20.55, the 2.6 percentage point decline in the average marginal tax rate leads to a 3.5 percent increase in the after-tax hourly wage. Applying a wage elasticity of 0.1 suggests an increase of less than 0.5 per-

TABLE 3-3

PREDICTED IMPACT OF EGTRRA/JGTRRA ON HOURS WORKED

	% Δ Net Wage (Wage Elasticity)	Δ Hours Worked (%, Level)	% Δ Net Income (Income Elasticity)	Δ Hours Worked (%, Level)	Total Effect (Hours, Earned Income)
All	+3.5% (0.20)	0.7% (14)	+2.8% (–0.10)	–0.3% (–5.2)	8.8 ($180)
Secondary Earners	+5.0% (0.65)	3.2% (55)	+3.4% (–0.25)	–0.9% (–11.5)	43.5 ($750)
Household Heads	+5.1% (0.20)	1.0% (19)	+2.7% (–0.10)	–0.3% (–4.0)	15.0 ($175)

SOURCE: Data come from the 2001 March CPS.
NOTES: The sample includes all prime-age (23–59) individuals. Tax rates are calculated using the NBER TAXSIM model, and assume all married couples file jointly and all household heads take the standard deduction. The tax rates are calculated for 2000, and then again for 2004 (by inflating all income components using the CPI). Δ represents the difference between the actual rate and what it would have been under the 2004 tax law.

cent in hours worked by all workers (or eleven hours per year). This positive substitution effect would be offset by the increase in disposable income resulting from the tax cut, and would result in an overall increase of just under nine hours per year. Though the overall effect on hours worked is small, there is substantial heterogeneity in the expected effects among different demographic groups. Among married women, for example, the impact is predicted to be much larger, because both their net wage increase and their behavioral response are greater. An uncompensated hours-of-work elasticity of 0.65 for married women with a 5 percent increase in their after-tax hourly wage would lead to 54 more hours worked per year due to the substitution effect, and a net increase of 43.5 hours worked ($750). For female household heads, the predicted impact is a mere 15 hours ($175) per year, less than 1 percent. These modest results for impact on hours worked are consistent with CBO's (2007) findings on the effects of the expiration of the Bush tax cuts, which do account for the heterogeneous effects on individual taxpayers.

Figures 3-4a–3-4c present the unconditional distribution of hours worked by prime-age males, married women, and female household heads, respectively. All else equal, the tax cuts should have shifted the distributions

FIGURE 3-4a

ANNUAL HOURS OF WORK, KERNEL DENSITY, PRIME-AGE MALES

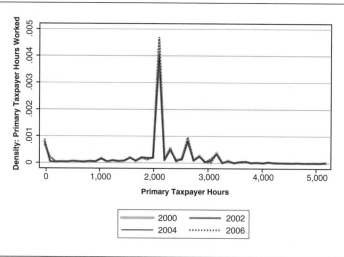

SOURCE: 2001–2007 March CPS.

FIGURE 3-4b

ANNUAL HOURS OF WORK, KERNEL DENSITY, MARRIED WOMEN

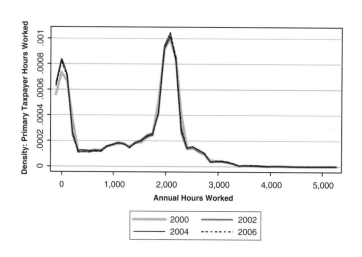

SOURCE: 2001–2007 March CPS.

FIGURE 3-4c

ANNUAL HOURS OF WORK, KERNEL DENSITY, SINGLE MOTHERS

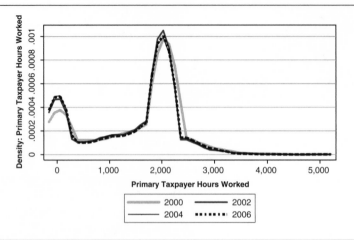

SOURCE: 2001–2007 March CPS, prime age (25–39).

to the right, and reduced the mass at zero hours worked. The data show, however, that hours worked by prime-age males remained effectively unchanged over this period, while the distributions for females generally shifted left, reflecting a decline in females' employment population ratios and hours of work. To infer any tax effect here requires a counterfactual set of distributions, which would account for general economic trends during this period. That is beyond the scope of this chapter, but it is worth noting that economic growth is likely to have reinforced any tax effect after 2002. While the gross domestic product's annual growth rate fell from 3.7 in 2000 to 0.8 in 2001, it rose back to 3.6 percent by 2004 and hovered around 3 percent through 2006.

Uncertainty about the labor supply effect of the tax cuts is substantial for several reasons, however, including uncertainty about the size (and composition) of the labor supply elasticity and the limited evidence on other margins of labor supply responsiveness (including occupational choice, human capital decisions, and compensation choices). The next section discusses issues in the evaluation of taxes and labor supply, and the section after that reviews the existing empirical evidence, including the evidence on intertemporal responsiveness.

Taxes and Labor Supply

Estimating the effects of taxes on labor supply is notoriously difficult, because of the joint determination of labor supply and taxes with nonproportional tax schedules, because of unobserved tastes for work, and because of measurement error in both the marginal tax rate and the wage. This difficulty explains the vast empirical literature on the subject and the divergent labor supply estimates that abound. Several extensive reviews of labor supply and taxation discuss the set of conceptual and methodological problems in the literature (Hausman 1985; Blundell and MaCurdy 1999). This section focuses on two issues central to evaluating the impact of the tax cuts: the budget set and identification.

The Budget Set. A worker filing a tax return in 2000 faced a federal income tax schedule with five brackets, with rates ranging from 15 to 39.6 percent. These rates applied to taxable income, so some earnings were shielded from federal income taxes by personal exemptions and the standard deduction (or itemized deductions). For a taxpayer with two children, the exemptions were $18,550 if filing jointly and $14,850 if filing as head of household. In addition, this taxpayer would face either no state income tax (in Florida or Texas) or as much as a 9 percent state income tax (in California, Oregon, and Iowa). This taxpayer would also have paid payroll taxes of 7.65 percent on her first dollar of earnings (and bear the burden of her employer's share).

Figures 3-5a–3-5c show the 2000 federal income tax schedule for three hypothetical taxpayers, each with two children: a primary earner filing jointly, a primary earner filing as head of household, and a secondary earner. Tax filers with children qualify for the child tax credit, a dependent-care deduction, and the Earned Income Tax Credit. The effective tax schedule accounts for the EITC, state taxes, and payroll taxes, but does not incorporate the child tax credit (which adds two other tax brackets at the bottom of the income distribution and an additional nonconvexity in the schedule for the head-of-household filers). For a married secondary earner with two children, the marginal tax rate on the first dollar of earnings is –26 percent (because of the EITC), but the rate then rises to +55 percent at $20,000 of earned income (because of the phaseout of the EITC and the 15 percent rate in the first bracket); it then falls to 34 percent at $35,000 of earned income

FIGURE 3-5a

2000 INCOME TAX SCHEDULE: MARRIED COUPLE, TWO CHILDREN

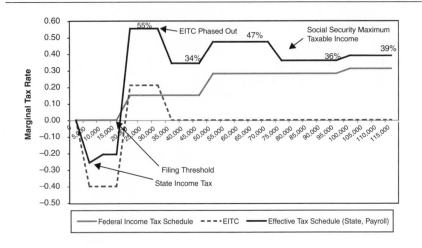

SOURCE: Author's diagram.

FIGURE 3-5b

2000 INCOME TAX SCHEDULE: HEAD OF HOUSEHOLD, TWO CHILDREN

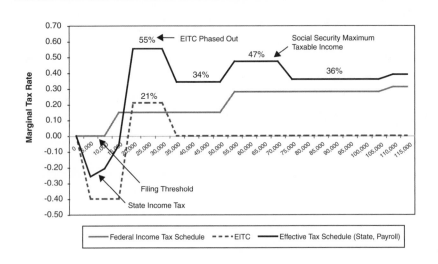

SOURCE: Author's diagram.

FIGURE 3-5c

2000 INCOME TAX SCHEDULE: SECONDARY EARNERS, TWO CHILDREN

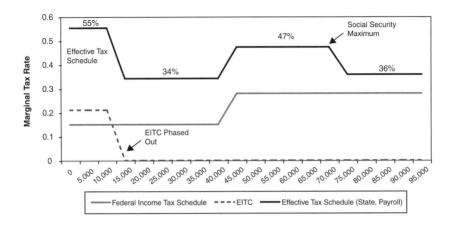

SOURCE: Author's diagram.

(because of the end of the EITC). Tax-filing units with income below $115,000 therefore face numerous tax brackets, but notably those at the very bottom face some of the lowest and highest marginal tax rates in the tax code.

It is worth noting that for head-of-household tax filers (figure 3-5b), the budget set would be complicated even further by the transfer system, which adds implicit marginal tax rates on the order of 60–70 percent from the Temporary Assistance for Needy Families (TANF) program, 25 percent from food stamps, and a notch from loss of Medicaid. Even absent these features, the tax schedule shows the complexity of the budget set. In fact, the budget set faced by secondary earners further down the income distribution looks strikingly similar to that created by the tax-transfer system (figure 3-5c). The phaseout of the EITC, combined with federal income, payroll, and state income taxes, can easily lead to a 55 percent marginal tax rate for the first dollar of earnings. Marriage penalty tax relief lowers this rate for some—though far from all—secondary earners.

The budget sets for these hypothetical taxpayers are consistent with those in Kotlikoff and Rapson (2006). This study concludes that "the patterns by age and [income] of marginal tax rates on earnings . . . can be summarized with one word— bizarre" (4).

The implication of such complicated budget constraints cannot be underestimated. Conceptually, they dramatically alter the behavioral response of taxpayers, including sticky responses at kink points and discrete jumps across budget segments. Recognition of this impact was the motivation for the nonlinear-budget set methods (see discussion below). But perhaps the more fundamental concern is that, in practice, they affect taxpayers' ability to understand the incentives they face.

Evidence abounds that individuals have a limited understanding of the actual tax schedules they face (de Bartolome 1995; Liebman and Zeckhauser 2004; Feldman and Katuščák 2006). Most of this work shows that taxpayers typically perceive their actual tax schedules crudely, and respond to what Liebman and Zeckhauser refer to as a "schmedule." De Bartolome shows, in an experimental setting, that people confuse actual and marginal rates, and often use the average tax rate as if it were the marginal tax rate. There is further evidence of such confusion in the context of labor supply: using variation in the child tax credit, both Liebman and Zeckhauser and Feldman and Katuščák present evidence that individuals respond to average income tax rates rather than marginal tax rates. In a different context, empirical evidence on the behavioral response to EITC expansions also suggests that taxpayers fail to recognize the marginal incentives in the tax schedule, since this evidence has failed to show any reduction in the hours worked by single mothers in the phaseout of the EITC (Eissa and Hoynes 2006), where effective marginal tax rates rise to as high as 55 percent.

Figure 3-6 shows that EGTRRA and JGTRRA did little to simplify the tax schedule. If anything, the addition of a new 10 percent bracket and the increase in the refundability of the child credit added to the complexity. The tax cuts also were unusual because they phased in different provisions at different rates and at different times. While the 10 percent bracket took effect immediately in 2002, other marginal rates were legislated to decline by one percentage point each year for three years, except for the top (39.6) percent rate, which was scheduled to decline by 2.6 percentage points in the third year. The child tax credit was scheduled to increase by $100 in 2006, remain constant in 2007, and then increase by $100 in each year

FIGURE 3-6

EFFECT OF TAX CUTS ON THE EFFECTIVE MARGINAL TAX SCHEDULE:
MARRIED COUPLE, TWO CHILDREN

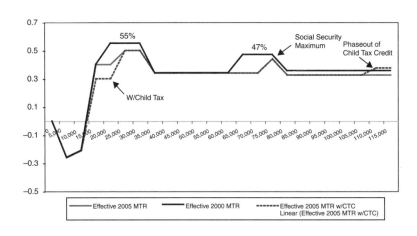

SOURCE: Author's diagram.

though 2010. These legislated changes are likely to have limited even further taxpayers' understanding of their actual tax schedules over the period.

This discussion is not meant to suggest that the complexity of (or changes in) tax schedules leads workers to ignore taxes altogether. Workers do respond, but to a tax schedule that is inaccurately perceived. Two points are worth noting here. First, such misperceptions have implications for equilibrium tax rates (government spending) and the welfare effects of taxation (Chetty, Kroft, and Looney 2007; Finkelstein 2007). Second, there may be substantial differences in misperceptions across the income distributions. Higher income tax-filers (with incomes over $100,000) face a flatter and less complicated tax schedule than those with lower incomes (CBO 2007).

Identification of Labor Supply and Tax Effects. Estimating labor supply responses to taxation faces two main—and well-known—problems. The first problem results from the nonlinearity of the tax schedule, which causes the worker's marginal tax rate to be jointly determined with her hours of work. Moreover, identification of the tax effect is rendered tenuous because the marginal tax rate is then a function of determinants of labor supply behavior. The second problem is also related to nonlinearity of the budget set, namely that tax changes can lead to unexpected and seemingly irrational labor supply responses.

More recent work on labor supply and taxes has largely focused on the former concern of identifying the tax effect with joint determination of hours worked and taxes. This is partly because of difficulties that arose with the estimation of (earlier) models that address nonlinear budget sets. I review both methods of estimating labor supply responses briefly below, and argue that both approaches involve tradeoffs; ultimately, a useful avenue for empirical tax and labor supply research would be to marry the focus on identification with careful modeling of the institutional features of the tax system.

Nonlinear Budget Sets. The main advantage of the nonlinear budget set approach is that it explicitly recognizes two things: institutional features of tax transfer systems induce important nonlinearities in the tax schedule; and these in turn complicate the analysis of the behavioral response. For example, some taxpayers located in the 28 percent bracket will reduce their hours of work and fall into the 15 percent bracket (even if the reduction to 25 percent would imply more hours worked). This occurs because of the income effect induced by the five percentage point cut in the marginal tax rate on earning in the 10 percent bracket. Therefore, the tax cut in the first bracket induces an income effect beyond the first bracket and can reduce total hours worked by taxpayers in higher brackets, even as their marginal rates are declining. Tax changes with a nonlinear budget set can also lead to "sticky" behavior at kink points—no behavioral response even if underlying elasticities are large—and to discrete jumps—large behavioral responses when underlying elasticities are small.

Though this approach is conceptually attractive, empirical evaluation of the EITC's labor supply effects has generally shied away from it. The main advantage of the nonlinear budget set approach has to be weighed against shortcomings that cast doubt on the reliability of the estimates. These shortcomings include lack of knowledge of the exact budget constraint, restrictions on underlying preferences, and strong exogeneity assumptions

(Heckman 1983). Because survey data provide no information on taxes, the tax schedule has to be imputed using reported income and demographic information. Errors in self-reported income along with very limited information on itemized deductions can cause substantial errors in the imputed tax schedule. Early work using this approach that showed sizable compensated wage elasticities for males (Hausman 1981) was found to be highly sensitive to constraints imposed to make the empirical models tractable, namely that the income effect must be nonnegative. Triest (1990) and MaCurdy, Green, and Paarsch (1990) showed that this constraint was binding, and that it heavily influenced the estimated elasticities for males.

More recent work has attempted to address these criticisms. Blomquist and Newey (1997) propose a nonparametric estimator that relaxes some of the restrictions imposed by parametric estimates. They model labor supply as a function of the entire tax schedule, and develop an estimator that includes the entire budget set in the regression. While they attempt to reduce the dimensionality, their approach does not readily generate a single elasticity of labor supply.

Tax Reforms as Quasi-Experiments. It is instructive to briefly clarify the different sources of variation in individual tax rates that identify the effects of taxes on labor supply. All individuals face the same statutory tax *schedule* at any point in time, though they face different tax *rates* based on their characteristics (family size, amount of nonlabor income, amount of earned income). In addition, multiple provisions in the code, such as phaseouts, phase-ins, and income tests for certain tax provisions, create deviations between effective and statutory marginal tax rates (Barthold, Koerner, and Navratil 1998). If the very social and economic characteristics that lead to variation in work incentives also have an independent effect on labor supply decisions, there is essentially no independent variation in tax rates left to identify the behavioral response to taxation.

To overcome this problem, researchers have relied on variation in tax schedules, and therefore rates, that arises over time with policy reforms. Typically, this quasi-experimental approach has focused on variation in tax rates at the group level (children in the case of the EITC; high-income spouses in the case of the Tax Reform Act of 1986). This approach assumes that all relevant wage and income changes are captured by *group-level* variation in the grouping variable (presence and number of children; other household income) and time. To the extent that marginal tax rates, wages, and incomes are measured with error, a grouping approach also has the advantage of reducing measurement error bias in the coefficients of interest.

Clearly, policy reforms have nonneutral effects within groups and allow use of *individual* variation in wages, income, and federal personal income taxes. An alternative approach would therefore rely not only on cross-sectional variation in demographic characteristics and taxes but also on time variation to identify the effect of taxes on labor supply. This approach yields more efficient estimates by using all available information, and should yield the same behavioral response as the grouping estimate if the experiment is valid.

The quasi-experimental approach has been criticized for lacking structure and imposing strong assumptions for identification (Blundell and MaCurdy 1999), but it often represents a useful starting point and is appealing because of its simplicity and transparency. Recent work by Blundell, Duncan, and Meghir (1998) has attempted to apply this approach to estimate models that account for the nonlinearity of the budget set. This research estimates labor supply responses to tax reforms in the United Kingdom, extending the approach to account for the effects of changes in labor force composition and discontinuities in the British tax system. This approach is attractive because it accounts for the institutional features of the tax system, and because it tackles the identification problem seriously. Applying this approach to U.S. tax reforms would be a useful exercise, though likely far more complicated because of the U.S. tax transfer schedule.

What Do We Know about Taxes and Labor Supply?

The literature on the impact of taxation on labor supply is extensive, and spans different data, methods, and time periods. Table 3-4 summarizes selected empirical studies on the effect of taxation on male (3-4a) and female (3-4b) labor supply. The traditional empirical approach, followed in both the labor and public finance fields, was to posit a linear budget constraint and estimate a structural labor supply equation. Generally, ordinary least squares and two-stage least squares were used. The empirical work through the early 1980s has been reviewed extensively elsewhere (see Hausman 1985). For the most part, this work suggested that male labor supply is insensitive to taxes, while the labor supply of married women is more responsive.

It is helpful to state up front the thought experiment behind "standard" analyses of taxes and labor supply. For the most part, the microeconometric literature does not account for the uses of government revenues (or the financing of tax cuts), and estimates the "partial" effect of a change in the after-tax wage and nonlabor income (an exception is Conway 1997). This partial effect is theoretically ambiguous, because income and substitution effects offset each other. Tax cuts can also be revenue neutral, however, in which case only the substitution effect operates. An example here (at least in design) is the Tax Reform of Act of 1986. More generally, the impact of taxes under budget balance can also be characterized by the substitution effect—under simplifying assumptions about preferences for public spending, private consumption, and labor supply. Conway (1997) estimates labor supply responses to income taxes that account for federal and state government spending. Her findings suggest that ignoring the spending side can bias downward the labor supply response to taxes, and that more attention should be paid to the interaction of public spending and private consumption in individual preferences.

Male Labor Supply. With the exception of a study by Hausman (1981), which found that male labor supply is sensitive to taxes, the literature has found consistently that hours worked by males do not show much of a response to taxes. In one respect, Hausman's finding—of a very small (0.03) net-wage elasticity—was consistent with the literature. His large elasticity was a compensated elasticity and was driven by the large income effect (see table 3-4a). Both Triest (1990) and MaCurdy et al. (1990), however, found essentially no income effect.

Three exceptions to the low elasticity of response by men are worth noting. Moffitt and Wilhelm's (2000) analysis of the effects of the 1986 Tax Reform Act on the labor supply decisions of high-income men presents an especially intriguing set of results. Using Survey of Consumer Finances

TABLE 3-4a

EMPIRICAL STUDIES ON THE IMPACT OF TAXATION ON MALE LABOR SUPPLY

Author (date)	Data (years)	Sample (men)
Hall (1973)	Survey of Income Opportunity (SEO) (1967)	Married, Single, aged 20–59
Hausman (1981)	PSID (1975)	Working Married, 25–55
MaCurdy (1981)	PSID (1967–1976)	Married
Altonji (1986)	PSID (1968–1981)	Married
MaCurdy, Green, and Paarsch (1990)	PSID (1975)	Working, Married, 25–55
Triest (1990)	PSID (1983)	Working, Married, 25–55
Moffitt and Wilhelm (2000)	Survey of Consumer Finances	High-Income

SOURCES: Blundell and MaCurdy 1999, author's summary.

TABLE 3-4b

EMPIRICAL STUDIES ON THE IMPACT OF TAXATION ON FEMALE LABOR SUPPLY

Author (date)	Data (years)	Sample (men)
Rosen (1976)	Survey of Work Experience (1976)	White Married, 30–44
Cogan (1980)	PSID (1976)	Married
Heckman and MaCurdy (1980)	PSID (1968–75)	Married
Hausman (1981)	PSID (1975)	Married
Triest (1990)	PSID (1983)	Working, Married, 25–55
Eissa (1995)	CPS (1983–1985 and 1989–1991)	Married, 99th %tile vs. 75th %tile
Meyer and Rosenbaum (2001)	CPS (1984–1996)	Single mothers 19–44 yrs.
Eissa and Hoynes (2004)	CPS (1984–1996)	Married mothers, fathers 25–54

SOURCES: Blundell and MaCurdy 1999, author's summary.

| | | Labor Supply Elasticity | | |
Analysis	Functional Form	Uncompen-stated wage	Income	Wage
Cross-section	Step Function		weak	0 (positive, small for black husbands)
Cross-section	Linear, hours worked	0.03	−1	
Life cycle	Intertemporal labor supply			0.15
Life cycle	Intertemporal labor supply			0.17
Cross-section	Linear Labor Supply (piece wise linear/differentiable constraints)	0	−0.01	
Cross-section	Linear labor supply, hours	0.05	0	
Panel	Linear labor supply, hours	0	0	

| | | Labor Supply Elasticity | | |
Analysis	Functional Form	Uncompen-stated wage	Income	Wage
Cross-section	Hours	2.3		
Cross-section	Hours	2.45		
Life cycle	Leisure demand (hours worked)			−0.41 (1.61)
Cross-section	Linear, labor supply	1	−0.12	
Cross-section	Linear labor supply, hours	1	−0.33	
TRA86	Participation Hours	0.4 0.4		
EITC and welfare	Tax effects	Weekly employment up 4.4%; annual employment up 7%		Smaller effects in the 1990s
EITC, federal and state taxes	Participation	0.27 (women) 0.032 (men)	−0.04 (women) −0.01 (men)	

(SCF) data from 1983 and 1989, they examine the response to the substantial tax cuts in TRA86 (which lowered the top federal marginal income tax rate from 50 to 28 percent), and find a dramatic surge in wage and salary income reported by high-income men. This is intriguing because Moffitt and Wilhelm find "essentially no evidence of any response" in the hours worked by these men over the period of the tax cuts, leaving a surge in hourly wages as the most likely explanation. More broadly, the evidence gathered on the effects of TRA86 suggests other aspects of labor supply (such as self-employment, employment at a job with different compensation schemes, etc.) are important elements of the behavioral response.

A second exception to the general finding of low elasticities by males is the evidence that entrepreneurial activity is sensitive to the marginal tax rate—and to the progressivity of the tax schedule (Gentry and Hubbard 2005). These results suggest that the negative effect of tax convexity is not limited to more educated individuals, but rather that it discourages entry into self-employment at all levels of education. Cullen and Gordon (2007) provide further evidence. They estimate the effects of taxes on entrepreneurial activity using IRS data from individual tax returns from 1964 to 1993. Their results imply that a drop of five percentage points in personal tax rates in each bracket would lead to over a 20 percent fall in entrepreneurial activity.

Yet another exception is the evidence on the labor supply behavior of less-skilled men. Data show the labor market participation rate of less-skilled males has been steadily declining over the past several decades: prime-age males with less than a high school education were a full twelve percentage points less likely to participate in the labor market in 2005 than in 1970. Even high-school graduates (with no college degree) reduced their participation by about ten percentage points over this period (Mosisa and Hipple 2006). Empirical evidence suggests that for most of this period, declining labor market opportunities (wages) are the primary reason for the decline in work (Juhn 1992).

Female Labor Supply. The empirical work on the impact of taxation of female labor supply is summarized in table 3-4b.

Married Women. Earlier surveys of married women's labor supply response to taxes placed the range of elasticities between –0.2 and 2.3 (Hausman

1985). Hausman (1981) uses data from the 1975 Panel Study of Income Dynamics (PSID) and estimates a net wage elasticity of approximately 1 for married women.

Various studies have applied this methodology to data for the United States and different countries (see Moffitt 1990). Triest (1990) uses the 1984 PSID data to estimate a labor supply elasticity of 1.1 for married women. For working women, Triest estimates an elasticity of 0.2 for hours of work, suggesting that the participation decision is more responsive to changes in the net wage than are hours conditional on working. It is interesting to note that Mroz (1987) also finds similar results in his sensitivity analysis of married women's labor supply.

Several studies evaluate the impact of tax reforms in the 1980s (Burtless 1991; Bosworth and Burtless 1992; Eissa 1995), and find that married women's labor supply responded to the tax cuts. Burtless (1991) and Bosworth and Burtless (1992) both find a significant break in the labor supply trend of married women starting in 1981, which they attribute to the Economic Recovery and Tax Act of 1981. In addition, Burtless (1991) finds evidence that the impact of the tax reforms is on hours of work, rather than labor force participation, though his results are sensitive to the specification used. Eissa (1995) finds a sizable response by women married to very high-income men (in the ninety-ninth percentile of the CPS distribution) when compared to women further down the income distribution (at the seventy-fifth percentile) following TRA86. Her analysis suggests an overall elasticity of hours worked of around 0.8, half of which is due to participation. Recent work by Liebman and Saez (2006) evaluates the response of married women to the 1986 and 1993 tax acts using data from the Survey of Income and Program Participation matched to Social Security earnings records from 1981 to 1999, and comes to a different conclusion. This study finds wives of high earners having little to no behavioral response—and in fact finds a decline in labor force participation—to both the 1986 and 1993 tax changes, which we attribute to the surge in primary earnings at the top.

A related set of studies examining the response to expansions of the Earned Income Tax Credit suggests the response may be more specific to married mothers. Eissa and Hoynes (2004) estimate a difference-in-difference model comparing married mothers to married women without children and find that the 1993 EITC expansion led to a one percentage point reduction in the participation rate of married mothers. A higher tax credit reduces labor force participation by married women through the income effect, as the husband's employment generates more disposable income. These findings support earlier evidence in Ellwood (2000), which compares married mothers in high- and low-wage quartiles and also finds that expansion of the EITC is associated with reductions in the employment of married mothers.

EITC expansions have also been found to reduce hours worked by working married women, though the effect is small (Eissa and Hoynes 2007; Heim 2008). Eissa and Hoynes (2007) estimate standard hours-worked models, and instrument for the after-tax wage using tax parameters (in the spirit of Blomquist and Newey's [1997] proposed estimator). They find that the increase in the maximum credit from $500 in 1984 to $3,556 in 1996 reduced hours worked by working married mothers by only 1 to 4 percent. Their analysis is comprehensive in that it incorporates all income tax changes over this period, but it suffers from changes in the composition of working women and of mothers over this period, as well as the endogeneity of work more generally.

Single Mothers. A related body of evidence has found overwhelmingly that the EITC encourages work among single mothers. Perhaps most striking about these findings is their consistency across different empirical methods—including quasi-experimental methods (Eissa and Liebman 1996; Ellwood 2000; Hotz, Mullin, and Scholz 2005; Meyer and Rosenbaum 2000; Rothstein 2008) and more structural methods (Dickert, Houser, and Scholz 1995; Meyer and Rosenbaum 2001)—and across different reforms evaluated. These findings are consistent with incentives created by the EITC, which transfers income conditional on work, thereby encouraging entry into the labor market.

Data show, however, that most workers are in regions of the credit that discourage hours worked, and so the credit is predicted to reduce hours for the majority of those already in the labor force. Evaluations of the large federal expansions in the credit in 1986, 1990, and 1993 typically use difference-in-difference models and compare changes for a treated group (e.g., single women with children) to a control group (e.g., single women without children). These models seem to work well and provide robust

FIGURE 3-7
ANNUAL EMPLOYMENT RATE FOR WOMEN BY MARITAL STATUS AND
PRESENCE OF CHILDREN, 1984–2003

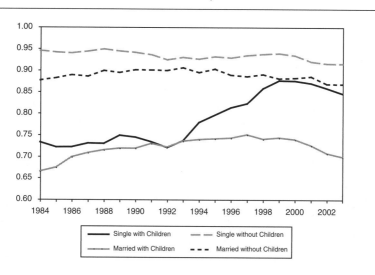

SOURCE: Eissa and Hoynes 2006.

estimates for the impact of the EITC on participation, but may be less well suited for estimating the impacts on hours worked. Analyzing the determinants of hours worked is more complicated due to the changes in the composition of the working sample and selection into work more generally.

Labor Force Participation. To illustrate the findings from the difference-in-difference literature, figure 3-7 presents annual employment rates for women by marital status and presence of children for 1983–2006.[6] The figure shows the dramatic increase in employment rates for single women with children compared to single women without children. Most of this change occurred between 1992 and 1999, when employment rates for single women with children increased by sixteen percentage points. This is during the period of the largest expansion in the EITC due to the Omnibus Budget Reconciliation Act of 1993. Over this same period, there was little change in employment rates of single women without children. Others have shown that the groups with the most to gain from EITC expansions (e.g., single women or women with lower wages, lower education levels, or more children) experienced larger gains in employment rates (Ellwood 2000; Meyer and Rosenbaum 2000; Rothstein 2008).

Overall, evaluations of the effects of the EITC suggest a strong positive relationship between taxes and the employment rates of single women with children. In terms of the magnitude of the effects, Eissa and Liebman (1996) find that the 1986 expansion of the EITC led to a 2.8 percentage point increase in participation for single mothers. Meyer and Rosenbaum (2001) find that 60 percent of the 8.7 percentage point increase in annual employment for single mothers between 1984 and 1996 is due to the EITC. They find that a smaller amount of the increase in participation between 1992 and 1996—35 percent—is due to the EITC (with the remainder due to welfare reform and other changes). Hotz and Scholz (2003) compare the implied elasticities of participation with respect to net income to these and other studies and find the range to be quite narrow—between 0.69 and 1.16.[7]

Hours of Work. While the EITC is expected to increase labor force participation, it is expected to reduce hours worked for those already in the labor force. But there is little evidence from the literature that is consistent with this prediction.

Very few papers have examined the impact of the EITC on the hours worked by single mothers. This is fundamentally a harder empirical problem because of the selectivity of those who are working. Eissa and Liebman (1996) apply their difference-in-difference model to annual hours worked (conditional on working) and find a small positive (and marginally significant) impact on all single mothers and a zero impact on single mothers with less education. Meyer and Rosenbaum (2001) find mixed (positive and negative) but insignificant impacts of the EITC on hours worked (conditional on working). Rothstein (2008) finds no difference between single mothers and childless single women in weekly hours worked (conditional on working) across the wage distribution. Keane and Moffitt (1998) estimate a structural model of labor supply choice and simulate the effect of the EITC on total hours but do not break down the estimate for those already working. Another source of evidence builds on the prediction from labor supply theory that taxpayers should be bunched at the kinks in the EITC schedule (and should be less present at the end of the EITC schedule). Liebman (1998) and Saez (2002a) use tax return data and find no evidence consistent with these predictions.

Reasons for participation effect but no hours-worked effect. The finding of greater tax sensitivity of labor market entry and exit (relative to hours of work) is consistent with a wide set of estimates in the empirical literature (Triest 1990; Mroz 1987; Robins 1995). Yet few studies suggest that we should observe no hours-worked response to the phaseout of the EITC. Below, I seek to shed some light on why we observe a response by labor force participation but none by hours worked.

One possibility is that workers are bound by institutional restrictions or norms that push them either to part-time or full-time work, so they cannot freely choose their hours of work.[8] Figure 3-8 presents the distribution of annual hours worked for our CPS sample of single mothers in 1986, 1990, 1993, and 2000. Two important observations emerge from this figure. First, annual hours of work are highly concentrated—while some workers are working part-time, the majority of workers have full-time full-year working hours. Second, the increase in employment at the end of this period (seen in the smaller mass at zero hours) is matched almost fully by an increase in full-time, full-year hours of work.

A second possibility is that the estimated effects are biased by measurement error in the survey data. Bound, Brown, and Mathiowetz (2001) find evidence suggesting measurement error for both annual hours of work— calculated as the product of weeks worked last year and usual hours worked per week—and hourly wages. Moreover, they find evidence that errors in the measurement of standard labor market variables are not "classical," but are negatively correlated with their true values.

Third, taxpayers may not fully understand the EITC and income-tax schedules. A substantial share of EITC recipients use tax preparers and nearly all receive a lump-sum payment with their annual tax return. As a result, they have little opportunity to learn about the features of the credit that matter for the hours-worked response. This stands in contrast to the situation of workers in welfare programs, where there is monthly reporting, and to workers in low-wage jobs, where there are (bi)weekly pay periods;

FIGURE 3-8

KERNEL DENSITY ESTIMATE: ANNUAL HOURS, SINGLE MOTHERS

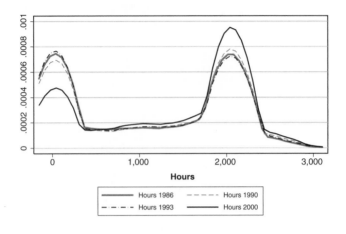

SOURCE: Eissa, Kleven, and Kriener 2008.

these workers have more opportunities to learn about ordinary income taxes (which are still poorly understood). Further, the available evidence from informal and formal surveys suggests that the knowledge about the EITC is relatively high but certainly not universal among the eligible population (Liebman 1998; Phillips 2001; Smeeding, Phillips, and O'Connor 2000; Romich and Weisner 2000). For example, Phillips finds that about 66 percent of families nationally had heard of the EITC. There is scant evidence, however, on what is known about the structure of the EITC, such as the point at which the credit begins to be phased out.

Intertemporal Responses. The sunset of the Bush tax cuts brings front and center the question of workers' willingness to substitute work over time. If workers fully expect taxes to rise in January 2011, they should be willing to substitute work to prior years (given the interest rate, impatience, habit formation, etc.). The elasticity relevant for evaluating the behavioral response to anticipated wage changes is the marginal-utility-of-wealth constant or the Frisch elasticity. Theory suggests that labor supply responses to such anticipated (evolutionary) changes in the after-tax returns to work are larger than those implied by the Marshallian (income constant) elasticity (Blundell and MaCurdy 1999). It therefore represents an upper bound to the wage elasticity reviewed earlier, which keeps unearned income constant.

Most reforms of the tax (and transfer) system can arguably be characterized best as one-time unanticipated shifts in the life-cycle wage profile itself (Blundell 1998). Here, however, the Frisch elasticity would not be appropriate for evaluating effects on labor supply, because it ignores the wealth effect from the one-time shift in the net-wage profile and therefore overestimates the impact of tax changes. Yet a key difficulty in the empirical evaluation of intertemporal response is the distinction between anticipated and unanticipated changes in the wage profile. Card (1994) argues that the existing literature sheds little light on the very questions that motivated the life-cycle model, including how labor supply responds to tax-induced changes in the wage. This is in no small part due to the literature's tendency "to concentrate on one aspect of intertemporal hours-of-work variation (the response to wage growth along a known lifecycle trajectory) and to ignore another (the response to wage innovations that lead to revised expectations about future wage points)" (Card 1994, 1). For the most part, earlier reviews of empirical work dismissed intertemporal labor supply responses (MaCurdy 1985), though recent work has generally been more favorable to such responses. Still, it is notable that estimates of the Frisch elasticity, while larger than traditional estimates, remain fairly moderate for males (Mulligan 1995; Blundell, Meghir, and Neves 1993; Kimmel and Kniser 1998; Ziliak and Kniesner 1999; Kniesner and Ziliak 2005, 2006).

Mulligan (1995) presents an exhaustive review of the evidence on the intertemporal elasticity of substitution (from aggregate time-series and life-cycle patterns, individual panel data, time-diary studies, seasonal cycles, and other temporary episodes), and argues against the consensus that intertemporal responses are trivial. In fact, his preferred intertemporal elasticity of labor supply is 2.

Kniesner and Ziliak (2005) use a canonical life-cycle model of consumption and labor supply, with uncertainty and intertemporal separability. They estimate the model using PSID data on male household heads spanning the 1981, 1986, 1990, 1993, and 1997 tax acts that together lowered the number of tax brackets from sixteen to four, the top marginal tax rate from 70 percent to 39.6 percent, and the lowest rate from −7.65 to −40 percent (due to the EITC). Their estimates suggest a Frisch-substitution elasticity of labor supply of 0.54, and fairly moderate intertemporal shifting of hours worked by male household heads to the anticipated increase in the real after-tax wage.

Overall, recent evidence suggests that intertemporal responses to the Bush tax cuts may be significant. The size of the elasticity suggests as well the potential for nontrivial welfare gains from higher after-tax wages resulting from revenue-neutral tax reform (Kniesner and Ziliak 2006). I explore the welfare effects of tax cuts in the next section, focusing exclusively on the impact of the prominence of discrete labor supply responses.

Implications for Welfare Evaluation of Tax Reform

The finding that labor force participation responses are more significant than hours-worked responses has several important implications for the design of tax transfer programs and for the welfare evaluation of taxation. Recent work by Saez (2002b) has shown that accounting for labor force participation responses can change the optimal transfer program. In particular, Saez shows that with sufficiently high participation elasticities, the optimal tax transfer scheme can be similar to the EITC—with negative marginal tax rates at the bottom of the earnings distribution. An EITC would, on the other hand, be inefficient in a standard model with only intensive (hours worked) responses.[9]

Liebman (2002) extends this work by examining more closely the optimal design of the EITC. He uses a microsimulation model calibrated to 1999 CPS data to illustrate the trade-offs in the design of an EITC—including the optimal maximum credit, and phase-in and phaseout rates—with fixed costs and participation effects. Liebman finds that the efficiency cost of transferring income through the EITC is substantially lower than previous studies have found, in large part because of the participation response of single mothers and the associated reduced welfare spending. His simulations suggest a cost of less than $2 to provide a transfer worth $1 to EITC recipients.

Eissa, Kleven, and Kreiner (2008) examine the impact of participation responses on the welfare evaluation of actual tax reforms. They extend the standard framework for welfare evaluation of tax reforms to account for discrete labor market entry by way of nonconvexities in preferences and budget sets. Such nonconvexities are significant because they allow first-order welfare effects along the extensive (participation) margin. Eissa, Kleven, and Kreiner show that the marginal deadweight burden of tax reform is given by the effect that behavioral responses have on government revenue, where the behavioral revenue effect is related to the two different margins of labor supply response. The first effect captures the revenue effect from the change in the optimal hours of work for those who are working. The second effect captures the effect on revenue brought about by the tax-induced change in labor force participation. While the second effect on efficiency is related to the tax rate on labor force participation, the efficiency effect from changed working hours depends on the tax burden on the last dollar earned:

$$
\frac{\partial EB/\partial\theta}{\sum_{i=1}^{N} w_i \bar{h}_i P_i(\tilde{q}_i)} = \sum_{i=1}^{N} \left[\frac{m_i}{1-m_i} \frac{\partial m_i}{\partial\theta} \varepsilon_i + \frac{a_i}{1-a_i} \frac{\partial a_i}{\partial\theta} \eta_i \right] s_i
$$

Here w is the wage, h is hours, m is the marginal tax rate, a is the average tax rate, ε is the hours elasticity, η is the participation elasticity, θ is the reform, and s is the wage share for individual i.

Eissa, Kleven, and Kreiner (2008) simulate the effects of the 1986, 1990, 1993, and 2001 tax acts in the United States (incorporating all federal income tax changes, not just the EITC) and show that each had different effects on tax rates along the intensive and extensive margins (see figure 3-9). The 1993 expansion, for example, reduced the tax rates on labor force participation, but increased the marginal tax rates on hours worked for most workers. The authors show that conflating these two tax rates in welfare analysis can be fundamentally misleading. For tax reforms that change average tax rates differently from how they change marginal tax rates (such as the 1993 expansion of the EITC), ignoring the participation margin can lead even to the wrong sign of the welfare effect.

Their analysis shows that the 2001 tax cut generated substantial welfare gains (of $1.40 per dollar reduction in the tax burden for their central elasticity estimate of 0.5) due to the strong participation response. Their estimates suggest that the 2001 tax cuts have created pure efficiency gains,

FIGURE 3-9

CHANGES IN MARGINAL AND PARTICIPATION TAX RATES

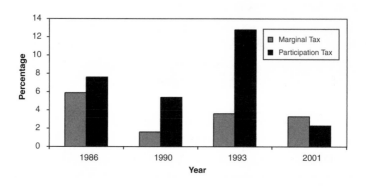

SOURCE: Eissa, Kleven, and Kriener 2008.
NOTE: The changes in marginal and average tax rates reflect only changes at the federal level, calculated as the difference between the post- and pre-reform rates. The pre-reform tax rate is calculated for the years 1985, 1990, 1993 and 2000, respectively. The post-reform tax rates is imputed for federal tax rules that apply in 1988, 1993, 1996, and 2002, respectively, to allow for the phase-in of the reforms. Tax rate changes are calculated as an average for all individuals in the sample. Data come from the March Current Population Surveys.

such that the tax cuts could potentially be justified even with distortionary financing and without incorporating social welfare weights that are higher for single mothers than for the rest of the population. That is, if one were to finance the tax cuts through lump-sum taxation, which involves a marginal cost of funds less than or equal to 1, the reforms would increase aggregate utilitarian welfare.[10]

More recently, Eissa and Hoynes (2008) examine the welfare effects of changing EITC schedule parameters for single mothers. Table 3-5 presents their findings on expanding the EITC by reducing the phaseout (panel A) and then by raising the subsidy rates (panel B) from their current levels by one percentage point. The table shows that the welfare effects arise both on the extensive and intensive margins (columns 1 and 2), and that they can move in opposite directions (panel B). Eissa and Hoynes (2008) show that reducing the phaseout rate is welfare improving, and for high elasticities could be justified without appealing to any welfare weights for single mothers (column 4). Changing the subsidy rate, on the other

TABLE 3-5

WELFARE EFFECTS OF PHASE-OUT RATE CHANGES ON SINGLE PARENTS

		Efficiency Gains				
	Elasticity Composition	Intensive	Extensive	Total	Traditional	Welfare Gain per Dollar Revenue
A. Marginal Reform 1: 2004 EITC with lower phaseout rate						
Low	ε=0, η=0.2	0.000	0.019	0.019	0.043	1.120
Middle	ε=0.1, η=0.3	0.022	0.029	0.050	0.086	1.391
High	ε=0.2, η=0.4	0.043	0.039	0.082	0.129	1.834
Middle [reversed]	ε=0.3, η=0.1	0.065	0.010	0.074	0.086	1.706
B. Marginal Reform 2: 2004 EITC with higher phaseout rate						
Low	ε=0, η=0.2	0.000	–0.018	–0.018	0.100	1.118
Middle	ε=0.1, η=0.3	0.050	–0.026	0.023	0.199	0.877
High	ε=0.2, η=0.4	0.100	–0.035	0.064	0.299	0.721
Middle [reversed]	ε=0.3, η=0.1	0.149	–0.009	0.140	0.199	0.542
C: Marginal Reform 3: 2004 EITC with lower subsidy rate						
Low	ε=0, η=0.2	0.000	–0.024	–0.024	0.129	1.080
Middle	ε=0.1, η=0.3	0.065	–0.035	0.029	0.258	0.916
High	ε=0.2, η=0.4	0.129	–0.047	0.082	0.388	0.796
Middle [reversed]	ε=0.3, η=0.1	0.194	–0.012	0.182	0.258	0.637
D. Marginal Reform 4: 2004 EITC with higher subsidy rate						
Low	ε=0, η=0.2	0.000	0.024	0.024	–0.021	1.080
Middle	ε=0.1, η=0.3	–0.011	0.036	0.026	–0.043	1.086
High	ε=0.2, η=0.4	–0.021	0.049	0.027	–0.064	1.091
Middle	ε=0.3, η=0.1	–0.032	0.012	–0.020	–0.043	0.943

SOURCE: Authors' tabulations of the 2005 March CPS.

NOTES: The participation elasticity is given by η and the compensated hours of work elasticity is given by ε. The welfare gain is measured in percentage of wage income. The total welfare gain is calculated as the sum of the intensive and extensive gains. The "traditional" welfare gain is calculated assuming that the total labor supply elasticity is entirely along the intensive margin. The welfare gain per dollar spent equals RTB/(RTB–EG), where EG is the efficiency gain and RTB is the reduction in tax burden.

hand, generates smaller welfare gains, and so could be justified only with substantial weights on the welfare of single mothers. Workers in the subsidy region receive a lower marginal rate, but their gains are offset by the losses of workers further up the income distribution who now face the high marginal tax rates in the phaseout region.

Comparing the results for the two instruments, Eissa and Hoynes find welfare effects per dollar spent are more sensitive to the size of the labor supply elasticity when the phaseout rate is changed. More generally, even given its current size, expansions of the credit (lower phaseout/higher subsidy) generate greater welfare gains than contractions (characterized by higher phaseout/lower subsidy).

Conclusions

The overall effect of the Bush tax cuts on labor supply behavior depends in large part on which margins of labor supply are evaluated. An extensive body of work evaluating the effects of taxes on labor supply suggests hours worked by working taxpayers are not responsive to taxes, even for married women. A careful reading of the evidence, however, suggests that labor market entry and exit are very sensitive to taxes, especially for female household heads but also for married women. This finding is suggested by early work on the Negative Income Tax Experiments (Robins 1985), statistical models of labor supply (Mroz 1987), nonlinear estimation methods (Triest 1990), and quasi-experimental evaluation of behavioral responses to tax cuts (see reviews in Hotz and Scholz 2003 and Eissa and Hoynes 2006). Eissa and Hoynes (2006) point to two main lessons learned from evaluations of behavioral responses to EITC expansions: first, the evidence confirms that real responses to taxes are important, and second, it shows that the labor supply response is concentrated along the extensive (entry) margin. This evidence suggests that the effects of the tax cuts on this narrow measure of labor supply may be seen more in the participation decision of females.

The concentration of labor supply responses along the extensive margin has important implications for the welfare evaluation of tax reforms. Tax changes have different effects on the participation and hours margins that can move in opposite directions (for example, with an expansion of the

EITC). This distinction, along with the different behavioral responses along the two margins of labor supply, can lead to errors in estimates of the efficiency effects of tax changes. Eissa, Kleven, and Kreiner (2008) show that the 2001 tax cuts create pure efficiency gains for single mothers, and that most of the gains occurred along the participation margin.

Labor supply, however, is more than hours worked and labor force participation; it includes occupational choice and human capital formation. Direct evidence on broader measures of labor supply is limited, but several observations suggest that these measures are responsive to taxes. An especially interesting result that speaks to this point is the surge in reported wage and salary earnings of high-income men following TRA86 with no corresponding change in their hours of work (Moffitt and Wilhelm 2000). Another piece of evidence comes from findings that the marginal tax rate and the progressivity of the tax schedule reduce entry into self-employment and entrepreneurial activity (Gentry and Hubbard 2005).

An especially unusual feature of the tax cuts is their extensive use of phase-ins and the legislated sunset of all the tax cuts in 2010. On the one hand, gradual phase-in of small changes in tax rates may mute the response if taxpayers fail to perceive the changed incentives. Yet an intriguing question is to what extent the sunset of the tax cuts generates intertemporal responses that work in the opposite direction.

Notes

1. See the discussion in Romer and Romer (2008).

2. The child tax credit offsets federal income tax liability and encourages work; it therefore expands the returns to work for eligible parents.

3. The results are qualitatively similar if all tax-filing units are assigned the expected value of itemized deductions (by filing status and by income class).

4. These average rates are larger than expected because of the assumption that tax filers itemize only their state income taxes.

5. The increase in after-tax income could be interpreted as the change from its pretax cut level.

6. These tabulations are calculated using the 1984–2007 March Current Population Surveys. The sample includes all women aged nineteen to forty-four who are not in school or disabled. We also drop the relatively small number of women who report working positive hours but have zero earnings or report positive earnings but zero hours. For these calculations, employment is defined by any work over the (prior) calendar year.

7. This range excludes the estimates from Hotz, Mullin, and Scholz (2002). Their studies differ from the others in that their sample is limited to current or past welfare recipients.

8. An opposing view is that workers choose an hours-wage package and can choose to change jobs in response.

9. Saez (2002b) shows that the optimal program is instead a classical negative income tax program, with a substantial income guarantee that is phased out at a high rate.

10. The marginal cost of funds for lump-sum taxation is generally below 1 because, assuming that leisure is a normal good, such taxes make individuals work more (Ballard and Fullerton 1992). In the absence of income effects (quasi-linear utility), the marginal cost of funds is exactly 1.

References

Altonji, J. G. 1986. Intertemporal substitution in labor supply: Evidence from micro data. *Journal of Political Economy* 94 (part 2): S176–S215.

Auten, Gerald, Robert Carroll, and Geoffrey Gee. 2008. The 2001 and 2003 tax rate reductions: Overview and a look at the taxable income response. *National Tax Journal* 61: 345–64.

Ballard, Charles L., and Don Fullerton. 1992. Distortionary taxes and the provision of public goods. *Journal of Economic Perspectives* 6: 117–31.

Barthold, Thomas A., Thomas Koerner, and John F. Navratil. 1998. Effective marginal tax rates under the federal individual income tax: Death by one thousand pin pricks? *National Tax Journal* 51 (3): 553–64.

Blomquist, N.S., and W. Newey. 1997. Nonparametric estimation of labor supply functions generated by piecewise linear budget constraints. Working Paper No. 1997:24, Department of Economics, Uppsala University, Sweden.

Blundell, Richard. 1998. Consumer demand and intertemporal allocations: Engel, Slutsky, and Frisch. In *Econometrics and economic theory in the 20th century: The Ragnar Frisch Centennial Symposium*, ed. S. Strøm, 147–66. Cambridge: Cambridge University Press.

Blundell, Richard, and Thomas MaCurdy. 1999. Labor supply: a review of alternative approaches. In *Handbook of labor economics.* Vol 3a, ed. O. Ashenfelter and D. Card, 1559–1695. Amsterdam: Elsevier Science.

Blundell, Richard, Costas Meghir, and Pedro Neves. 1993. Labor supply and intertemporal substitution. *Journal of Econometrics* 59 (1): 137–60.

Blundell R. W., A. Duncan, and C. Meghir. 1998. Estimating labor supply responses using tax policy reforms. *Econometrica* 66: 827–61.

Bosworth, Barry, and Gary Burtless. 1992. Effects of tax reform on labor supply, investment, and saving. *Journal of Economic Perspectives* 6 (1): 3–25.

Bound, John, Charles Brown, and Nancy Mathiowetz. 2001. Measurement error in survey data. In *Handbook of econometrics.* vol. 5, ed. E. E. Lerner and J. J. Heckman, 3705–3843. New York: North Holland Publishing.

Burtless, Gary. 1991. The supply side legacy of the Reagan years: Effects on labor supply. In *The economic legacy of the Reagan years: Euphoria or chaos?* ed. A. P. Sahu and Ronald Tracy, 43-63. New York: Praeger, 43–63.

Card, David. 1994. Intertemporal labor supply: An assessment. In Christopher Sims, ed., *Advances in econometrics, Sixth World Congress.* New York: Cambridge University Press.

Chetty, Raj, Kory Kroft, and Adam Looney. 2007. *Salience and taxation: Theory and evidence.* NBER Working Paper No. 13330, Cambridge, MA.

Cogan, John. 1981. Fixed costs and labor supply *Econometrica* 49 (4): 945–63.

Congressional Budget Office (CBO). 2007. *The effect of tax changes on labor supply in CBO's microsimulation tax model.* Washington, DC: CBO.

Conway, Karen Smith. 1997. Labor supply, taxes, and government spending: A microeconometric analysis. *Review of Economics and Statistics* 79, no. 1: 50–67.

Cullen, Julie Berry, and Roger H. Gordon. 2007. Taxes and entrepreneurial activity: Theory and evidence for the U.S. *Journal of Public Economics* 91 (7): 1479–1505.

de Bartolome, Charles. 1995. Which tax rate do people use: Average or marginal? *Journal of Public Economics* 56: 79–96.

Dickert, Stacy, Scott Houser, and John Karl Scholz. 1995. The earned income tax credit and transfer programs: A study of labor market and program participation. In *Tax policy and the economy*. Vol. 9, ed. James Poterba, 1–50. Cambridge, MA: MIT Press.

Eissa, Nada. 1995. *Taxation and labor supply of married women: The Tax Reform Act of 1986 as a natural experiment*. NBER Working Paper No. 5023, Cambridge, MA.

Eissa, Nada, and Hilary Hoynes. 2004. Taxes and the labor market participation of married couples: The Earned Income Tax Credit. *Journal of Public Economics* 88 (August): 1931–58.

_____. 2006. Behavioral responses to taxes: Lessons from the EITC and labor supply. *Tax policy and the economy*. Vol. 20, ed. James M. Poterba, 74–110. Cambridge, MA: MIT Press.

_____. 2007. The hours of work response of married couples: Taxes and the Earned Income Tax Credit. In *Tax policy and labor market performance*, ed. Jonas Agell and Peter Birch Sørensen, 187–227. Cambridge, MA: MIT Press.

_____. 2008. Redistribution and tax expenditures: The Earned Income Tax Credit. NBER Working Paper No. 12924, Cambridge, MA.

Eissa, Nada, Henrik Kleven, and Claus Kreiner. 2008. Evaluation of four tax reforms in the United States: Labor supply and welfare effects for single mothers. *Journal of Public Economics* 92, no. 3-4: 795–816.

Eissa, Nada, and Jeffrey Liebman. 1996. Labor supply response to the Earned Income Tax Credit. *Quarterly Journal of Economics* 111: 605–37.

Ellwood, David. 2000. The impact of the Earned Income Tax Credit and social policy reforms on work, marriage and living arrangements. *National Tax Journal* 53 (4), part 2: 1063–1106.

Feldman, Naomi E., and Peter Katuščák. 2006. Should the average tax rate be marginalized? CERGE Working Paper No. 304, Czech Republic.

Finkelstein, Amy N. 2007. E-ZTax: Tax salience and tax rates. NBER Working Paper No. 12924, Cambridge, MA.

Gentry, William, and R. Glenn Hubbard. 2005. "Success taxes," entrepreneurial entry and innovation. In *Innovation policy and the economy*. Vol. 5, eds. Adam B. Jaffee, Josh Lerner and Scott Stern, 87–108. Cambridge, MA: MIT Press.

Hall, Robert E. 1973. Wages, income and hours of work in the U.S. labor force. In *Income maintenance and labor supply: Econometric studies*, eds. Glen Cain and Harold Watts, 102–62. Chicago: Rand McNally.

Hausman, J. 1981. Labor supply. In *How taxes affect economic behavior*, ed. H. Aaron and J. Pechman, 27–71. Washington, DC: Brookings Institution.

_____. 1985. Taxes and labor supply. In *Handbook of public economics*. Vol. 1, ed. A. Auerbach and M. Feldstein, 213–63. Amsterdam: Elsevier Science.

Heckman, James. 1983. Comment. In *Behavioral simulations in tax policy analysis*, ed. Martin Feldstein, 70–82. Chicago: University of Chicago Press.

_____. 2005. The effect of taxation on labor supply, education and the acquisition of skills in the workplace. Testimony before the President's Advisory Panel on Federal Tax Reform. Gleacher Center, Graduate School of Business, University of Chicago.

_____, and T. E. MaCurdy. 1980. A life-cycle model of female labour supply. *Review of Economic Studies* 47: 47–74.

Heim, Bradley. 2008. The impact of the Earned Income Tax Credit on the labor supply of married couples: Structural estimation and business cycle interactions. Unpublished manuscript.

Hotz, V. Joseph, and John Karl Scholz. 2003. The Earned Income Tax Credit. In *Means-tested transfer programs in the United States*, ed. Robert Moffitt, 141–97. Chicago: University of Chicago Press.

Hotz, V. Joseph, Charles H. Mullin, and John Karl Scholz. 2002. Welfare benefits, employment and income: Evidence from the California Work Pays Demonstration Project. Unpublished manuscript.

_____. 2005. Examining the Effect of the Earned Income Tax Credit on the Labor Market Participation of Families on Welfare. http://www.ssc.wisc.edu/~scholz/Research/EITC_Draft.pdf.

Juhn, Chinhui. 1992. Decline in male labor market participation: The role of declining market opportunities. *Quarterly Journal of Economics* 107 (February): 79–121.

Keane, Michael, and Robert Moffitt. 1998. A structural model of multiple welfare program participation and labor supply. *International Economic Review* 39 (3): 553–89.

Kimmel, Jean, and Thomas J. Kniesner. 1998. New evidence on labor supply: employment versus hours elasticities by sex and marital status. *Journal of Monetary Economics* 42 (2): 289–301.

Kniesner, Thomas, and James Ziliak. 2005. The effect of income taxation on consumption and labor supply. *Journal of Labor Economics* 23 (4): 769–96.

_____. 2006. Evidence of tax-induced individual behavioral responses. Paper presented at conference on tax reform, James A. Baker III Institute for Public Policy, Rice University, Houston, TX.

Kotlikoff, Laurence, and David Rapson. 2006. Does it pay, at the margin, to work and save? Measuring effective marginal taxes on Americans' labor supply and saving. NBER Working Paper No. 12533, Cambridge, MA.

Liebman, Jeffrey. 1998. The impact of the Earned Income Tax Credit on incentives and the income distribution. In *Tax policy and the economy*. Vol. 12, ed. James Poterba, 83–119. Cambridge, MA: MIT Press.

_____. 2002. The optimal design of the Earned Income Tax Credit. In *Making work pay: The Earned Income Tax Credit and its impact on American families*, ed. Bruce D. Meyer and Douglas Holtz-Eakin, 196–233. New York: Russell Sage Foundation.

_____, and Emmanuel Saez. 2006. Earnings responses to increases in payroll taxes. Mimeo, Kennedy School of Government, Harvard University, Cambridge MA. http://www.hks.harvard.edu/jeffreyliebman/liebman_saez_october.15.2006.pdf.

_____, and Richard J. Zeckhauser. 2004. Schmeduling. Working paper, Kennedy School of Government, Harvard University, Cambridge, MA.

MaCurdy, Thomas E. 1981. An empirical model of labour supply in a life-cycle setting. *Journal of Political Economy* 89(6): 1059–85.

_____. 1985. Interpreting empirical models of labor supply in an intertemporal framework with uncertainty, In *Longitudinal analysis of labor market data*, ed. James Heckman and B. Singer. Cambridge: Cambridge University Press.

MaCurdy, T., D. Green, and H. Paarsch. 1990. Assessing empirical approaches for analyzing taxes and labor supply. *Journal of Human Resources* 25: 415–90.

Meyer, Bruce, and Dan Rosenbaum. 2000. Making single mothers work: Recent tax and welfare policy and its effects. *National Tax Journal* 53 (4), part 2: 1027–62.

_____. 2001. Welfare, the Earned Income Tax Credit, and the labor supply of single mothers. *Quarterly Journal of Economics* 116, no. 3 (August): 1063–1114.

Moffitt, Robert. 1990. Introduction. *Journal of Human Resources* 25 (3): 313–16.

_____, and Mark O. Wilhelm. 2000. Taxation and the labor supply decisions of the affluent. In *Does Atlas shrug? The economic consequences of taxing the rich*, ed. Joel Slemrod. Cambridge, MA: Russell Sage Foundation and Harvard University Press.

Mosisa, Abraham, and Steven Hipple. 2006. Trends in labor force participation in the United States. *Monthly Labor Review* 129 (10): 35–57.

Mroz, Thomas. 1987. The sensitivity of an empirical model of married women's hours of work to economic and statistical assumptions. *Econometrica* 55: 765–99.

Mulligan, Casey. 1995. The intertemporal elasticity of work: What does the evidence say? Paper presented at the annual meeting of the Population Association of America, San Francisco, California.

Ohanian, Lee, Andrea Raffo, and Richard Rogerson. 2006. *Long-term changes in labor supply and taxes: Evidence from OECD countries, 1956–2004.* Research Working Paper 06-16, Federal Reserve Bank of Kansas City, Economic Research Department.

Phillips, Katherin Ross. 2001. *Who knows about the Earned Income Tax Credit?* Urban Institute, New Federalism, National Survey of America's Families, Series B, No. B-27. http://www.urban.org/UploadedPDF/anf_b27.pdf.

Prescott, Edward. 2004. Why do Americans work so much more than Europeans? *Federal Reserve Bank of Minneapolis Quarterly Review* 28 (1): 2–13.

Robins, P. 1985. A comparison of the labor supply findings from the the Negative Income Tax Experiments. *Journal of Human Resources* 20: 567–82.

Romer, Christina, and David Romer. 2008. A narrative analysis of postwar tax changes. Working paper, University of California at Berkeley, Department of Economics.

Romich, Jennifer L., and Thomas Weisner. 2000. How families view and use the EITC: Advance payment versus lump sum delivery. *National Tax Journal* 53 (4), part 2: 1245–1265.

Rosen, Harvey S. 1976. Taxes in a labor supply model with joint wage-hours determination. *Econometrica* 44: 485–507.

Rothstein, Jesse. 2008. *The unintended consequences of encouraging work: Tax incidence and the EITC.* Working paper, Princeton University, Princeton, NJ. http://www.princeton.edu/~jrothst/workingpapers/rothstein_eitc_may122008.pdf.

Saez, Emmanuel. 2002a. Do taxpayers bunch at kink points? Mimeo, University of California, Berkeley, and NBER. http://elsa.berkeley.edu/~saez/bunch.pdf.

———. 2002b. Optimal income transfer programs: Intensive versus extensive labor supply responses. *Quarterly Journal of Economics* 117: 1039–73.

Smeeding, Timothy, Katherin Ross Phillips, and Michael O'Connor. 2000. The EITC: Expectation, knowledge, use, and economic and social mobility. *National Tax Journal* 53 (4), part 2: 1187–1210.

Triest, Robert 1990. The effect of income taxation on labor supply in the United States. *Journal of Human Resources* 25: 491–516.

U.S. House of Representatives. Committee on Ways and Means Report No. 107-007. 2001. Economic growth and tax reflief act of 2001. http://frwebgate.access. gpo. gov/cgibin/getdoc.cgi?dbname=107_cong_reports&doc d=f:hr007.107.pdf.

Ziliak, James P., and Thomas J. Kniesner. 1999. Estimating life cycle labor supply tax effects. *Journal of Political Economy* 107 (2): 326–59.

4

A Response to Nada Eissa

Steven J. Davis

The chapter by Nada Eissa provides a timely evaluation of tax cuts on labor income during the presidency of George W. Bush. The cuts were moderate in size and extended across the income distribution. Eissa calculates that legislation enacted in 2001, 2002, and 2003 lowered marginal federal income tax rates by 2.6 percentage points on average across households, and lowered average income tax rates by 2.7 percentage points. One goal of the chapter is to gauge the likely impact of these tax cuts on labor supply.

Some of the evidence reviewed by Eissa suggests that the Bush tax cuts had a very modest effect on labor supply. According to the illustrative calculations in table 3-3, for example, the Bush tax cuts raised hours worked by a mere nine hours per person (twenty-three through fifty-nine years old) per year. These calculations neglect heterogeneity among workers in tax changes and response behavior, however, and they do not disentangle responses on the hours and employment margins. Whether—and how much—these simplifications understate the overall response of hours worked to the Bush tax cuts is unclear. The chapter acknowledges these issues but does not tackle them directly.

Other evidence suggests that labor supply is highly responsive to taxes for some demographic groups on some margins. Thus Eissa writes in her conclusion that a "careful reading of the evidence . . . suggests that labor market entry and exit are very sensitive to taxes, especially for female household heads but also for married women." Eissa also notes that labor supply responses to taxes are not limited to decisions about how many hours to work and whether to get a job.

Micro and Macro Studies of Labor Supply Responses to Taxes

In her review of empirical evidence, Eissa focuses on studies of individual labor supply responses to tax changes. These studies typically find small elasticities of hours worked in response to tax rate changes for most demographic groups. Small elasticities multiplied by the moderate size of the Bush tax cuts yield the small overall hours effect reported in table 3-3.

Several recent studies find larger elasticities of hours worked with respect to country-level changes and differences in tax rates. Examples include Prescott (2004), Davis and Henrekson (2005), Rogerson (2006), and Gordon (2007). One reason these macro studies find bigger elasticities is that they capture government spending-side responses to tax changes, responses that are usually ignored in studies of individual labor supply. Spending-side responses matter for labor supply outcomes, perhaps as much as or more than the direct effects operating on the tax side.

To see the implications of spending-side responses, consider a hike in labor income tax rates that increases government revenues. It is helpful to distinguish three cases:

A. Use the extra revenues to fund government purchases of goods and services that are not substitutable with private spending. Military spending is the leading example that approximately satisfies this requirement.

B. Use the extra revenues to fund lump-sum transfers to households. "Lump sum" means that the transfers are not means tested or otherwise dependent on the recipient's behavior or circumstances.

C. Use the extra revenues to fund government safety net and social insurance programs. Leading examples include government programs for Medicaid, food stamps, unemployment insurance, and disability payments.

In case A, the extra government spending has no effect on household resources or incentives, and not much is lost by ignoring spending-side responses. In this case, the tax hike affects labor supply through direct effects of tax rates on individual work incentives and through general equilibrium responses. The individual work incentives involve the substitution and income effects that are staples of micro-oriented labor supply studies. Thus the basic approach taken by Eissa and other micro-oriented studies (CBO 2007, for example) captures the full effect of tax rate changes on aggregate hours worked when (a) the government spending-side response approximates the conditions of case A, and (b) there are no important general equilibrium effects on labor supply.

In case B, the extra government spending reduces individual work incentives through an income effect. The lump-sum transfer payments make households richer, so they work less. To a first approximation, this income effect on the spending side cancels out the income effect on the tax side. On net, we are left with a pure substitution response to the tax hike. According to table 2 in CBO (2007), the substitution elasticity is 78 percent greater than the total wage elasticity that captures both income and substitution effects.[1] Thus, using CBO assumptions, the tax hike lowers aggregate hours by 78 percent more in case B than in case A.

In case C, the tax hike lowers aggregate hours by an even larger amount, because the benefit side of social insurance programs discourages work activity through means testing, other eligibility requirements, and phaseout provisions. The available evidence indicates that labor supply elasticities with respect to benefits for unemployment insurance, worker compensation, and disability insurance are substantially higher than those found in traditional labor supply studies (Krueger and Meyer 2002). If this pattern holds broadly for government transfer payments, then the effect of a tax hike on aggregate hours in case C may be more than twice as large as in case A.

Most government spending in the United States and other rich countries is for transfer payments to households. Differences among rich countries in the fraction of gross domestic product (GDP) devoted to government spending are also mainly the result of transfer payments. Likewise, transfer payments largely account for the more rapid growth of government spending relative to GDP in Western Europe than in the United States since the 1960s. These facts suggest that the data variation used in macro studies of rich-country tax responses is closer to case C than case A.

These observations lead me to three conclusions. First, spending-side responses to tax changes are an important determinant of the overall response of hours worked. Second, macro-oriented studies find bigger labor supply responses to tax changes than micro-oriented studies, partly because the macro studies capture the spending-side responses of government behavior. Third, if future tax hikes lead to bigger government, they will discourage labor supply by substantially more than the micro-oriented studies suggest.

Longer-Run and Equilibrium Responses to Taxes

Traditional micro-oriented studies of labor supply behavior also understate the longer-run response to tax rate changes for another set of reasons. At the individual level, an adjustment in hours worked may require a job switch, a change in child-care arrangements, or other significant lifestyle changes. Bringing about such changes often involves large fixed costs and some time. As a result, the full response of hours worked to tax rate changes involves lumpy adjustments at the individual level, and unfolds slowly over time in the population. Most micro-oriented studies of labor supply behavior are not designed to effectively capture this type of dynamic response.

Equilibrium responses to tax changes are also likely to unfold slowly over time and to involve effects not captured by micro-oriented studies.[2] Consider the example of underground economic activity motivated by a desire to evade taxes. High tax rates on labor income encourage households to supply labor and procure goods and services in the underground economy. Tax evasion of this sort requires cooperation between at least two persons, a buyer and a seller. A key point is that it becomes easier to find a willing accomplice for off-the-books exchange in a higher-tax environment. When taxes are high generally, more people seek accomplices to help evade taxes. In this respect, the underground economy is a network that becomes more attractive as more people participate. Such networks are slow to evolve and, once in place, can be difficult to eradicate.

Two conclusions follow from this brief discussion of taxes and the underground economy. First, micro-oriented studies do not capture the network effect sketched above, because they rely on individual-specific variation to identify the effect of taxes on labor supply. For this reason, they understate the extent to which taxes lead to an expansion of the underground economy at the expense of the legal market economy. Second, because networks are slow to evolve and dissipate, taxes have a slow-working effect on the amount of labor supplied to the underground economy.

Schneider and Enste (2000) and Davis and Henrekson (2005) review evidence on taxes and the underground economy and provide references to the literature. Davis and Henrekson also stress that micro-oriented labor supply studies are unlikely to capture the full effect of taxes on substitution between market activity and home production, e.g., eating in a restaurant versus eating a meal prepared at home. Lindbeck (1995) discusses other reasons for delayed responses to the economic disincentives created by high tax rates and generous social insurance programs.

Labor Supply Responses on Other Margins

In her review of the evidence, Eissa focuses on the decision of whether to work, and how many hours to work when employed. This focus mirrors most of the literature and available evidence. Many, many studies investigate the response of employment and hours worked to taxes. As Eissa acknowledges, labor supply responses on other margins are harder to measure and, as a result, are much less studied. Of course, that does not mean that other response margins are small or unimportant, or that we can safely ignore them in forming judgments about tax policy.

A fundamental point is the following: the negative impact of income taxes on economic efficiency is potentially large even when hours and employment are not very responsive to taxes. What matters for efficiency under reasonable conditions is the elasticity of taxable income, as shown by Feldstein (1999). Chetty (2008) generalizes the Feldstein analysis to cover situations where part of the cost of tax evasion and tax avoidance involves a transfer of resources to other persons in the economy. The chapter by Giertz in this volume reviews what we know about the elasticity of taxable income.

The study of taxable income elasticities is attractive because of its promise to capture the full range of labor supply responses to tax changes without the need to identify and isolate every important response margin. However, the taxable income approach presents its own problems, and the literature in this area has not reached anything approaching a consensus. For this reason, among others, it is important to directly investigate other labor supply response margins such as schooling and training, occupational choice, the form of compensation, immigration and emigration, the choice between market provision and home production, and the choice between legal activities subject to personal taxes and underground activities that evade taxes.

Eissa mentions two recent studies that investigate tax effects on entrepreneurial activity. Gentry and Hubbard (2005) stress the potential for high tax rates and a progressive tax schedule to discourage risk-taking activities by acting as a tax on "success." Because of tax progressivity, a risk-neutral investor requires a higher pretax expected return to undertake a risky project or business enterprise. The effect is to discourage risk-taking business activities. Cullen and Gordon (2007) point out that the option to incorporate weakens or reverses this effect when the corporate income tax rate is lower than the personal tax rate. In this case, the option to incorporate effectively allows the entrepreneur to choose a lower tax rate ex post in the event that the enterprise succeeds. Cullen and Gordon also analyze other channels through which the tax system affects entrepreneurship and risk taking. The overall effect of tax changes on risk taking depends very much on the details. For example, a five percentage point across-the-board reduction in personal tax rates discourages risk-taking activity, according to their analysis, but a move to a Hall-Rabushka flat tax (Hall and Rabushka 1995) with a 20 percent tax rate encourages it.

A progressive income tax schedule also penalizes other types of "success." I will give one example. Like many forms of human capital investment, attending college involves an important tradeoff between income now and income later. If the extra future income attributable to college pushes the individual into a higher tax bracket, then tax progressivity reduces the after-tax rate of return to a college education. In this way, a progressive tax schedule discourages investments in a college education. The same point applies to other human capital investments that involve a tradeoff between income now and income later. I am not aware of studies that directly examine the response of college enrollment rates to tax progressivity, but many studies find that college enrollment rates are sensitive to the rate of return to education. See, for example, Fredriksson and Topel (2007), who document a close relationship between the returns to college and college enrollment rates.

Summary

The chapter by Eissa offers a useful discussion of how work hours respond to labor income tax rates. Like most of the literature, her discussion focuses on micro-oriented studies of individual labor supply behavior. These studies are highly useful, but they neglect several aspects of the broader labor supply response to taxes.

With respect to hours worked, the full impact of a change in labor income tax rates is bigger than suggested by micro-oriented studies for several reasons. First, the micro-oriented studies typically neglect government-spending responses to tax changes and the impact of government spending on labor supply. Second, most micro-oriented studies are not designed to effectively capture the longer-term effects of taxes on individual labor supply decisions. Third, studies of individual labor supply do not capture equilibrium responses to tax rate changes.

Notes

1. The figures in the top row of Eissa's table 3-3 imply that the pure substitution response is 59 percent greater than the "total" response, where the 59 percent figure is computed as 100 (14-8.8) / 8.8.

2. My discussion here does not cover the full range of potentially important equilibrium labor supply responses to taxes.

References

Chetty, Raj. 2008. Is the taxable income elasticity sufficient to calculate deadweight loss? The implications of evasion and avoidance. NBER Working Paper No.13844, Cambridge, MA.

Congressional Budget Office. 2007. *The effect of tax changes on labor supply in CBO's microsimulation tax model.* Washington, DC: CBO. April.

Cullen, Julie Berry, and Roger H. Gordon. 2007. Taxes and entrepreneurial activity: Theory and evidence for the U.S. *Journal of Public Economics*, 91: 1479–1505.

Davis, Steven J., and Magnus Henrekson. 2005. Tax effects on work activity, industry mix and shadow economy size: Evidence from rich-country comparisons. In *Labour supply and the incentives to work in Europe*, ed. Ramón Gómez-Salvador et al., 44–104. Cheltenham, UK: Edward Elgar.

Feldstein, Martin. 1999. Tax avoidance and the deadweight loss of the income tax. *Review of Economics and Statistics* 81, no. 4: 674–80.

Fredriksson, Peter, and Robert H. Topel. 2007. Wage determination and employment in Sweden since the early 1990s—Wage formation in a new setting. Paper prepared for Reforming the welfare state: Recovery and beyond in Sweden, NBER conference, Stockholm. http://www.nber.org/chapters/ c5360.pdf.

Gentry, William M., and R. Glenn Hubbard. 2005. "Success taxes," entrepreneurial entry, and innovation. In *Innovation policy and the economy* 5, eds. Adam B. Jaffee, Joshua Lerner, and Scott Stern, 87–108. Cambridge, MA: MIT Press.

Gordon, Robert J. 2007. Issues in the comparison of welfare between Europe and the United States. Paper presented to Bureau of European Policy Advisers, Brussels. http://faculty-web.at.northwestern.edu/economics/gordon/BRU_ 071125.pdf.

Hall, Robert E., and Alvin Rabushka. 1995. *The Flat Tax.* 2nd ed. Stanford, CA: Hoover Institution.

Krueger, Alan B., and Bruce D. Meyer. 2002. Labor supply effects of social insurance. In *Handbook of public economics.* Vol. 4, ed. Alan J. Auerbach and Martin Feldstein. Amsterdam: Elsevier Science.

Lindbeck, Assar. 1995. Hazardous welfare state dynamics. *American Economic Review* 85, no. 2: 9–15.

Prescott, Edward. 2004. Why do Americans work so much more than Europeans? *Federal Reserve Bank of Minneapolis Quarterly Review* 28, no. 1: 2–13.

Rogerson, Richard. 2006. Understanding differences in hours worked. *Review of Economic Dynamics* 9 (3): 365–409.

Schneider, Friedrich, and Dominik H. Enste. 2000. Shadow economies: Size, causes, and consequences. *Journal of Economic Literature* 38 (1): 77–114.

5

The Elasticity of Taxable Income: Influences on Economic Efficiency and Tax Revenues, and Implications for Tax Policy

Seth H. Giertz

Taxes are frequently so much more burdensome to the people than they are beneficial to the sovereign.
                                   –Adam Smith, *The Wealth of Nations*

While research into the elasticity of taxable income (ETI), which measures the responsiveness of reported taxable income to changes in tax rates, dates back to at least Lindsey (1987), recognition of its importance as a central parameter for tax policy design did not begin to take hold until the second half of the 1990s.[1] In fact, a 1998 survey to determine public and labor economists' views on key policy parameters (Fuchs, Krueger, and Poterba 1998) included no questions on the ETI.[2] I suspect that a 2008 survey would include such questions, just as I suspect that a 1998 conference entitled "Tax Policy Lessons from the 1990s" would have no session on the elasticity of taxable income. The two 1998 survey questions most likely to provide some insight into the views public economists then held of the ETI asked about the effect of the Tax Reform Act of 1986 (TRA86) and the Omnibus Budget Reconciliation Act of 1993 (OBRA93) on long-run (steady-state) gross domestic product (GDP). For TRA86, a fundamental

The author would like to thank David Weiner and Ed Harris for helpful comments.

reform that broadened the tax base and substantially lowered marginal tax rates, the median response was that steady-state GDP would rise by 1 percent. However, the interquartile range was large, from 0.20 to 3 percent of GDP. For OBRA93, which raised marginal tax rates for primarily upper-income groups, the median response was zero, with an interquartile range from –0.5 to 1 percent of GDP. It is noteworthy that half of public economists surveyed thought that raising marginal tax rates for the highest-income groups (in 1993) would not result in decreased steady-state GDP.

Disagreement among public economists as to the effect of taxes on the economy is embodied by the views of two former chairmen of the president's Council of Economic Advisors (CEA). One former chairman, Martin Feldstein (1995b, 1999), estimated that the 1993 tax increases substantially increased deadweight loss (DWL) and that repealing the rate increases could actually *increase* tax revenue because positive behavioral responses would more than offset the mechanical revenue loss—that is, the loss in tax revenue absent any behavioral responses. Another former CEA chairman, Joseph Stiglitz (2004), viewed the 1993 tax increases in a quite different light: "The Clinton experience showed that raising taxes on the rich does not have the adverse effects that the critics claimed" (4). Additionally, Stiglitz is very critical of the Bush tax cuts, while Feldstein supports the lower marginal tax rates.[3] One could argue that the two former CEA chairmen take such different positions on recent tax policy because of differing political ideologies or party allegiance. However, a more plausible explanation is that they hold very different views of how responsive individuals are to changes in tax rates. Feldstein's estimates for the effects of repealing OBRA93, for example, rest on an ETI estimate that is toward the high end of the literature—although not implausible.[4] Stiglitz, on the other hand, while not directly speaking to the ETI, believes that behavioral responses to tax rates are small (at least for high-income individuals). If the ETI is very small, then the revenue and efficiency implications from repealing OBRA93 would be quite different from those estimated by Feldstein.

Developments in Assessing the Efficiency Implications of Taxation

Economists have long recognized that taxation creates economic inefficiency by distorting the price of leisure relative to that of all other goods in the economy. Even a broad-based income tax can have substantial efficiency costs, so long as leisure remains untaxed. Harberger (1964) uses this as motivation for comparing the efficiency implications of direct versus indirect taxation and in so doing shows how labor supply elasticities can be used to measure the efficiency implications of income taxation. Harberger's analysis won over the profession and led to increased research into labor supply elasticities, which were seen as proxies for the efficiency costs from taxation.[5] More than two decades later, Lindsey (1987) examined the ETI, as opposed to the labor supply elasticity. However, Lindsey emphasized the revenue implications of the ETI and not its efficiency implications.

In addition to producing ETI estimates, Feldstein (1995b) described the behaviors that could affect taxable income and argued that many of these behaviors were not captured by labor supply elasticities. Thus, it is more accurate to state that taxation creates economic inefficiency not only by distorting the relative price of labor and leisure, but more broadly by distorting the relative price of goods or activities that are taxed and those that are not taxed, since leisure is not the only untaxed activity. For example, in response to taxes, not only work hours but also work effort might change. Compensation can shift from taxed forms to nontaxed forms. When tax rates are higher, more compensation is paid in tax-exempt fringe benefits instead of wages, and economic activity may shift from jurisdictions with more burdensome taxes to others where taxes are more favorable. Evasion is another response to taxation that confers DWL, but does not imply increased leisure. In response to higher tax rates, people are more likely to understate their incomes and to overstate their deductions. Over the long run, taxes also influence investment decisions, including how much education to pursue and in what occupations to specialize.

Feldstein (1999)[6] shows that one parameter, the ETI, can capture this wide array of behavioral responses and can then be used to calculate both the efficiency and revenue implications from a change in tax rates. In fact, Feldstein shows that the ETI, along with information on marginal tax rates and income, is all that is necessary to calculate changes in both tax revenue and efficiency.[7] In Harberger's (1964) model, labor is the only source of income, all income is taxed when earned, taxable income thus equals labor income, and the ETI with respect to the tax rate is the same as the labor supply elasticity—or at least the elasticity of labor earnings, since labor hours and labor *earnings* may be imperfectly correlated due to factors such as work effort.[8] Feldstein's model is more complex, recognizing that income comes from many sources and that those sources are taxed differently (or sometimes not taxed at all). Taxpayers can shift income, as well as alter their tax deductions, exclusions, and credits; some of those behaviors result in income escaping the tax base (going untaxed), while others allow taxpayers to shift when and under what base (for example, individual versus corporate) income is reported and taxed. Taxpayers also have some discretion over what share of their income is reported to the tax authorities. In this more realistic setting, taxable income and labor income (and their corresponding tax elasticities) can differ substantially.

The remainder of this chapter is structured as follows: In the next two sections I focus on important developments in ETI research, both empirical and theoretical, over the first decade of the twenty-first century and relate them to important tax issues that the United States will face over the next few years. Next, I examine the two most important Bush tax cuts, the Economic Growth and Tax Relief Reconciliation Act of 2001 (EGTRRA) and the Jobs Growth and Tax Relief Reconciliation Act of 2003 (JGTRRA), which changed our tax system in many ways, including lowering individual marginal tax rates. The tax changes, however, are not permanent—that is, for the most part, the federal tax system will, after 2010, revert to its 2001 state unless additional legislation is enacted. Thus I go on to use a range of ETI estimates from the literature to show how allowing the individual income tax rate cuts to expire might affect economic efficiency and tax revenues.

I find that, based on 2005 data, returning individual income tax rates to their 2001 levels would raise revenues by $98.6 billion, assuming no behavioral responses.[9] At an ETI of 0.2, $15.6 billion of this mechanical increase ($12.2 billion from the federal income tax and $3.4 billion from payroll and state taxes) would be lost due to reductions in taxable income. At an ETI of 0.8, $62.4 billion of the mechanical revenue gain ($48.8 billion from the federal income tax and $13.6 billion from payroll and state taxes) would be lost. The DWL per dollar of additional revenue from the federal income tax is also highly sensitive to the ETI, ranging from $0.18 at an ETI of 0.2 to $1.25 at an ETI of 0.8.[10]

I also calculate Laffer curves (which show the relationship between marginal tax rates and tax revenue) under a range of different ETI assumptions, with special attention focused on the top tax bracket. There is considerable debate about the degree to which changes to tax rates affect revenues. My analysis is not intended to settle this debate, but rather to show what ETI assumptions are implicitly associated with the different points of view. Again, estimates are quite sensitive to the ETI. At an ETI of 0.2, the estimated Laffer tax rate for the top tax bracket is 78 percent; at an ETI of 1, the estimated Laffer rate is just 41 percent—or slightly higher than the current effective marginal tax rate for this group.

Developments in ETI Research since 2000

Slemrod (2002) presents a taxonomy of the ways in which people respond to taxation and the costs associated with this behavior. These can be condensed to four broad areas:

1) *Real behavior.* This involves individuals changing their consumption or the amount they work, for example, by moving away from taxed goods or activities toward those that are untaxed or more lightly taxed. It also includes the shifting of income across tax bases or to jurisdictions where tax rates are more favorable. The labor supply elasticity (which measures the trade-off between time spent on labor and leisure) captures only a portion of that response.

2) *Timing of income receipt.* Sammartino and Weiner (1997) show overall patterns of adjusted gross income (AGI) that are consistent with large transitory shifting at the top of the income distribution surrounding OBRA93. The timing of executive compensation has also been shown quite responsive to OBRA93 (Goolsbee 2000).[11] Changes to the tax treatment of capital gains in 1987, 1997, and 2003 all appear to have had a large short-term influence on realization behavior. (Even the timing of marriages, births, and deaths appears to be influenced by tax considerations.)

3) *Circumvention.* This includes both illegally (evasion) and legally (avoidance) bypassing the tax system. In the case of evasion,

income is concealed or at least not reported to the tax authorities. (See Slemrod and Yitzhaki 2002 and Slemrod 2007.) In the case of avoidance, income is shifted (intertemporally or between sources) so that a taxpayer receives more favorable tax treatment. Diverting income into a tax-deferred retirement account is an example of avoidance. Higher tax rates generally increase the benefits from evasion and avoidance.[12]

4) *Response to administration and compliance policy.* Rigorous enforcement of tax laws and low compliance costs should limit evasion and lead to smaller income responses of reportable taxable income to tax changes. However, the benefits from such polices must be weighed against the government's additional costs of administering and enforcing the tax system, since these costs also represent a loss to society. In contrast, lax enforcement and high compliance costs will tempt taxpayers to hide income, and thus result in larger changes in taxable income when rates change. That implies that, instead of structural parameters, taxable income elasticities are endogenous and a function of institutions. The time and money that taxpayers spend complying with tax laws and regulations are also a substantial source of deadweight loss (Guyton et al. 2003).

Behavioral changes have efficiency implications. To assess them accurately requires that we differentiate real behavioral changes that affect resource allocation from mere accounting maneuvers that simply re-label income. It requires that we distinguish between the shifting of activity from inside to outside the tax base on the one hand, and the shifting of income from one tax base to a different tax base on the other For example, following the Tax Reform Act of 1986, which set the tax rate on Subchapter S income below that on Subchapter C income, Subchapter S income increased nearly threefold as income was shifted from Subchapter C corporations to Subchapter S corporations. That shift of income was simply a transfer from one tax base to another, but since individuals do not report Subchapter C income, only half of the picture was in view: the increase in Subchapter S income. Thus, without information on the drop in

Subchapter C income, the relationship between the marginal income tax rates and taxable personal income can have misleading implications for both economic efficiency and tax revenues.

Issues That Complicate Estimation. The primary methodological objective in the empirical literature is to devise a method for separating the response of taxable income to changes in tax rates from responses to the many other factors that also affect taxable income. Tax changes take place in a changing economic environment, and the changes to that environment affect income growth. Adequately controlling for those non-tax-induced trends in taxable income poses a major challenge to estimating elasticities. In addition, a sound methodology must address several other important issues, including mean reversion, tax rate endogeneity, institutional changes (which often coincide with changes in the rate structure), and the distinction between transitory (or temporary) and permanent (or longer-term) responses. Finally, some behavioral responses involve externalities or transfers between economic agents which alter how the efficiency implications of the ETI should be interpreted. Some of the issues that complicate estimation are discussed in more detail below.

Exogenous Shifts in the Income Distribution and Mean Reversion. The distribution of reported income has widened over the past thirty years. That trend accelerated in the 1980s, especially at the very top of the distribution. According to Piketty and Saez (2003), the share of income reported by the top 10 percent of filers rose by more than 40 percent, from 33 percent in 1979 to 46.8 percent in 2006, with nearly two-thirds of that increase accruing to the top 1 percent of taxpayers.[13] The share of income reported by the top one-half of 1 percent more than doubled, the share reported by the top one-tenth of 1 percent nearly tripled, and the share reported by the top one-hundredth of 1 percent more than quadrupled. Because people with the highest income pay a disproportionate share of taxes—the top 1 percent pays nearly 39 percent of all federal income taxes—their behavior is especially important.[14] Not fully accounting for the portion of income growth unrelated to tax policy can result in large biases. For example, the cuts in marginal tax rates in the 1980s were greatest at the top of the income distribution and were thus inversely correlated with the great income growth at the very top of the distribution. The fact that the income growth at the top of the income distribution is jagged (while following a decidedly upward trend) makes controlling for it even more difficult. If the non-tax-related portion of that income growth is not fully accounted for, that trend will bias ETI estimates in a positive direction when tax rates fall (and in a negative direction when tax rates rise).

Mean reversion is another issue that complicates estimation. Over a person's lifetime, income often follows a general path with many fluctuations. After a period when income is particularly high or low, it will often revert to a more normal path. That phenomenon is especially pronounced at the tails of the distribution. Those at the extreme right of the income distribution are often not there for long, and will likely have a substantial drop in income (that is unrelated to tax policy). At the other extreme, those in school (or not employed) will often have large increases in income upon entering the workforce. Not accounting for that mean reversion at the tails of the distribution can substantially bias estimated elasticities. More specifically, not fully controlling for mean reversion will erroneously count both non-tax-related increases (by those below their lifetime path) and non-tax-related decreases in taxable income (by those above their life-time path) as responses to changes in tax rates. Those factors will bias ETI estimates in opposite directions, depending on whether tax rates are raised or lowered, but there is no reason to believe that the biases will cancel each other out. Partly for that reason, many studies exclude those with very low earnings. Those at the high end cannot be so easily dis-carded, since they are responsible for a large share of both taxable income and tax revenues.

These issues are even further complicated by the fact that the size of tax-able income elasticity appears to vary across the income distribution. That is, estimated ETIs are generally larger (sometimes much larger) for higher-income groups. In such cases, Navratil (1995) shows that some of the early differences-in-differences approaches will produce biased estimates for each group. Additionally, if the ETI does in fact vary with income, a single over-all elasticity will not be applicable when considering the impact of rate changes that target only part of the income distribution or that differ in magnitude across the distribution.

Endogeneity of the Tax Rate. Because of the federal tax system's progressivity, it is almost axiomatic that a simple cross-section regression will show a direct relationship between tax rates and taxable income. Even with longitudinal data, an individual's tax rate rises with taxable income. In order to isolate the impact of taxes on taxable income, tax rates should be imputed based on an instrumented (or exogenous) measure of taxable income. After instrumenting, the correct relationship between taxable income and the tax rate should be achieved for each individual, but that method does not address the cross-sectional correlation between taxable income and tax rates. Studies using cross-sectional variation for identification generally must also include differencing methods (which transform the key dependent variable to the change in the tax rate).

Institutional Factors: Contemporaneous Tax Policy Changes. If institutional changes to the tax system take effect contemporaneously with rate changes, they could affect reported taxable income, biasing estimated elasticities, or at least complicating the estimation. In fact, Slemrod (1996) shows that changes to the underlying tax base may result in substantially different elasticities before and after a tax change. Most regression techniques yield a weighted average of the two elasticities.

Most elasticity measures also assume policies toward tax evasion and avoidance as given, when in fact those too are choices that policymakers can change. Recent work emphasizes the role of institutional factors (Slemrod and Kopczuk 2002, Kopczuk 2005) and shows that the elasticity of taxable income is not a structural parameter, but rather a function of the tax system. Taxpayers are more responsive when opportunities to avoid taxes are more prevalent (or less costly). Possible influences on responses to taxes include the availability of substitutable forms of compensation (such as the ability of firms to use nontaxable fringe benefits as opposed to taxable compensation) and the expected penalties for evasion.

The definition of taxable income itself may influence results. Changes to the tax system may alter that definition. Using the concurrent definition for taxable income (that is, the definition that was in effect when the income was received) will confound responses to tax rates with statutory changes to the tax base. But even if a consistent measure is chosen, Slemrod (1998) shows that estimates may depend on the definition used and that even a constant-law definition can yield biased results. And Heim (2007) shows that taxable income elasticities will be biased if the definition of taxable income changes, unless there are cross-price elasticities of zero between goods whose tax status changes and those that are always taxable.

Transitory versus Permanent Responses and Income Shifting. Permanent, or longer-term, behavioral responses to tax changes are of primary importance; transitory responses are a lesser concern. For illustration, suppose that in 1986 taxpayers knew that the tax rates were set to fall in 1987. In the short term, some may have delayed the receipt of income from December 1986 to January 1987. That response would not have affected real economic behavior and would not have influenced long-term taxable income. By contrast, a longer-term response like a persistent change in investment or labor market behavior would have affected the allocation of resources and taxable income for years to come. That is not to say that transitory behavior is always small or trivial. For example, capital gains realizations rose by over 96 percent from 1985 to 1986 in anticipation of less-favorable treatment of capital gains set to begin in 1987.

Separating transitory from permanent responses is often difficult. Measuring changes in taxable income in the year prior to and the years succeeding a tax change will likely yield a combination of permanent and transitory responses. Phase-in periods and taxpayer expectations about future tax legislation also matter. For example, if rate cuts phase in, people not only divert income (on paper) to the future, but also may substitute leisure in the short term for work in the future when the rates are fully lowered. In that instance, intertemporal substitution could result in a near-term understatement and a longer-term overstatement of the ETI.

A related issue is the relationship between tax policy and long-term career and investment decisions. Tax policy can affect investment in both human and physical capital, which over time can influence taxable income. That long-run response is important in measuring the true response to tax changes, but may not be fully observed for many years following a tax change, leading to an understatement of the ETI.

Transfers between Economic Agents. Chetty (forthcoming) warns that the large elasticities found for high-income groups may overstate the efficiency implications of this group's behavior. Chetty suggests that behavioral responses by upper-income filers are more likely to involve "fiscal externalities"—i.e., behavioral responses may reflect the shifting of economic activity to other agents in the economy, or in some cases sheltering income has external transfer costs—and thus implying a difference between the private and social costs of avoiding taxes. Carroll (1998) notes the possibility of income shifting between economic agents. For example, a highly paid lawyer may reduce his workload in response to a tax increase targeted at high earners, but his reduction may shift business to lawyers in lower tax brackets. As an example of transfer costs, Chetty suggests that an executive may be deterred from taking a larger share of compensation in the form of fringe benefits because doing so would require offering more fringe benefits to other employees in the firm. Another case of transfer costs involves the potential for fines imposed by the IRS. The expected value of these fines represents a cost to a subset of taxpayers. However, this is not a deadweight loss to society as a whole because the cost to those evading taxes is exactly offset by additional revenues "transferred" to the government.

Recent ETI Estimates. As the obstacles to identification have become better recognized, more sophisticated methods and richer datasets have been used to estimate the ETI. A striking result is that ETI estimates, while remaining quite sensitive to a wide array of factors, have tended downward from the earliest estimates by Feldstein (1995a) and Lindsey (1987). These first studies reported estimated ETIs of between 1 and 3. More recent studies report estimates closer to 0.4, but estimates still range from close to 0 to greater than 1. In addition to displaying this sensitivity to specification decisions, estimates have been found to vary across time and across the income distribution.[15]

An influential study by Gruber and Saez (2002) examines taxable income responses to the tax cuts of 1981 and 1986 using a panel of tax returns for years 1979 through 1990. This approach lays the groundwork for papers by Kopczuk (2005), Giertz (2006, 2007), and Heim (2007, forthcoming). Gruber and Saez calculate constant-law income using 1990 law excluding capital gains and using the National Bureau of Economic Research's TAXSIM model to estimate federal and state tax rates. They then apply two-stage least squares, regressing the log of the income growth (over three-year intervals) against the log change in the net-of-tax rate plus year fixed effects and dummies for marital status.[16] Recognizing the possibility of mean reversion and secular trends in income, they explore two additional specifications, 1) the log of initial period income as an independent variable; and 2) a ten-piece spline of the log of initial period income.

They are most confident in an income-weighted estimated ETI of 0.40 from the model that includes a ten-piece spline based on the natural log of initial period income. The spline allows the functional relationship between the dependent variable and the independent variables to vary by decile. Gruber and Saez's (2002) corresponding elasticity for a broader measure of income is much smaller, 0.12, suggesting that much of the taxable income response comes through deductions, exemptions, and exclusions, rather than changes in labor supply.

Kopczuk (2005) uses the same panel as Gruber and Saez to estimate the ETI and to test the hypothesis that the ETI is not a structural parameter, but rather a function of the tax system's structure. Kopczuk models taxable income as a function not just of tax rates, but also of the interaction between tax rates and the size of the tax base, which is used as a proxy for the cost of shifting funds outside the tax base. Additionally, Kopczuk treats mean reversion and divergence within the income distribution as separate phenomena by including separate variables to control for them. Kopczuk's estimates are extremely sensitive to both sample selection and model specification. However, he does find evidence of a relationship between the size of the tax base and the ETI—favoring a specification which finds that a one percentage point increase in the tax base lowers the ETI by 0.79 percent.

Giertz (2007) uses a panel of tax returns from 1979 to 2001 (that heavily oversamples high-income filers) in order to estimate taxable income and broad income elasticities. Applying the methods of Gruber and Saez (2002), he reports an estimated ETI for the 1980s that is slightly larger than that in Gruber and Saez, but the analogous estimate for the 1990s is less than half as large (0.20). Following Kopczuk (2005), Giertz includes separate and nonlinear controls for mean reversion and divergence within the income distribution. This explains about one-third of the difference between the estimates for the 1980s and the 1990s, lowering the 1980s estimate to 0.40 and raising the 1990s estimate to 0.26. Additionally, Kopczuk's work implies that changes to the tax base since 1986 could account for a portion of the remaining difference.

Heim (2007) and Giertz (2006) use a variety of approaches to estimate taxable income elasticities for years covering the OBRA90 and OBRA93 tax increases. Heim's preferred specification yields estimated ETIs ranging from 0.46 to 0.58 depending on the length of the interval over which income changes are measured. Both papers attempt to control for adjacent-year income shifting when measuring behavioral changes over intervals of several years. When measuring behavioral responses from 1991 to 1994, for example, controlling for adjacent-year shifting recognizes that 1991 income may have been influenced by income shifting between 1990 and 1991 (since tax rates rose in 1990), and that 1994 income may have been influenced by shifting between 1993 and 1994 (since tax rates rose in 1993). Both papers report estimates that are quite sensitive to an array of factors. Heim concludes that the range of estimates reported in the paper often "resulted from small changes in the specification, [and] includes most a priori educated guesses as to what the taxable income elasticity would be . . . suggest[ing] that it may never be possible to pin down the taxable income elasticity with any reasonable degree of accuracy" (33).

Heim (forthcoming) is one of the first to look at responses to the 2001 and 2003 tax cuts. The paper uses a panel of individual tax returns spanning years 1999 to 2005. Heim measures responses over three-year intervals, employing controls common to the literature since Gruber and Saez (2002), and reports a "best estimate" of around 0.25 when not accounting for adjacent-year income shifting. However, much smaller and statistically insignificant estimates are reported when accounting for adjacent-year shifting, causing him to conclude that most of the response to the tax changes was intertemporal (or transitory) income shifting. The large estimated coefficients on the adjacent-year tax rates are somewhat puzzling in this instance. With tax rates rising, there is an incentive to shift income to an earlier period. This would likely involve shifting of income from 2003 to 2002. Marginal tax rates for moderate- and upper-income groups fell only slightly prior to 2003, but fell substantially in 2003 when JGTRRA passed, expediting the rate cuts that had been scheduled to phase in over the next few years. However, the 2003 rate cuts were a surprise. For such an unanticipated drop in rates, there would be no (or very little) opportunity to shift income backward.

Auten, Carroll, and Gee (2008) also use tax return data from 1999 to 2005 to measure behavioral responses to the 2001 and 2003 tax cuts. They compare behavior over two-year intervals and restrict their sample to filers ages twenty-five to sixty-one with more than $50,000 in taxable income.

Instead of controlling for mean reversion and divergence in the income distribution by using a function of base-year (or lagged) taxable income, they include variables on financial income, proxies for entrepreneurship, and regional and occupational dummies. In addition, they include functions of age and number of children in the family. They report a population-weighted estimated ETI of 0.35 (almost identical to their income-weighted estimate). Including taxpayers over age sixty-one lowers their estimate to 0.28. Restricting the sample to those with incomes over $200,000 raises their ETI estimate to 1.09.

In another paper looking at recent tax changes, Singleton (2007) focuses on EGTRRA's provision designed to reduce the marriage penalty. He uses Current Population Survey data linked to Social Security earnings records to examine behavioral responses to this provision, which substantially lowered marginal tax rates (MTRs) for married couples with taxable income ranging from $46,700 to $54,193 (in 2002 dollars). This provision did not alter MTRs for single filers or filers with incomes above or below this range. Singleton reports overall estimated elasticities that range from 0.16 to 0.66, with estimates varying by education and other demographics. These estimates are for earned income and not fully taxable income.

Most of the recent empirical ETI research has relied on panel data. An exception is Saez (2004), who builds on work by Slemrod (1996) and Feenberg and Poterba (1993) by using aggregated time-series data spanning 1960 to 2000. Saez uses a consistent definition of income (that more closely approximates AGI less capital gains, as opposed to taxable income) and average marginal tax rates for different income groups. Saez's study does not focus primarily on a single tax change, but examines the responses to all tax changes over the past four decades.

Regressing the log of taxable income against the log of the net-of-tax rate plus a time-trend polynomial results in a statistically insignificant estimated ETI of 0.20. For the top 1 percent of the taxable income distribution, Saez reports a much larger and statistically significant ETI estimate of 0.50. Corresponding ETI estimates for the bottom 99 percent of the distribution are negative (but not statistically different from 0).

Saez reports estimated ETIs that vary greatly over some subsets of the forty years examined. For example, dividing the change in log income between 1981 and 1984 by the change in logged net-of-tax rates between the same two years yields an estimated ETI of 0.77. The same analysis comparing 1985 to

1988 yields a much larger estimated ETI, 1.7. Comparing 1991 with 1994 yields an estimated ETI of about 0. The variation in ETIs over time is consistent with Goolsbee (1999) and Giertz (2007), who both find very different elasticities when employing identical techniques to different time periods.

Saez (2004) also employs a regression framework that uses taxable income shares to estimate ETIs for different segments of the taxable income distribution. Special attention is paid to the top 1 percent of filers. For the various taxable income groups, Saez regresses the log of the group's share of taxable income against the log of the net-of-tax rate. Without any time trends, that regression yields an estimated ETI of 1.58 for the top 1 percent. Including both the time trend and square of the time trend yields an estimated ETI of 0.62. Saez expresses confidence in the 0.62 estimate because that regression has an adjusted coefficient of determination of 0.98, and the fitted values do an excellent job of tracking the trend in the share of income reported by the top 1 percent.

Further segmentation of the income distribution shows that, even among the top 1 percent of the distribution, estimated ETIs vary greatly by income. In fact, the same approach that yields 0.62 for the top 1 percent yields an estimated ETI of 1.09 for the top 0.01 of 1 percent. For those in the ninetieth to ninety-fifth percentiles, the same approach yields a negative (although statistically insignificant) estimated ETI.

Applying the ETI for Tax Policy

Saez (2004) presents a method for assessing the revenue and efficiency implications resulting from changes in marginal tax rates. That method is described in this section and applied in the following section.[17] Saez, building on the work of Feldstein (1999), breaks the change in revenues resulting from an increase in tax rates on the top tax bracket into a mechanical and behavioral response, such that

$$\Delta revenue = N \cdot \Delta EMTR \cdot (z - \bar{z}) \cdot \left[1 - ETI \cdot \left(\frac{z}{(z - \bar{z})} \right) \cdot \left(\frac{EMTR}{1 - EMTR} \right) \right]^{[18]} \quad (1)$$

Here, z is average taxable income for those in the top rate bracket, $\bar{z}$ is the level of taxable income where the top tax rate kicks in, and N is the number of taxpayers in the top bracket. *EMTR* is the effective marginal tax rate—the share of an additional dollar of income that is paid to the government— and *ETI* is the elasticity of taxable income. The first part of equation (1), $N \cdot \Delta EMTR \cdot (z - \bar{z})$, equals the *mechanical response*, or the change in tax revenue assuming no behavioral responses. Thus, if *ETI* equals 0, there is no behavioral response, and tax revenue increases linearly with the tax rate. The second piece inside the brackets,

$$ETI \cdot \left(\frac{z}{(z - \bar{z})} \right) \cdot \left(\frac{EMTR}{1 - EMTR} \right),$$

is the share of the mechanical response that is offset by changes in behavior. If this share is greater than 1, it implies a Laffer response—that is, an increase in the MTR results in a decrease in tax revenue. Note that the Laffer (or revenue-maximizing) rate equals

$$\left(\frac{1}{\left[1 + \left(\frac{z}{z - \bar{z}} \right) \cdot ETI \right]} \right)$$

Note also that rearranging equation (1) to highlight revenue changes from the mechanical and behavioral responses yields

$$\Delta Revenue = \overbrace{N \cdot \Delta EMTR \cdot (z - \bar{z})}^{\text{Mechanical Response}} - \overbrace{ETI \cdot \Delta EMTR \cdot N \cdot z \left(\frac{EMTR}{1 - EMTR} \right)}^{\text{Behavioral Response or Marginal Deadweight Loss}}. \quad (2)$$

Finally, the behavioral response is also exactly equal to the change in DWL resulting from the tax rate change.[19] The behavioral response from equation (2) encompasses revenue changes from the federal, payroll, and state tax bases combined—even for a tax increase in just the federal rate— because the bases overlap. By imputing income at the new tax rates, z', where

$$z' = z \cdot \left[1 - ETI \cdot \left(\frac{dt}{1 - MTR} \right) \right], \quad (3)$$

one can calculate the overall revenue offset to the individual income tax separately from the overall change in revenues. Thus, when behavioral responses are accounted for, the change in federal income tax revenue from raising the rate on the top income tax bracket can be expressed such that

$$\Delta Federal\ Revenue = N \cdot \left[\Delta EMTR \cdot (z' - \bar{z}) - federal\_EMTR \cdot (z - z') \right] \quad (4)$$

Note that total efficiency costs from the tax system, as opposed to the incremental costs of a change in rates, can be expressed such that

$$Deadweight\ Loss = 0.5 \cdot \left(\frac{EMTR^2}{1 - EMTR} \right) \cdot ETI \cdot \sum_{i=1}^{N} (z - \bar{z}), \qquad (5)$$

which is analogous to the usual Harberger DWL formula. Other things being equal, tax increases for upper-income groups will result in greater DWL because these groups face higher EMTRs and because the DWL increases by the square of the tax rate.

Data and Institutional Background

One of the most significant economic policy initiatives of the Bush administration has been lowering marginal tax rates on ordinary individual income, as well as rates on capital gains and dividends. In order to garner enough political support for the tax cuts, the administration agreed to labyrinthine legislation, in which most of the provisions phase in and phase out (or end abruptly) between 2001 and 2011. These tax changes remain a hotly contested issue, in part because they are set to expire after 2010, at which time tax rates will revert to their 2001 levels, but also because of America's long-term fiscal outlook: absent substantial changes, government expenditures are projected to exceed revenues at an unprecedented rate.

The centerpiece of the Bush tax cuts was the Economic Growth Tax Relief and Reconciliation Act of 2001, which lowered marginal tax rates and expanded allowable credits and deductions. This was followed by the 2003 Jobs Growth and Tax Relief Reconciliation Act, which accelerated the marginal rate cuts from EGTRRA that were not set to fully phase in until 2006. Additionally, JGTRRA substantially lowered tax rates on capital gains and dividends. Another provision of EGTRRA reduced the marriage penalty by expanding the size of the 15 percent tax bracket for married filers only.[20] Table 5-1 shows the marginal tax rate schedules (for the individual income tax) before EGTRRA and after JGTRRA. For those at the 28 percent statutory rate and above, marginal income tax rates are scheduled to rise by roughly 10 percent after 2010. The consequences of letting these tax cuts expire (as measured both in terms of tax revenue and in terms of economic efficiency) is the focus of the next section.

TABLE 5-1

FEDERAL INDIVIDUAL INCOME TAX SCHEDULE (IN 2005 DOLLARS)

2000 & 2011 Tax Rates	2003–2010 Tax Rates	Single Filers	Married Filing Jointly[a]	Married Filing Separately	Head of Household
15%	10%	0–$7,300	0–$14,600	0–$7,300	0–$10,450
15%[b]	15%	$7,301–$29,700	$14,601–$59,400	$7,301–$29,700	$10,451–$39,800
28%	25%	$29,701–$71,950	$59,401–$119,950	$29,701–$59,975	$39,801–$102,800
31%	28%	$71,951–$150,150	$119,951–$182,800	$59,976–$91,400	$102,801–166,450
36%	33%	$150,151–$326,450	$182,801–$326,450	$91,401–$163,225	$166,451–$326,450
39.6%	35%	$326,451 or more	$326,451 or more	$163,226 or more	$326,451 or more

SOURCE: IRS tax schedules.
NOTES: a. The same schedule applies to qualifying widows/widowers; b. This assumes that the marriage penalty relief will be extended.

The difference between the projected 2011 rate schedule and the schedule for 2003–2010 is the percentage point change in the tax rate for each group of taxpayers. More specifically, this is the change in statutory MTRs. Because I am looking at the effect of allowing the individual rates to rise while maintaining other features of the tax system, I assume that this also represents the projected change in the effective marginal tax rate. However, the EMTR—as noted earlier, the share of an additional dollar of income that is paid to the government—is often somewhat different from the statutory MTR because the EMTR takes into account phase-ins, phaseouts, and other interactions with the IRS code. These other factors affect the actual share of income that the government receives.

Consider the personal exemption phaseout (PEP), which requires taxpayers to reduce their personal exemption by 3 percent for each dollar that their income exceeds the phaseout floor (until the personal exemption is reduced to zero). Thus, taxable income increases by $103 for every additional

TABLE 5-2
EFFECTIVE MARGINAL TAX RATES FOR 2005 (PERCENTAGES)

Statutory Bracket	Federal EMTR	Payroll EMTR	State EMTR	Total EMTR
0	−1.6	13.5	0.9	12.7
10	14.8	12.8	2.6	30.2
15	16.3	12.5	6.1	34.9
25	26.3	10.0	3.7	40.0
28	30.1	5.3	3.7	39.0
33	34.7	3.2	3.5	41.3
35	34.7	2.5	3.4	40.7

SOURCE: CBO 2005.

$100 of income within the phaseout range. The EMTR is then equal to the MTR plus 0.03 times the MTR, or for someone in the 35 percent tax bracket, 36.05 percent (that is, 1.03 times 35). According to CBO (2005), when all the intricacies of the tax code are taken into account, the range of EMTRs for the individual income tax is from −1.6 percent (for those often not paying income tax, but sometimes receiving refundable tax credits such as the Earned Income Tax Credit) to almost 35 percent (for the top two statutory tax brackets). These findings are presented in table 5-2. Table 5-2 also shows what happens when payroll and state taxes are included. While the individual income tax hits upper-income groups the hardest (at the margin), federal payroll taxes (used to finance Social Security and Medicare) hit lower-income groups the hardest. EMTRs for state taxes are greatest for middle-income groups. When these three taxes are combined, EMTRs range from just over 30 per-cent for the 10 percent bracket to over 41 percent for the 33 percent bracket.[21]

While these EMTRs account for the intricacies of the tax system, they are based on standard convention, which assumes that marginal income is earned income. (I exclude filers whose top MTR is from capital gains.) However, marginal rates could differ from imputed EMTRs, if behavior at the margin includes changes to fringe benefits, perquisites, itemized deductions or business income. For example, with respect to earned income, payroll taxes are likely relevant at the margin, but payroll taxes would not be relevant for responses to itemized deductions or many (but not all) fringe benefits. If a portion of behavioral responses includes some of

TABLE 5-3

2005 INDIVIDUAL INCOME AND TAX REVENUES BY TAX BRACKET

Statutory MTR (%)	Income Total	Income at MTR	Tax Revenue Total	Tax Revenue at MTR
10	130,864	107,061	12,612	10,706
15	1,028,305	589,969	132,330	88,495
25	1,411,064	241,641	237,515	60,410
28	503,828	36,360	104,491	10,181
33	387,519	79,067	92,352	26,092
35	1,094,230	565,392	315,443	197,887
Total	4,555,810	1,619,489	894,743	393,772

Source: IRS 2007.
NOTE: Dollar values are in millions.

these changes, then true EMTRs would be lower than those reported in table 5-2. However, it is unlikely that this would have much effect on prospective *change* in MTRs resulting from the expiration of EGTRRA and JGTRRA after 2010.

In addition to the information on EMTRs by tax bracket, two other pieces of information are crucial for employing the formulae (laid out earlier) that estimate the revenue and efficiency implications of allowing the individual tax rates to expire. We need to know both the ETI and the corresponding information on the amount of taxable income that is reported in each of the individual income tax brackets. The income information is published by the IRS and is summarized in table 5-3.[22]

Table 5-3 shows nearly $4.6 trillion in (modified) taxable income and nearly $900 billion in total tax revenue for 2005. These numbers are somewhat smaller than the actual totals for 2005 because they exclude filers whose top MTR is for income from capital gains.[23]

The final piece of information, the ETI, is the trickiest. As discussed above, the empirical literature on the ETI suggests a wide range of plausible estimates, and considerable disagreement surrounds the size of this parameter. Thus the next section shows how the expiring cuts in individual MTRs might affect revenue and efficiency under a range of different ETIs. This approach aims to show what implicit views of the ETI may underlie different views on tax policy—especially views on the relationship between rate changes and revenues. Additionally, it highlights the sensitivity of revenue estimates to a range of ETI assumptions.

Before proceeding, some caveats are in order. The results that follow are not from a full microsimulation model with behavioral responses made at the individual level. There are a number of reasons why results from such an exercise might differ from those presented in the next section. First, EMTRs differ within a statutory tax bracket, while here the average EMTR is applied to aggregated taxable income for each of the respective tax brackets. Second, some individuals are close to the bottom of their tax bracket, which would likely censor behavioral responses to a rise in the bracket's tax rate. Saez (2002) finds that while taxpayers by and large do not bunch at the kinks, there are still some who are near kink points. Because I am not using individual-level data, I do not censor responses. Third, income measures are taken from table 3.4 of IRS (2007), which groups filers by their top MTR. I exclude taxpayers whose top tax rate is for capital gains income. Some taxpayers, however, have capital gains income that is taxed at a rate lower than their top rate. This income may be included in my measure. Finally, I apply EMTRs for labor (that is, earned) income when estimating behavioral responses. The EMTR may be the best choice here, but it is imprecise. Some income, at the margin, may result from realizing capital gains; other income, at the margin, may be business income that is exempt from payroll taxes. Even if responses represent changes to earned income, EMTRs can vary depending on which member of the tax unit is reporting the additional income. Moreover, responses may reflect changes to itemized deductions, in which case the EMTR should exclude payroll taxes. The decision to use EMTRs for earned income may disproportionately bias responses for top tax brackets, since a larger share of this group's income comes from sources other than labor. However, the EMTR from the payroll tax is just 2.5 percent for high-income groups, whereas it exceeds 12.5 percent for the bottom two brackets. The choice of which EMTR to use is problematic even when using individual-level panel data.

Despite these caveats, this is a useful exercise that illustrates the range of revenue responses and efficiency consequences resulting from the expiration of the Bush tax cuts. It also shows that these questions can be broached even by those who do not have access to confidential tax returns—in other words, the vast majority of scholars.

Revenue and Efficiency Implications of Expiring Tax Legislation

The mechanical change in revenues from allowing the individual rates to expire—that is, the change in individual income tax revenues assuming no behavioral responses—is estimated here at $98.6 billion.[24] (See table 5-4.) That is 13 percent greater than actual 2005 revenues.[25] For the mechanical calculation, only revenues from the individual income tax change, since the mechanical calculation ignores taxable income responses to the change in rates. Behavioral responses, though, lower revenues from the individual income tax and from payroll and state taxes (which further offsets revenue increases from the individual income tax), since these bases overlap. About 38 percent of the mechanical revenue increase results from changing the 10 percent tax bracket back to 15 percent. This has the biggest effect both because the rate on this bracket is scheduled to undergo the largest percentage point increase, and because the increase in rates increases revenues not just from those facing this marginal rate, but also from filers in all the higher brackets (who pay this rate on some of their income). The 35 percent rate bracket, which is slated to rise to 39.6, is the second most important in terms of the expected mechanical increase in revenues. This bracket accounts for nearly 23 percent (or $26 billion) of the expected increase in revenues. In contrast to what occurs when the 10 percent bracket is raised, here, all the additional revenue is from filers in this marginal rate bracket. Although less than 1 percent of filers face this top bracket, this group reported over half of one trillion dollars in 2005 taxable income (IRS 2007).

Projecting tax revenues under a range of ETI estimates shows the extent to which behavioral responses might reduce the mechanical gain in tax revenues. Recall that this difference between the mechanical and actual change in revenues is also equal to the efficiency cost (or deadweight loss) resulting from the tax increase. As figure 5-1, figure 5-2, and table 5-5 show, a modest ETI of 0.2 would lower the gain in federal income tax revenues by more than 12 percent (or $12.2 billion, from $98.6 billion to $86.5 billion) compared to the mechanical gain. (When payroll and state taxes are accounted for, the revenue offset and total DWL rise nearly 28 percent, to $15.6 billion.) A large ETI of 1.0 would wipe away 62 percent (or $60.9 billion) of the revenue gain, and an additional 17 percent (or $17 billion) would be lost from payroll and state revenues. Revenues from filers in the

TABLE 5-4

EFFICIENCY CONSEQUENCES OF LETTING THE BUSH
INDIVIDUAL INCOME TAX CUTS EXPIRE

2005 MTR	Mechanical Δ Revenue	Behavioral Response = Change in DWL ETI=					
		0.2	0.4	0.5	0.6	0.8	1.0
10%	43,015	555	1,100	1,473	1,745	2,290	2,835
15%	N/A	N/A	N/A	N/A	N/A	N/A	N/A
25%	17,293	5,364	10,708	13,376	16,053	21,398	26,742
28%	5,772	1,719	3,440	4,307	5,167	6,888	8,602
33%	6,522	1,567	3,123	3,901	4,689	6,246	7,808
35%	26,041	6,392	12,795	15,972	19,157	25,535	31,907
Total	98,643	15,596	31,167	39,029	46,811	62,357	77,894

SOURCE: Author's calculations.
NOTES: Dollar values are in millions of 2005 dollars; N/A = not applicable.

FIGURE 5-1

CHANGE IN TAX REVENUES RESULTING FROM THE EXPIRATION
OF CUTS IN INDIVIDUAL MARGINAL TAX RATES

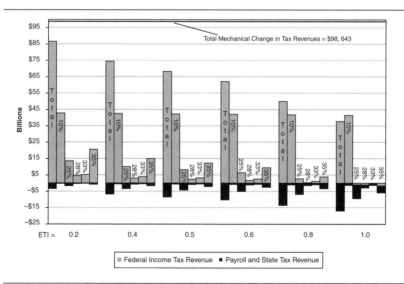

SOURCE: Author's calculations.

FIGURE 5-2

CHANGE IN DEADWEIGHT LOSS RESULTING FROM THE EXPIRATION OF
CUTS IN INDIVIDUAL MARGINAL TAX RATES

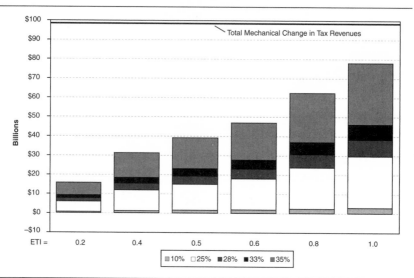

SOURCE: Author's calculations.

15 percent bracket rise by $21.9 billion under each scenario, even though their MTR is not scheduled to change when the cuts expire.[26] Members of this group pay more in taxes because their taxable income that was below the 15 percent rate was taxed at 10 percent, but would be taxed at 15 percent. It is assumed that there are no income effects and thus that this group does not change its behavior. At an ETI of 0.5—halfway between the extremes already discussed—the increase in federal revenues from the tax increase is 45 percent (or $30.5 billion) smaller than under the mechanical case, and an additional 28 percent (or $8.5 billion) would be lost from payroll and state revenues. As shown in table 5-5, the one-year revenue gain in federal income taxes from the expiration of the cuts in individual tax rates would equal $98.6 billion with no behavioral response; $86.5 billion when assuming an ETI of 0.2; and $37.8 billion when assuming an ETI of 1.

In each case, 36 percent of the reduction in federal income tax revenues (compared to the mechanical case) results from behavioral responses by those 0.7 percent of filers in the top income tax bracket. Forty-four percent

TABLE 5-5

REVENUE CONSEQUENCES OF LETTING THE BUSH
INDIVIDUAL INCOME TAX CUTS EXPIRE

2005 MTR		Mechanical Δ Revenue	Total Revenue Change = Mechanical Change − DWL					
			ETI=					
			0.2	0.4	0.5	0.6	0.8	1.0
10%	Income tax	43,015	42,732	42,449	42,208	42,066	41,783	41,501
	Other bases	N/A	−272	−534	−666	−796	−1,058	−1,321
15%	Income tax	N/A	N/A	N/A	N/A	N/A	N/A	N/A
	Other bases	N/A	N/A	N/A	N/A	N/A	N/A	N/A
25%	Income tax	17,293	13,641	10,000	8,178	6,348	2,708	−937
	Other bases	N/A	−1,712	−3,415	−4,261	−5,108	−6,812	−8,512
28%	Income tax	5,772	4,411	3,055	2,378	1,700	343	−1,013
	Other bases	N/A	−358	−724	−912	−1,095	−1,458	−1,817
33%	Income tax	6,522	5,192	3,863	3,198	2,534	1,205	−123
	Other bases	N/A	−237	−465	−578	−701	−929	−1,163
35%	Income tax	26,041	20,480	14,909	12,183	9,417	3,887	−1,647
	Other bases	N/A	−831	−1,663	−2,114	−2,533	−3,381	−4,219
	Income tax	98,643	86,456	74,277	68,145	62,065	49,925	37,780
Total	Other bases	N/A	−3,409	−6,801	−8,531	−10,234	−13,639	−17,032

Source: Author's calculations.
NOTES: Dollar values are in millions of 2005 dollars; N/A = not applicable.

of the reduction in federal income tax revenues is attributable to the 1.8 percent of filers in the top two tax brackets. If the ETI increases with income, as the empirical literature suggests, these shares would be even larger. Some have suggested returning rates to their 2001 levels for just the top two tax brackets. At an ETI of 0.5, this would imply just $15.4 billion more in annual revenues (from the federal income tax) and $19.9 billion in increased DWL. At an ETI of 0.2, federal income tax revenues would be expected to increase by $25.7 billion, with $8 billion in additional DWL. At an ETI of 1, the tax increase would move the top two tax brackets past their Laffer (or revenue-maximizing) rate. Thus this would actually lead to a reduction in overall revenues and an increase in DWL.

Marginal Deadweight Loss. The changes in revenues and in DWL from changes in tax policy can be combined into a measure that captures the increase in DWL associated with a one-dollar increase in revenues (or, for a tax cut, the reduction in DWL associated with a one-dollar reduction in revenues). This measure of marginal DWL simply equals the change in revenues divided by the change in DWL. As tables 5-6a and 5-6b show, ranges in ETI of 0.2 to 1 imply a tremendous range in the efficiency costs associated with raising additional revenue (by allowing MTRs to return to their 2001 levels). At an ETI of 0.2, for example, allowing the tax cuts to expire would result in a marginal DWL (per dollar of federal income tax revenue) of $0.18—that is, for each additional dollar the federal government receives in revenue, society would be worse off by $0.18. At an ETI of 1, the marginal DWL rises to $2.06 per additional dollar of income tax revenue raised. At an ETI of 0.5, this number is $0.57. When revenue offsets to the other tax bases are accounted for, the marginal DWL rises by just 4 percent at an ETI of 0.2, but by 82 percent at an ETI of 1.0.

For comparison, consider the use in Feldstein (1999) of an individual-level microsimulation model to assess the possible implications of a 10 percent increase in marginal tax rates. Feldstein concludes that, assuming an ETI of 1.04, behavioral responses would erase over two-thirds of the mechanical gain in tax revenues and that the marginal DWL would be over $2 per every additional dollar of revenue. Using more recent data and assuming an ETI of 0.4, Feldstein (2008) reports a marginal DWL of $0.76 per additional dollar of revenue raised. At an ETI of 0.4, my estimated DWL is smaller, at $0.42 per dollar of federal income tax revenue, but it rises to $0.62 when I account for revenue offsets to the payroll tax and to the states. Note that Feldstein is considering a case where rates for each bracket increase by the same percentage. The case examined here is different, since brackets change by different percentages and one group (those currently in the 15 percent bracket) experiences no change in its MTR.

For a given ETI, the efficiency implications of raising tax rates vary greatly across the brackets. Those in the 15 percent tax bracket drive down the overall DWL per dollar measure because this group is assumed to have no behavioral response (since its MTR does not change); but it does pay more in taxes because the 10 percent bracket rises to 15 percent. Raising the bottom (10 percent) tax bracket has only minor efficiency implications. The

TABLE 5-6a

MARGINAL DEADWEIGHT LOSS

(PER ADDITIONAL DOLLAR OF FEDERAL INCOME TAX REVENUE)

2005 MTR	ETI =					
	0.2	0.4	0.5	0.6	0.8	1.0
10%	0.01	0.03	0.03	0.04	0.05	0.07
15%	N/A	N/A	N/A	N/A	N/A	N/A
25%	0.39	1.07	1.64	2.53	7.90	N/A
28%	0.39	1.13	1.81	3.04	20.09	N/A
33%	0.30	0.81	1.22	1.85	5.19	N/A
35%	0.31	0.86	1.31	2.03	6.57	N/A
Total	0.18	0.42	0.57	0.75	1.25	2.06

SOURCE: Author's calculations.

TABLE 5-6b

MARGINAL DEADWEIGHT LOSS

(PER ADDITIONAL DOLLAR OF REVENUE INCLUDING
REVENUE OFFSETS FROM PAYROLL AND STATE TAXES)

2005 MTR	ETI =					
	0.2	0.4	0.5	0.6	0.8	1.0
10%	0.01	0.03	0.04	0.04	0.06	0.07
15%	N/A	N/A	N/A	N/A	N/A	N/A
25%	0.45	1.63	3.41	12.95	N/A	N/A
28%	0.42	1.48	2.94	8.54	N/A	N/A
33%	0.32	0.92	1.49	2.56	22.65	N/A
35%	0.33	0.97	1.59	2.78	50.49	N/A
Total	0.19	0.46	0.65	0.90	1.72	3.75

SOURCE: Author's calculations.

marginal DWL per dollar of revenue ranges from $0.01 at an ETI of 0.2 to $0.07 at an ETI of 1. This is partly because those in the lower tax brackets face a lower EMTR than those in the higher brackets and because the DWL increases by the square of the EMTR. Another reason for the low efficiency costs is that much of the additional revenue comes from those in higher tax brackets, who have income taxed in this bracket as well. Since the marginal income for these higher-income groups is in another tax bracket, their behavior is not affected by the rate changes (in lower brackets).[27]

For those in the 25 to 35 percent brackets, the marginal DWL measures are much larger. In a case where the tax cuts expire for only the top two brackets and we assume an ETI of 0.5, the result is a marginal DWL of $1.30 per dollar of revenue. However, at an ETI of 0.2, the marginal DWL is over 75 percent smaller. The marginal DWL per additional dollar of revenue is greatest for the 25 and 28 percent brackets. Raising rates on this group results in behavioral responses that lower revenues, while the "windfall" revenue from those in higher brackets (that is not associated with any additional DWL) is small because there are so few filers in the top two brackets.

Laffer Curves. It is widely accepted that behavioral responses to taxation (as measured by the ETI) act to offset revenue gains from an increase in tax rates and revenue losses from a decrease in rates. The degree to which this occurs, however, is a hotly contested issue. If higher tax rates cause less income to be reported, the result can be a net reduction in revenues. At one extreme, the government will receive no tax revenue at a 0 percent tax rate. At a tax rate of 100 percent, the government may also receive no (or at least very little) revenue. Thus, the revenue-maximizing, or Laffer, rate must be somewhere between 0 and 100. While the Laffer rate "optimizes" revenue collection (given other institutions in the economy), it should not be confused with an optimal tax rate, which economists use to describe the rate that raises a given amount of revenue with the fewest distortions to the economy.

The curve which shows the relationship between tax revenue and tax rates has borne the eponym "Laffer" for thirty years. The idea is much older, however. It was formally presented by French engineer and economist Jules Dupuit in the 1840s; and as early as the fourteenth century, the polymath Ibn Khaldun wrote: "At the beginning of the dynasty, taxation yields a large revenue from small assessments. At the end of the dynasty, taxation yields a small revenue from large assessments."[28]

Table 5-7 reports Laffer rates for each of the 2005 tax brackets under the various ETI assumptions. Laffer rates are very high at the bottom brack-

TABLE 5-7

LAFFER RATES UNDER A RANGE OF DIFFERENT ETI ASSUMPTIONS

2005 MTR	2005 EMTR	ETI =					
		0.2	0.4	0.5	0.6	0.8	1.0
10%	0.302	0.972	0.946	0.934	0.922	0.899	0.878
15%	0.349	0.871	0.772	0.731	0.695	0.631	0.579
25%	0.400	0.692	0.530	0.475	0.430	0.362	0.312
28%	0.390	0.693	0.531	0.476	0.431	0.363	0.313
33%	0.413	0.754	0.605	0.551	0.506	0.434	0.380
35%	0.407	0.775	0.634	0.581	0.536	0.464	0.410

SOURCE: Author's calculations.
NOTES: Rates that would maximize combined revenue from federal income taxes, state taxes, and payroll taxes.

ets because much of the revenue raised from these rates comes from filers in higher brackets. Laffer rates for the upper-income brackets are much lower and are quite sensitive to the ETI. At an ETI of 0.2, the revenue-maximizing rate from the top bracket is 77.5 percent—well above the current EMTR of 40.7 percent. At an ETI of 1, the picture is quite different, with the Laffer rate just slightly above the current EMTR. Note that these are the Laffer rates that would maximize combined tax revenue from the federal income tax, state income taxes, and federal payroll taxes. The rates that would maximize federal income tax revenue alone would be higher than those reported in table 5-7. This is especially true under the higher ETI assumptions, where offsetting revenues from an increase in federal rates can be substantial

Figure 5-3 plots the full Laffer curves for the top tax bracket under each of the ETI assumptions. The curves are generated under the assumption that the ETI is constant across all tax rates (on a given curve). In reality, little can be known about the ETI at rates far from those seen in the data. In any event, the curves illustrate the dramatic difference in the relationship between tax rates and tax revenues across a range of ETIs present in the literature. For comparison, the diagonal line shows the relationship with no

FIGURE 5-3

LAFFER CURVES FOR VARIOUS TAXABLE INCOME ELASTICITIES

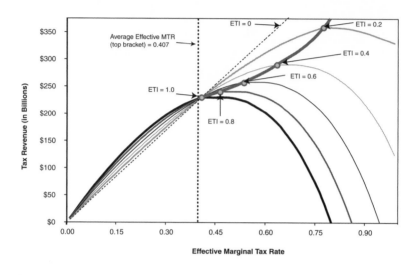

SOURCE: Author's calculations.

behavioral responses—implying that tax revenue increases linearly with tax rates, and no Laffer point is ever reached.

Conclusion

This chapter reviews recent literature on the ETI, highlighting important theoretical and empirical findings. In terms of theory, the ETI has been shown to be one of the central parameters for measuring the efficiency costs of the tax system and for measuring the revenue implications of tax changes. That said, recent research highlights instances when the ETI accurately captures the efficiency implications from a tax change and when the parameter may overstate or understate these consequences. Other research has shown that the ETI is not a structural parameter, but rather a function of institutional features that policymakers may have under their control. On the empirical side, recent research suggests that the ETI is substantially smaller than early estimates of it by Feldstein (1995a) and Lindsey (1987) and that the ETI increases with income. Recent research also finds ETI estimates to be quite sensitive to an array of factors, and the range of plausible estimates is therefore broad.

Based on 2005 data, I estimate that returning individual income tax rates to their 2001 levels would raise revenues by $98.6 billion dollars, assuming no behavioral responses. At an ETI of 0.2, $12.2 billion (or 12 percent) of this mechanical increase in federal income tax revenue would be lost due to reductions in taxable income. Another $3.4 billion in revenue would be lost from payroll and state taxes. At an ETI of 0.8, $48.8 billion (or 49 percent) of the mechanical revenue gain would be lost. Another $13.6 billion in revenue would be lost from payroll and state taxes. The DWL per dollar of additional revenue from the federal income tax is also highly sensitive to the ETI; it ranges from $0.18 at an ETI of 0.2 to $1.25 at an ETI of 0.8.

Laffer rates for each tax bracket and Laffer curves for the top tax bracket are sensitive to the range of ETI estimates found in the literature. An ETI of 0.2 implies a Laffer tax rate for the top tax bracket of 78 percent. On the other hand, at an ETI of 1, the estimated Laffer rate is just 41 percent, or slightly higher than the current effective marginal tax rate for this group.

Notes

1. Specifically, the ETI equals the percentage change in reported taxable income associated with a 1 percent increase in the net-of-tax rate, where the net-of-tax rate equals the share of the next dollar of reported taxable income that is not taxed, or 1 minus the marginal tax rate.

2. The survey did include questions on labor supply elasticities and narrower questions regarding behavioral responses to taxation.

3. Most tax legislation, and especially the Bush tax cuts, encompass more than simple changes to the rate structure. Some opposition, or support, for tax measures may be due to those other factors, and not necessarily to the changes to marginal tax rates.

4. While the estimate is toward the high end of the current literature, it was less so at the time Feldstein was writing.

5. Specifically, it is the compensated elasticity (or the substitution component of the overall elasticity) that is important for measuring efficiency. Compensated elasticities measure the portion of the overall response attributable to changes in relative prices (as opposed to the portion of the response due to changes in income). It is the distortion in relative prices that leads to losses in efficiency.

6. An NBER working paper version of the 1999 article was released several years earlier, in 1995. This earlier version influenced researchers prior to the publication of the 1999 version and contains different policy simulations than the later version.

7. There are exceptions when assessing efficiency and revenue implications from a tax change that is complex. For example, suppose tax rates rise and, in response, taxable income falls, but a portion of that drop in taxable income is due to increased charitable contributions (and suppose those charities produce positive externalities). Or, suppose that a tax increase is used to finance an underprovided public good. In instances such as those, where external costs or benefits are present, assessing efficiency implications is more complex.

8. However, Harberger does separately examine the effects of taxing savings.

9. This is not a revenue projection for 2011, but rather applies projected 2011 rates to 2005 data. A projection for 2011 would account for expected income growth through 2011, as well as other factors that would affect revenues.

10. When offsets to revenue from payroll and state taxes are taken into account, the range is from $0.19 to $1.72.

11. However, Hall and Liebman (2000) suggest that the large transitory response observed by Goolsbee (2000) could reflect the exercising of past stock options and stock appreciation rather than a response to changing tax rates.

12. Following Slemrod and Yitzhaki (2002), I use "avoidance" to mean avoiding the tax, but not avoiding the activity. For example, choosing leisure is one way to avoid paying income tax, but that decision falls under real substitution and not avoidance, because the consumption bundle has changed as a result of the tax.

13. For income shares updated to 2006, see www.econ.berkeley.edu/~saez/TabFig2006prel.xls.

14. See CBO (2007).

15. For a review of the empirical literature, see Giertz (2004).

16. An income effect variable is also discussed, but is left out of their most-preferred specification.

17. Note that this is a partial equilibrium approach, except to the extent that the ETI is influenced by indirect responses to tax changes occurring throughout the economy. For a general equilibrium approach to evaluating changes to tax rates, see CBO (2004).

18. Tax rate changes at lower brackets can be analyzed analogously by focusing on the group of taxpayers facing the marginal rates in the bracket whose rate is changing. However, with a tax rate increase there will also be a gain (and with a decrease in the tax rate there will also be a loss) in revenues from those with incomes in the higher brackets. In the section below, I assume that a change in tax rates for a lower tax bracket results in no behavioral responses by those in higher tax brackets, although it is possible that there could be a response to the income effect.

19. Again, for more detail on how these responses are calculated, see Saez (2004).

20. This subgroup is not broken out in IRS (2007). Thus, I assume that individual MTRs return to their pre-EGTRRA levels, except that marriage penalty relief is extended.

21. Note that EMTRs and MTRs can be very different from average tax rates, which simply represent total taxes divided by total income. For an analysis of average income tax rates across income groups and over time, see Piketty and Saez (2007).

22. See IRS (2007), table 3.4.

23. Total tax revenue includes some revenue from capital gains taxes, so long as capital gains were taxed at a lower rate than the filers' top rate on ordinary income.

24. Dollar values are expressed in 2005 terms unless otherwise noted. Compare CBO (2008), which reports that extending the cuts in individual rates, along with the child tax credit, would lower revenues by $96 billion for 2011 and $152 billion for 2012. Those estimates account for interactions with the AMT, which are ignored in this paper. The CBO numbers also account for some behavioral responses but assume that total GDP is not affected by the rate changes.

25. Total 2005 revenues for this paper are $894.7 billion, which is smaller than total 2005 individual income taxes because it excludes some capital gains revenues and revenues from the Alternative Minimum Tax.

26. Note that if EGTRRA truly expired, the upper-income limit for the 15 percent tax bracket for married filers would fall, raising tax rates over a small range from 15 to 28 percent. This change is ignored in the analysis.

27. Again, this assumes no income effects.

28. Quoted by Laffer (2004, 1-2). That the curve is named for Laffer is an example of Stigler's law of misonomy, which holds that no discovery is named after the person who initially makes it.

References

Auten, Gerald, Robert Carroll, and Geoffrey Gee. 2008. The 2001 and 2003 tax rate reductions: An overview and estimate of the taxable income response. *National Tax Journal* 61 (September): 345–64.

Carroll, Robert. 1988. Do taxpayers really respond to changes in tax rates? Evidence from the 1993 Act. U.S. Department of Treasury, Office of Tax Analysis Working Paper 78, Washington, DC.

Chetty, Raj. Forthcoming. Is the taxable income elasticity sufficient to calculate deadweight loss? The implications of evasion and avoidance. *American Economic Journal: Economic Policy.*

Congressional Budget Office. 2004. *Macroeconomic analysis of a 10 percent cut in income tax rates.* Washington, DC: Congressional Budget Office.

_____. 2005. *Effective marginal tax rates on labor income.* Washington, DC: Congressional Budget Office.

_____. 2007. *Historical effective federal tax rates: 1979 to 2005.* Washington, DC: Congressional Budget Office. December.

_____. 2008. *An analysis of the president's budgetary proposals for fiscal year 2009.* Washington, DC: Congressional Budget Office.

Feenberg, Daniel, and James Poterba. 1993. Income inequality and the incomes of very high income taxpayers: Evidence from tax returns. In *Tax policy and the economy.* Vol. 7, ed. J. Poterba, 145–77. Cambridge, MA: MIT Press.

Feldstein, Martin. 1995a. The effect of marginal tax rates on taxable income: A panel study of the 1986 Tax Reform Act. *Journal of Political Economy* 103, no. 3: 551–72.

_____. 1995b. Tax avoidance and the deadweight loss of the income tax. NBER Working Paper No. 5055, Cambridge, MA.

_____. 1999. Tax avoidance and the deadweight loss of the income tax. *Review of Economics and Statistics* 81, no. 4: 674–80.

_____. 2008. Effects of taxes on economic behavior. *National Tax Journal* 61 (March): 131–9.

Fuchs, Victor, Alan Krueger, and James Poterba. 1998. Economists' views about parameters, values, and policies: Survey results in labor and public economics. *Journal of Economic Literature* 36 (September): 1387–1425.

Giertz, Seth. 2004. Recent literature on taxable-income elasticities. CBO Technical Paper 2004-16, Washington, DC. December. www.cbo.gov/ftpdocs/60xx/doc6028/2004-16.pdf.

_____. 2006. The elasticity of taxable income during the 1990s: A sensitivity analysis. CBO Working Paper 2006-3, Washington, DC. www.cbo.gov/ftpdocs/70xx/doc7037/2006-03.pdf.

_____. 2007. The elasticity of taxable income over the 1980s and 1990s. *National Tax Journal* 60 (December): 743–68.

Goolsbee, Austan. 1999. Evidence on the high-income Laffer curve from six decades of tax reforms. *Brookings Papers on Economic Activity* 2: 1–47.

_____. 2000. What happens when you tax the rich? Evidence from executive compensation. *Journal of Political Economy* 108 (2): 352–78.

Gruber, Jonathan, and Emmanuel Saez. 2002. The elasticity of taxable income: Evidence and implications. *Journal of Public Economics* 84 (1): 1–32.

Guyton, John, John O'Hare, Michael Stavrianos, and Eric Toder. 2003. Estimating the compliance cost of the U.S. individual income tax. *National Tax Journal* 56 (3): 673–88.

Hall, Brian, and Jeffrey Liebman. 2000. The taxation of executive compensation. In *Tax policy and the economy*. Vol. 14, ed. J. Poterba, 1–44. Cambridge, MA: MIT Press.

Harberger, Arnold. 1964. Taxation, resource allocation, and welfare. In *The role of direct and indirect taxes in the federal revenue system*, ed. John Due, 25–80. Princeton, NJ: Princeton University Press.

Heim, Bradley. 2007. The elasticity of taxable income: Evidence from a new panel of tax returns. Working Paper, U.S. Department of the Treasury, Washington, DC.

_____. Forthcoming. The effect of recent tax changes on taxable income. *Journal of Policy Analysis and Management*.

Internal Revenue Service. Statistics of Income Division. 2007. *Individual income tax returns 2005—Publication 1304.* Washington, DC: Internal Revenue Service.

Kopczuk, Wojciech. 2005. Tax bases, tax rates and the elasticity of reported income. *Journal of Public Economics* 89 (11-12): 2093–2119.

Laffer, Arthur. 2004. The Laffer curve: Past, present, and future. Heritage Foundation. *Backgrounder* 1765. June. http://www.heritage.org/Research/Taxes/upload/64214_1.pdf/.

Lindsey, Lawrence. 1987. Individual taxpayer response to tax cuts: 1982–1984, with implications for the revenue maximizing tax rate. *Journal of Public Economics* 33(2): 173–206.

Navratil, John. 1995. The Tax Reform Act of 1986: New evidence on individual taxpayer behavior from panel tax return data. In *Essays on the impact of marginal tax rate reductions on the reporting of taxable income on individual tax returns*. PhD diss., Harvard University.

Piketty, Thomas, and Emmanuel Saez. 2003. Income inequality in the United States, 1913–1998. *Quarterly Journal of Economics* 118 (1): 1–39.

_____. 2007. How progressive is the U.S. federal tax system? A historical and international perspective. *Journal of Economic Perspectives* 21 (1): 3–24.

Saez, Emmanuel. 2002. Do taxpayers bunch at kink points? NBER Working Paper No. 7366, Cambridge, MA.

_____. 2004. Reported incomes and marginal tax rates, 1960–2000: Evidence and policy implications. In *Tax policy and the economy*. Vol. 18, ed. James Poterba, 117–73. Cambridge, MA: MIT Press.

Sammartino, Frank, and David Weiner. 1997. Recent evidence on taxpayers' response to the rate increases in the 1990s. *National Tax Journal* 50 (3): 683–705.

Singleton, Perry. 2007. The effect of taxes on taxable earnings: Evidence from the 2001–2004 U.S. federal tax acts. Working Paper, Syracuse University, Syracuse, NY.

Slemrod, Joel. 1996. High income families and the tax changes of the 1980s: The anatomy of behavioral response. In *Empirical foundations of household taxation*, eds. Martin Feldstein and James Poterba, 169–89. Chicago: University of Chicago Press.

_____. 1998. Methodological issues in measuring and interpreting taxable income elasticities. *National Tax Journal* 51 (4): 773–88.

_____. 2002. Tax systems. *NBER Reporter* (Summer). www.nber.org/reporter/summer02/slemrod.html.

_____. 2007. Cheating ourselves: The economics of tax evasion. *Journal of Economic Perspectives* 21 (1): 25–48.

_____, and Wojciech Kopczuk. 2002. The optimal elasticity of taxable income. *Journal of Public Economics* 84 (1): 91–112.

_____, and Shlomo Yitzhaki. 2002. Tax avoidance, evasion, and administration. In *Handbook of Public Economics*. Vol. 3, ed. J. Auerbach and M. Feldstein, 1423–70. Amsterdam: Elsevier Science.

Stiglitz, Joseph. 2004. The parties' flip-flops on deficit spending: Economics or politics? *Economists' Voice* 1 (1). www.bepress.com/ev/vol1/iss1/art2.

6

A Response to Seth H. Giertz

Daniel Feenberg

There are two aspects of Seth Giertz's excellent chapter that I want to talk about. One is slightly technical; I want to try to provide some explanation for why estimating elasticity of taxable income (ETI) is so difficult. I think this difficulty is unappreciated by nonspecialists, who are quick to latch onto a favorite estimate without understanding the weaknesses in the estimation. The other aspect is a bit more philosophical and addresses the different functions of the partial equilibrium analysis done here and the general equilibrium work done a few years back in the macro group at the Congressional Budget Office (CBO). Perhaps surprisingly, I strongly endorse the partial equilibrium approach taken here for the comparison of tax reforms.

There is a section of the chapter called "Issues That Complicate Estimation," but the complex solutions offered by the works Giertz cites may be raising standard errors more than they are reducing bias.

Figure 6-1 below shows the share of adjusted gross income going to the top half percent of taxpayers from 1960 to 2004; the data are from the public use files of the IRS's Statistics of Income division. Jim Poterba and I looked at an earlier version of this figure a decade ago and saw constancy before 1981 and after 1987, with a one-time jump for a transition. Figure 6-2 excludes capital gains—a more legitimate approach, in my opinion, but one that shows much the same thing. We thought the likeliest explanation for change from 1981 to 1987 was the series of Reagan tax cuts; these were sharp for the very well off and led to an increased willingness to realize taxable income within that class. We didn't think that such a quick change in the economy could be related to deunionization, globalization, or skill-biased technical change, because those are things that occur slowly.

FIGURE 6-1

SHARE OF AGI RECEIVED BY TOP 0.5 PERCENT OF AGI RECIPIENTS

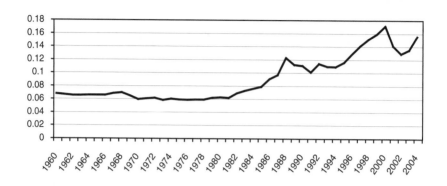

SOURCES: IRS-SOI and TAXSIM.

FIGURE 6-2

SHARE OF INCOME RECEIVED BY TOP 0.5 PERCENT OF
TAXPAYERS, RANKED BY NON-GAIN INCOME

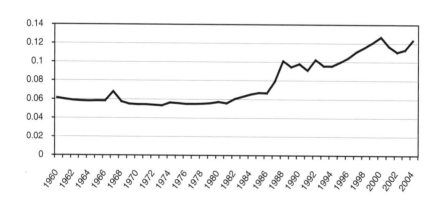

SOURCES: IRS-SOI and TAXSIM.

Of course, resting as it did on only two effective observations, our argument was not airtight. A variety of authors went ahead to use individual panel data; these are surveyed in Giertz's chapter. Hundreds of thousands or even millions of tax records should be more informative than one graph, but in fact they produce a disturbingly wide range of results.

Consider the problem of estimating the elasticity of taxable income using data from 2001 to 2005. There was a low-income group with no change in tax rate, a middle-income group with a small reduction in rates, and a high-income group with a larger reduction. It is certainly possible to treat this panel of taxpayers as a natural experiment. Regress the change in log income on the change in log net-of-tax share and you have a ready-made estimate of the elasticity of taxable income with respect to the net-of-tax share. Giertz mentions some of the problems with this regression, but I want to discuss the inadequacy of the available solutions.

Mean Reversion

Mean reversion is something that comes up in tax-price regressions but isn't much noticed in other contexts. This is not because mean reversion isn't universal—it largely is—but because it doesn't cause bias or inconsistency in the analysis of random cross-sections. But the studies cited here are mostly nonrandom panels. Those characteristics make mean reversion a problem. Consider a typical panel with 100 percent of base-year taxpayers of very high income, and one in ten thousand taxpayers with a modest income. Then the sample includes all the taxpayers going from high to low, but only one in ten thousand of those going from low to high. Even without stratification, there will still be a tendency for high-income taxpayers to be headed down, independent of the change in tax, and low-income taxpayers to be headed up. Given the correlation of income and change in rates, this will tend to bias the coefficient on the change in rates.

Moffitt and Wilhelm (2000) suggest controlling for base-period income. This makes some sense, intuitively. If high base-period income signals a likely decline in income, then adding base-period income as an explanatory variable can absorb the bias. This approach works if mean reversion is an AR-1 process with a coefficient that is constant across incomes and has meaningful independence from the change in tax rates. If mean reversion is AR-2, then using more early years could serve to control for reversion bias, but as far as I am aware this has never been done, nor has anyone tested for the structure of mean reversion.

Mean reversion may vary across incomes, so recent authors have followed Gruber and Saez (2002) in including more general functional forms, up to and including a ten-piece spline function of income. If a single (log) linear term in income steals variance and raises the standard errors, then a flexible function of income is far more problematic. With a ten-piece spline, it is difficult to imagine that there is much independent variation in tax rates left to measure. Now in the papers Giertz cites there are some other sources of variation—changes in state taxes, differences in itemized deductions or the alternative minimum tax (AMT), etc.—that do provide some non-income-related variation. It has become the norm in economics papers to be very explicit about what is controlled for, and let the reader figure out for himself what is left over to serve for identification. In these papers, very little is left over, and it isn't obvious that the leftover variance is more independent than what is controlled for. Giertz points out that various authors' best estimates are widely spread from 0 to perhaps 1, with large standard errors. With income so partialed out, these regressions are not strong evidence that the ETI is 0. A long panel, or several concatenated panels, could ameliorate this situation—it would have periods of stability and tax rate changes in both directions. Several authors have used this approach, but it hasn't achieved really tight results, and some authors have used the long time period to make separate ETI estimates for each reform—which rather defeats the purpose.

Inequality

Another problem that Giertz brings up is the potential effect of a long-term trend in income inequality. After a decade of stability, income inequality started to grow again in 1997 without the benefit of a tax cut. A variety of authors have argued that there is long-term trend growth in inequality independent of taxes, and that this should be controlled for in regression estimates of ETI. The cure seems to be roughly the same as the cure for mean reversion: add a measure of the taxpayer's place in the income distribution

FIGURE 6-3

SHARE OF WAGES ACCRUING TO THE TOP 0.5 PERCENT
OF EARNERS AND INCOME FROM NONQUALIFIED STOCK
OPTIONS AS A SHARE OF WAGES

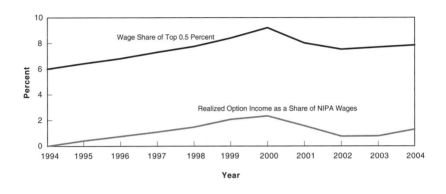

SOURCE: Congressional Budget Office using data from Scott Jaquette, Matthew Knittel, and Karl Russo, Recent Trends in Stock Options, OTA Working Paper 89 (Washington, D.C.: Department of the Treasury, Office of Tax Analysis, March 2003).
NOTES: Nonqualified stock options can be granted in unlimited amounts and, for purposes of the individual income tax, are treated the same as wages once they are exercised and the stock is purchased. NIPA = National Income and Product Accounts.

as an explanatory variable. Giertz mentions that you can't compensate for two sources of bias with one variable, which is true, but a ten-piece spline adds ten variables, so that shouldn't be a problem.

Personally, I don't think the spline is doing much that is good. My impression was always that the post-1997 increase in inequality was something new, and probably related to executive stock options. Most stock options are nonqualified and are taxed as wages to the recipient. This is the correct tax treatment, since they are deducted as wages from corporate income, but for the purpose of measuring inequality, they should really be looked at as capital gains. Data on stock options are not collected by the IRS, but the CBO (2008) produced this very interesting figure (reproduced here as figure 6-3). You can see that stock options increased by a startling amount just during the period of increased inequality, even to reproducing the downturn in 2001. So it is possible that the upturn in inequality is mostly an artifact of an overheated stock market, which can hardly become a long-term trend. If this is the case, the spline is merely absorbing variance that could usefully be pinning down the ETI. I should add that if you control for changes in income inequality, nothing of the evidence from the first figure contributes to the result.

What are we to conclude about the best choice of a value for ETI? If we don't know the true value, is it reasonable to use zero? I don't think so. I think Giertz is right to consider a range.

Partial versus General

Giertz takes a range of estimates for ETI and considers how they affect the forecast of revenue for several plausible tax reforms. He does this in the simplest way possible—multiplying the ETI by the relative change in marginal tax rates by the base-period income. Obviously this is partial equilibrium, and doesn't account for changes in relative prices or changes in individual and government savings that might result. The CBO macro group (CBO 2004) takes a full general equilibrium approach and provides forecasts for all major macroeconomic variables. These forecasts depend on assumptions about how taxpayers, bondholders, congressmen, and foreign countries will respond to the tax change and the resulting change in the deficit. A variety of assumptions yields a wide variety of forecasts; the common theme is that behavioral considerations—if they have any significance at all—involve increased effort by taxpayers preparing for future tax increases.

The partial equilibrium answer is not a forecast of the future, but more like a price list. We can think of a menu of possible tax and expenditure changes, each with a partial equilibrium cost estimate, and let the legislature pick a budget-consistent set of choices from that menu. If the legislature respects a budget-balance constraint, the general equilibrium considerations are minimal. This approach probably makes more sense than pricing every possible combination of expenditure and financing methods. An exception would be if there were significant interactions that make the cost of one program dependent on the cost of another. While there are always such interactions, are they significant enough to justify the complexity of the general equilibrium results? Are they even as large as the discrepancies arising from stacking order issues? Those don't seem to bother anyone.

Consider a pure spending program. When a new bridge is proposed, the cost is summarized by the quantity of resources times the price of resources. The funding source isn't considered. Should it be? It is just as significant as in a tax proposal of similar magnitude.

There is a good analogy to the benefits of money economies over barter economies. The existence of money prices reduces the need to find a coincidence of wants. The existence of revenue scores plays a similar role in simplifying government budget planning. The fact that the revenue score might not take into account financing decisions is not a mark against it, but of course not an excuse to ignore the effect of the overall deficit either.

Just to show how open-minded I am, I can make an argument in favor of general equilibrium analysis. Fifty years ago London was planning the Victoria subway line, and did a cost-benefit analysis showing that the benefits exceeded the costs. However, the construction was then financed with an increase in subway fares that so depressed patronage that the benefit of the new line was wiped out. I suppose if the inefficient financing had been known in advance, the line might not have been built. Of course, in the long run, the line was justified even with the inefficient financing, but that is a different story.

According to most people with whom I have discussed the general equilibrium analysis, that analysis proves that behavioral effects don't matter; but that isn't a fair summary of the implications for making tax policy. Using the methodology of Giertz's chapter, which is conventional in a large literature on the behavioral effects of income taxation, one can make interesting comparisons of tax reforms. For instance, Jim Poterba and I compared changing the top rate to changing the AMT. We found that changing the AMT had few behavioral consequences, because marginal rates were not much affected, while changing the top rate had significant behavioral effects that changed the revenue estimate substantially. The general equilibrium analysis is really about the effects of deficit policy, not tax policy.

In summary, I think Giertz's chapter is very well done, and I am pleased to see that, within the government, well-trained and thoughtful economists are writing papers for the open literature on these topics. It is a far distance from scholarship like this to the usual secretive alchemy of revenue scoring.

References

Congressional Budget Office. 2004. *Macroeconomic analysis of a 10 percent cut in income tax rates.* Washington, DC: CBO.

————. 2008. *Sources of the growth and decline in individual income tax revenues since 1994.* Washington, DC: CBO.

Gruber, Jonathan, and Emmanuel Saez. 2002. The elasticity of taxable income: Evidence and implications. *Journal of Public Economics* 84, no. 1: 1–32.

Moffitt, Robert, and Mark Wilhelm. 2000. Taxation and labor supply decisions of the affluent. In *Does Atlas shrug? The economic consequences of taxing the rich,* ed. Joel Slemrod, 193–234. Cambridge, MA: Russell Sage Foundation and Harvard University Press.

7

Welfare and Macroeconomic Effects of Deficit-Financed Tax Cuts: Lessons from CGE Models

John W. Diamond and Alan D. Viard

Tax cuts are often adopted with no explicit provision for offsetting the resulting revenue loss. The tax cut packages enacted on June 7, 2001, and May 28, 2003, were of this type. The decrease in revenue from such tax cuts initially increases the deficit, leading to a larger stock of government debt. However, the government's infinite-horizon budget constraint requires that offsets ultimately be adopted to service or retire that debt. Deficit-financed tax cuts have been controversial, with supporters often pointing to beneficial economic effects from reductions in distortionary taxes and opponents pointing to the adverse economic effects of deficits.

In view of these conflicting economic effects, an ultimate assessment of deficit-financed tax-cuts requires an estimate of the magnitudes of the various effects. Computable general equilibrium (CGE) models offer a natural way to obtain such estimates. In this chapter, we survey prior work on deficit-financed tax cuts in CGE models and present new results for a range of tax-cut experiments. Prior work has often emphasized the impact on macroeconomic variables, such as output, consumption, labor supply, and the capital stock. We report these impacts, but also emphasize the impact of deficit-financed tax cuts on the welfare of various generations in our overlapping-generations (OLG) framework. We find that even when deficit-financed tax cuts increase long-run output, they often reduce the welfare of future generations while increasing the welfare of present generations.

The chapter is organized as follows. We first provide the economic background for this topic, including the early results obtained by Auerbach and Kotlikoff (1987). We next survey the lessons learned from similar studies in the 2000s, describe the structure and calibration of the model that we use, and present our results. We then describe recent empirical work that investigates how actual deficit-financed tax cuts are ultimately paid for, and we briefly review the work that has been done in models of infinite-lived agents. Finally, we summarize our findings and suggest ways in which further research might extend our own.

Background

It is useful to review the basics of modeling OLG economies and the early work by Auerbach and Kotlikoff (1987) before we consider more recent research in this area.

Basic Theory in OLG Models. In an OLG model, the economic impact of a deficit-financed tax cut generally reflects both intergenerational redistribution and incentive effects.

In most cases, deficit-financed tax cuts lighten the fiscal burdens on older generations and increase those on younger generations, including those not yet born. The extent and distance of the shifting depend upon how rapidly the resulting debt is retired or serviced. It also depends, however, upon the ages of the affected taxpayers. A tax cut for the young financed by fiscal measures on the old may actually redistribute resources *toward* earlier generations, even if the financing measures are adopted later than the tax cut. Intergenerational redistribution from a deficit-financed tax cut is a zero-sum game; any gain that accrues to older or existing generations reflects a loss to younger or future generations.

The incentive effects depend upon how the initial tax cut and the financing measure affect distortions in the economy. For example, if a distortionary tax is reduced and the resulting debt is ultimately financed through a less distortionary fiscal instrument, a net improvement in the efficiency of the fiscal structure occurs.

These effects have an impact on the welfare of the affected generations and also alter (through income and substitution effects) their labor supply, consumption, and other decisions. Those decisions in turn determine the impact of the deficit-financed tax cut on the various macroeconomic variables.

Rationale for CGE Modeling. Some analyses have taken an ad hoc approach to the study of deficit-financed tax cuts, in which the various effects of deficits are discussed heuristically. This approach can easily lead to problems. For example, the analysis may assume that labor supply depends only upon the explicit marginal tax rate on labor, ignoring the impact of consumption and capital income taxes on labor supply. Dynamics may be handled in a very cursory manner, with little attention to the impact of incentives on the timing of work and other decisions. This approach cannot readily incorporate the simultaneity that is at the heart of general equilibrium analysis.

CGE models provide a more disciplined manner of proceeding. The models assume utility and profit maximization, with precise assumptions about the economic environment. The interaction of the effects is also taken into account. The direct income and substitution effects of the change in policy, for example, cause changes in factor prices, which in turn have income and substitution effects. CGE modeling therefore yields a coherent and self-consistent set of results. Of course, the ultimate validity of the results depends upon the extent to which the model accurately describes the actual economy.

Auerbach-Kotlikoff Results. The pioneering CGE modeling of deficit-financed tax cuts (among other policies) in an OLG framework was done by Auerbach and Kotlikoff (1987). We draw on their findings as background for the work that has been done in the 2000s.

Auerbach and Kotlikoff report the effects of broad-based income tax cuts that last one, five, and twenty years, followed by income tax increases that keep the debt-to-output ratio stabilized at its new, higher level. Their model features a (rather low) initial income tax rate of 15 percent. One experiment reduces the tax rate to 10 percent for twenty years, after which it is increased to maintain the ratio of debt to gross domestic product (GDP) at its year-twenty value. The required income-tax rate rises steadily over time, reaching a steady-state value of 30.4 percent. In the steady state, the capital stock is reduced 49 percent and labor supply is reduced 5 percent, causing output to fall by 19 percent and the wage rate to fall by 14 percent.

The dynamics are interesting. As Auerbach and Kotlikoff emphasize, the crowding out of capital proceeds in a very gradual manner, with much of it occurring after the tax cut has expired. After ten years, the capital stock has fallen only 2 percent. Even at the thirty-year mark, a decade after the tax cut has expired, the capital stock has fallen 20 percent, only two-fifths of the steady-state decline.

Auerbach and Kotlikoff identify two reasons for the slow pace. First, the income effect inducing additional consumption by the early generations is spread over their entire lifetimes, not just the period that the tax cut is in effect. Second, the substitution effect of the tax cut induces additional saving while it is in effect, because after-tax returns are higher during that period.

These policy experiments reduce steady-state welfare, but improve the welfare of earlier cohorts. Steady-state utility is reduced by more than 14 percent (measured by the fraction of lifetime resources that would have to be provided to compensate for the utility decline). The utility effects are largely redistributive, however, with utility gains for all generations already in the economy at the time the tax cut begins.

The duration of the deficit-financed tax cut has a sharply nonlinear effect. Compared to the five-year tax cut, the twenty-year tax cut causes ten times the increase in the steady-state income tax rate, seven times the steady-state crowding out of capital, nine times the steady-state labor supply reduction, and eleven times the steady-state welfare loss.

Auerbach and Kotlikoff noted that, in some respects, a longer tax cut is qualitatively different from a shorter one. During the period that the tax cut is in place, the substitution effects are equally large regardless of duration, but the income effects are larger for the longer tax cut. For example, they found that crowding out of capital begins immediately with the twenty-year tax cut because the income effect always outweighs the substitution effect. With the five-year tax cut, in contrast, there is initial crowding in of capital because the substitution effect outweighs the income effect within the five-year period.

Their results paint a dismal picture of the steady-state effect of deficit-financed tax cuts, as the short-run improvement in incentives from the initial tax cut is followed by a long-term deterioration due to the subsequent tax increase. In their words:

> Although temporary tax cuts may initially crowd in capital formation, there is no way to escape the long-run costs of short-run deficit finance. . . . Although one might think that, having crowded in capital through short-term tax cuts, one could adopt a painless policy for eliminating the accumulated debt (or simply meeting repayment commitments), such is not the case *when income taxes must be relied on*. One cannot postpone indefinitely raising tax rates, and once these rates are raised, the stimulus to saving through substitution effects is reversed; in addition, the cross-generational income effects that are at the heart of the crowding-out process ultimately play a decisive role in reducing national saving. (Auerbach and Kotlikoff 1987, 93; emphasis added)

Negative results are inevitable when the income-tax cut must ultimately be financed by income-tax increases.

Auerbach and Kotlikoff did not, however, consider deficit-financed tax cuts in which a reduction in one type of tax is ultimately financed by increasing a different type of tax or fiscal instrument that is potentially less distortionary. In that case, some, but not all, of the conclusions are modified. This approach has been developed in the 2000s and is the focus of our discussion below.

Lessons Learned in the 2000s

As CGE modeling has become more widespread, the number of studies examining deficit-financed tax cuts has increased. Although today's OLG models are broadly similar to Auerbach and Kotlikoff's (1987) early model, they are more likely to feature multiple production sectors, and they sometimes feature a rudimentary international sector.

Using the model described in the section below, Diamond (2005) considers a permanent extension of the 2001 and 2003 tax cuts. Financing begins after ten years and stabilizes the debt-output ratio at its new higher level. If the extension is financed by reductions in transfer payment, GDP is 0.8 percent higher in 2045–2054. If the extension is financed by a reduction in government consumption, GDP is 0.1 percent higher. If the extension is financed by an increase in tax rates, GDP is 0.2 percent lower. The differing impacts on GDP are largely due to differing impacts on capital accumulation; the corresponding changes in the 2045–2054 capital stock are 0.7 percent, 0.3 percent, and –1.2 percent.

A study by the U.S. Department of the Treasury (2006) employs a similar model to examine a permanent extension of the 2001 and 2003 tax cuts. This study finds that extending the cuts would raise long-run gross national product (GNP) and consumption by 0.7 percent if the extension was financed by a reduction in government consumption, but would reduce long-run real GNP by 0.9 percent if financed by an across-the-board increase in income tax rates. (In each case, the financing measure starts after 2017 and stabilizes the debt-to-output ratio at its new, higher level.) The difference again largely reflects a differing impact on capital accumulation, with the long-run capital stock rising 2.3 percent in the first case and falling 1.8 percent in the second case. The output impact in 2011–2016 is positive for both cases.

The study decomposes the effects of the tax cut extension into three components. Lowering the dividend and capital gains tax rate has long-run benefits under either financing mechanism, as does reducing the top four ordinary income tax rates. The gains, however, are larger under the government-consumption financing mechanism. Extending the remainder of the tax cuts generates long-run losses under either mechanism, although the losses are smaller when government consumption is reduced.

The Congressional Budget Office (CBO) produces annual dynamic analyses of the president's budget proposals. In recent years, these proposals have featured a net tax reduction, primarily reflecting a permanent extension of the 2001 and 2003 tax cuts. The most recent analysis (CBO 2008) considers two financing assumptions: a gradual reduction in government spending (both government purchases and transfer payments) and a gradual increase in marginal tax rates. In each case, the financing measures are phased in from 2019 through 2028. Using a closed-economy OLG model, CBO (2008) finds that the president's tax and spending proposals would increase 2009–2013 GNP by 0.4 percent and 2014–2018 GNP by 0.6 percent if they were financed by reducing government purchases. If the proposals were financed by raising tax rates, CBO finds GNP increases of 0.4 percent in each of the two time periods. Using an open-economy OLG model, CBO finds that the proposals would increase GNP by even larger amounts. With the government-spending adjustment, the increases for the two time periods are 0.8 percent and 1.2 percent; with the tax rate adjustment, they are 0.7 and 1.0 percent. CBO does not, however, examine the long-run effects.

Dennis et al. 2004 is another study by CBO economists. The study examines a 10 percent reduction in marginal tax rates, financed either by cuts in government spending or by increases in tax rates. The financing mechanisms start ten years after the tax cut is adopted and become fully effective after twenty years. In the OLG closed-economy model, steady-state GDP falls by 0.1 percent with the spending cut and by 1.5 percent with the tax rate increase. In the open-economy model, long-run GDP rises by 0.5 and 0.2 percent, respectively, but the more welfare-relevant GNP falls by 0.4 and 2.1 percent, respectively. Output always rises in the short run.

A study by the Joint Tax Committee (U.S. Congress 2006) considers a rate reduction in individual income taxes accompanied by base-broadening measures. In an OLG model, two different offsets to changes in government debt are used, one involving changes in transfer payments and one involving changes in individual income tax rates. Under either offset, the policy increases real GDP by 1.2 percent in 2006–2011. The 2007–2012 GDP increase is 1.9 percent with the transfer offset and 1.1 percent with the tax offset. The long-run increase in GDP is 2.6 percent with the transfer offset and 1.2 percent with the tax offset. The higher output growth is largely due to higher growth of the capital stock with the tax offset; long-run capital growth is 4.5 percent with the transfer offset and 1.8 percent with the tax offset. The long-run growth in consumption is 1.6 percent with the transfer offset and 1.0 percent with the tax offset.

Auerbach (2002) examines extension of the 2001 and 2003 tax cuts, though he considers a somewhat different policy experiment than most of the other studies. The other recent studies generally make those tax cuts permanent and then layer a financing mechanism on top of the tax cuts. (Of course, when the financing mechanism is a tax rate increase, layering on the tax increase effectively undoes the tax cuts in whole or in part.) Following the approach of Auerbach and Kotlikoff (1987), Auerbach instead considers experiments in which the 2001 and 2003 tax cuts remain in place for ten, fifteen, or twenty years before expiring, after which the debt-to-output ratio is stabilized using either increases in wage taxes or capital income taxes. Output increases while the tax cuts are in effect, but falls after the tax cuts expire. The long-run output decline is greater when the tax cut lasts longer, causing more debt to be accumulated, and when the financing is done through higher taxes on capital income. The negative effects are diminished if part of the revenue loss is offset by reducing government purchases during the time that the tax cuts are in effect.

In summary, the studies generally find that both the form of the initial tax cut and the financing method matter. An increase in steady-state output is most likely if the initial tax cut is targeted toward marginal rate reduction, if the financing method does not raise marginal rates and has income effects that encourage work (reduced transfer payments are ideal for those purposes), and if the financing is implemented quickly. The impact on steady-state output is generally driven by the impact on the steady-state capital stock rather than steady-state labor supply.

Although previous studies have offered valuable insights, their results are generally limited by the range of policy experiments and the extent of the welfare analysis undertaken. The papers have drawn from a somewhat limited set of initial tax cuts, generally across-the-board income tax cuts or extension of the 2001 and 2003 tax laws. Also, despite the early example set by Auerbach and Kotlikoff (1987), the more recent studies tend not to report the welfare impacts on the various generations.

To explore the welfare effects of various tax policy options, such as rate changes for wage, capital income, and corporate income taxes, we report some new results for a range of deficit-financed tax cuts.

Model Structure and Calibration

We use a dynamic OLG life-cycle computable general equilibrium model that explicitly calculates reform-induced changes in all asset values that would accompany a debt-financed tax cut. The model has three production sectors—owner-occupied housing, rental housing, and a composite good sector that includes all nonhousing goods and services. The time path of investment demands in all three sectors is modeled explicitly, taking into account capital stock adjustment costs. On the consumption side, the current tax advantage of owner-occupied housing relative to other assets is taken into account in modeling the demands for the three goods.

The model allows for a fairly detailed description of the transitional and long-run macroeconomic effects of debt-financed tax cuts and an examination of the intergenerational welfare effects. The model does not allow for multiple income groups within each generation.

This section outlines the basic structure of the model, which combines various features from Auerbach and Kotlikoff (1987) and other similar and well-known models constructed by Goulder and Summers (1989), Goulder (1989), Keuschnigg (1990), Fullerton and Rogers (1993), and Hayashi (1982). A detailed description of the model is provided in the appendix, and an even more complete description is provided in Diamond and Zodrow (2005).

Production. Firms in the composite good production sector produce output using a CES (constant elasticity of substitution) production function with capital and labor as inputs. Firms choose the time path of investment to maximize the present value of firm profits or, equivalently, to maximize firm value, net of all taxes and subject to quadratic costs of adjusting the capital stock. Total taxes in the composite good production sector include the corporate income tax and state and local property taxes. Each firm maintains a fixed debt-asset ratio and in each period pays out as dividends a constant fraction of earnings after taxes and depreciation, consistent with the old view of dividend taxation.

The model assumes individual-level arbitrage, which implies that the after-tax return to bonds must equal the after-tax return received by the shareholders of the firm. The value of the firm in the composite good sector equals the present value of all future net distributions to the owners of the firm.

Housing is produced in the owner-occupied and rental housing production sectors. Following Goulder and Summers (1989) and Goulder (1989), the model assumes that rental housing is produced by noncorporate landlords, and owner-occupied housing is produced by the owners. We assume that the technology used in the production of both rental housing and owner-occupied housing is identical, with capital and labor combined in the same CES production function. Landlords and owner-occupiers are also assumed to choose time paths of investment to maximize the equivalent of firm value, net of total taxes.

In the rental housing sector, the firm is modeled as a noncorporate firm, which implies that landlords are simply taxed at the individual level. In the owner-occupied housing sector, the measurement of the tax burden takes into account the fact that imputed rents are untaxed and that maintenance expenditures are not deductible, while mortgage interest and property taxes are deductible. The optimal investment path is calculated as above.

Individual Behavior. On the individual side, the model has a dynamic overlapping-generations framework, with fifty-five generations alive at each point in time. There is a representative individual for each generation, who has an economic life span (which begins upon entry into the workforce) of fifty-five years, with the first forty-five of those years spent working and the last ten years spent in retirement. Individual tastes are identical, so that differences in behavior across generations are due solely to differences in lifetime budget constraints. An individual accumulates assets from the time of "economic birth" that are used to finance both consumption over the life cycle, especially during the retirement period, and the making of bequests. The model includes a joy-of-giving bequest motive so that the real values of bequests change with changes in income and other economic variables.

The consumer is assumed to choose the time paths of consumption and leisure to maximize rest-of-life utility, which is a discounted sum of annual utilities, subject to a lifetime budget constraint that requires the present value of lifetime wealth, including inheritances, to equal the present value of lifetime consumption, including bequests. Annual utility is assumed to be a CES function of consumption of an aggregate consumption good and leisure. The aggregate consumption good is modeled as a CES function of the composite good and aggregate housing services (including a minimum-purchase requirement for both goods), with aggregate housing services in turn modeled as a CES function of owner-occupied and rental housing services.

In addition, the model includes a simple social security system, government purchases of the composite good, transfer payments, a humpbacked wage profile over the life cycle, a progressive tax on wage income, and constant average marginal tax rates applied to interest income, dividends, and capital gains. Transfer payments, excluding those funded by the payroll tax, are modeled as going disproportionately to younger generations, with the youngest 25 percent of the population receiving 31 percent of benefits. The progressive wage tax is modeled using a quadratic wage tax function similar to the method of Auerbach and Kotlikoff (1987). The model assumes a closed economy, no uncertainty, and perfect competition in every sector of the economy.

Calibration. The model is calibrated by choosing a number of parameter values and economic variables so that the initial income tax steady state in the base year, which is the year of reform, closely resembles the prevailing features of the U.S. economy in 2007. Parameter values are chosen to be consistent with empirical estimates and with parameter values used in other CGE studies, especially Altig et al. (2001), Auerbach and Kotlikoff (1987), Auerbach (1996), and Fullerton and Rogers (1993). The values for economic variables are generally chosen to be consistent with estimates from the National Income and Product Accounts.

Table 7-1 shows the values of the model parameters that are the most important in terms of determining individual and firm behavioral responses. The rate of time preference, ρ, is set equal to 0.005. In CGE models, the rate of time preference (or discount rate) is typically chosen in tandem with the intertemporal and intratemporal elasticities of substitution to generate reasonable levels of saving, investment, and labor supply in the initial steady state. Using the Euler equation approach, Ziliak and Kniesner (1999) estimate the rate of time preference under two specifications, obtaining values of 0.001 and 0.013. Jorgensen and Yun (2001) estimate a higher value of 0.02. The value we choose is at the low end of these estimates but is consistent with those in other CGE studies such as Altig et al. (2001).

The elasticity of intertemporal substitution (EIS) σ determines the willingness of consumers to substitute consumption across periods in response to changes in the relative prices of consumption, and it therefore plays a critical role in establishing the responsiveness of saving to tax changes. Empirical studies using aggregate consumption data typically find that the EIS is between 0 and 1, as noted in Diamond, Gunning, and Zodrow (forthcoming). The range of assumed values for the EIS used in CGE models is quite small, primarily because the chosen value must generate a steady-state capital stock that is consistent with the data and the assumed value of the pure rate of time preference. Auerbach and Kotlikoff (1987), Fullerton and Rogers (1993), Jorgenson and Yun (2001), Altig et al. (2001), and Diamond and Zodrow (2008) all assume a value of the EIS between 0.25 and 0.50,

TABLE 7-1

UTILITY FUNCTION PARAMETER VALUES

Symbol	Consumers	Value	Source
ρ	Rate of time preference	0.005	AAKSW
σ	Intertemporal elasticity of substitution	0.33	AAKSW, FR
ε	Intratemporal elasticity of substitution	0.8	FR
σ_{CH}	Elasticity of substitution for composite good and housing	0.8	N/A
σ_{TN}	Elasticity of substitution for taxed and non-taxed goods	0.5	N/A
σ_{RO}	Elasticity of substitution for rental and owner-occupied housing	2.0	N/A
α_E	Utility weight on leisure	0.23	N/A
α_C	Utility weight on composite consumption	0.77	N/A
α_G	Utility weight on composite non-housing consumption	0.78	N/A
α_H	Utility weight on composite housing consumption	0.22	N/A
α_{GT}	Utility weight on taxed non-housing consumption	0.56	N/A
α_{GN}	Utility weight on non-taxed non-housing consumption	0.44	N/A
α_O	Utility weight on owner-occupied housing	0.75	N/A
α_R	Utility weight on rental housing	0.25	N/A

SOURCES: FR = Fullerton and Rogers 1993; AAKSW = Altig et al. 2001.

depending partly on the interaction of the EIS with the choice of the pure rate of time preference parameter. We assume that the EIS is equal to 0.33.

The intratemporal elasticity of substitution ε and the percentage of the endowment devoted to leisure are key parameters that determine the compensated and uncompensated wage elasticities. For a given intratemporal elasticity of substitution, there is a larger percentage increase in labor supply associated with an increase in the wage rate if the share of the initial time endowment devoted to leisure is greater. The intratemporal elasticity of substitution determines consumer willingness to substitute between labor supply and leisure in response to changes in their relative prices, and it is therefore critical in determining the labor supply response to a change in the after-tax wage. We assume that the intratemporal elasticity of substitution is equal to 0.8 and that the share of the time endowment devoted to leisure is 0.3.[1]

TABLE 7-2

TECHNOLOGICAL PARAMETER VALUES

Symbol	Technology	Value	Source
N	Population growth rate	0.01	AK, FR
G	Technological growth rate	0.01	AK, FR
α_1	Capital share in composite good production	0.25	N/A
α_2	Capital share in housing production	0.98	N/A
β_X	Composite good adjustment cost parameter	5	N/A
β_{rh}	Rental housing adjustment cost parameter	5	N/A
β_{oh}	Owner-occupied housing adjustment cost parameter	5	N/A
μ_X	Composite good adjustment cost parameter	0.1001	$\delta + 0.0201$
μ_h	Housing adjustment cost parameter	0.0386	$\delta_h + 0.0201$
ζ	Dividend payout ratio in the composite good sector	0.68	NIPA
b_X	Debt-to-capital ratio in composite good sector	0.35	FR
b_{rh}	Debt-to-capital ratio in the rental sector	0.35	FR
b_{oh}	Debt-to-capital ratio in the owner-occupied sector	0.35	NIPA
δ	Economic depreciation in the composite good sector	0.1	N/A
δ_h	Economic depreciation in the housing sector	0.04	N/A

SOURCES: AK = Auerbach and Kotlikoff 1987; FR = Fullerton and Rogers 1993; NIPA = National Income and Product Accounts.

The elasticities of substitution between the composite good and aggregate housing consumption σ_{CH} and between rental and owner-occupied housing σ_{RO} are chosen so that the values of the compensated own-price elasticities of owner-occupied and rental housing are both roughly –0.8 as reported in Rosen (1985).[2] The various weighting parameters in the production functions and utility function are set to replicate as closely as possible the actual pattern of aggregate production and consumption for the three goods in the model.

Table 7-2 shows the technological parameter values. The rate of population growth is equal to 0.01 and the rate of technological growth is equal to 0.01, so that the economy grows at a 2 percent annual rate in steady state. The size of adjustment costs is also important in determining the effects of debt-financed tax cuts. We assume that the adjustment cost parameter β_X in the nonhousing production sector is equal to 5, meaning

TABLE 7-3
INITIAL STEADY-STATE BASE-YEAR VALUES (BILLIONS OF DOLLARS)

	Non-Housing	Rental Housing	Owner-Occupied Housing	Total
Output	11,760	536	1,547	13,844
Capital	14,799	3,734	12,956	31,489
Wages	8,820	10	417	9,490
Firm value	9,209	2,420	8,421	15,640
Investment	1,481	144	500	2,126
Earnings	2,368	N/A	N/A	2,368
Services	N/A	138	472	610

SOURCE: National Income and Product Accounts.

that an increase of one percentage point in the ratio of investment to the capital stock is associated with an increase of five percentage points in q. This value is a compromise between the estimates presented in Cummins, Hassett, and Hubbard (1994) and Shapiro (1986), and the earlier and considerably larger estimates presented in Summers (1981). In the absence of data on the values of the adjustment cost parameters in the owner-occupied and rental housing sectors, these values are assumed to equal the value of the adjustment cost parameter in the composite good sector, although there is no economic reason why these values would need to be the same.

Table 7-3 shows the initial steady-state values for output, the capital stock, firm value, investment, and earnings in each sector, which are calibrated to data from the U.S. Bureau of Economic Analysis (2007).

Table 7-4 shows the initial steady-state values for federal taxes in the base year. The federal tax system raises $2,609 billion in total tax revenue in the base year; federal income taxes raise $1,660 billion, and social security payroll taxes raise $949 billion, which is assumed to equal the amount of social security benefits. Total federal income taxes are 18.9 percent of GDP. Federal government expenditures are 19.5 percent of GDP. Government debt is assumed to be 30 percent of annual GDP. This ratio is constant in the initial steady state.

Table 7-5 shows the federal tax rates in the initial steady state. Under the progressive wage tax, the income-weighted average marginal wage tax rate is

TABLE 7-4

INITIAL STEADY-STATE BASE-YEAR TAXES AND TARGETS

(BILLIONS OF DOLLARS)

	Base-Year Values	Source
Federal Taxes	2,609	NIPA
Income	1,660	NIPA
Payroll	949	NIPA

SOURCE: NIPA = National Income and Product Accounts.

TABLE 7-5

INITIAL STEADY-STATE FEDERAL TAX RATES

Symbol	Description	Value
τ_{wmarg}	Income-weighted marginal wage tax rate	0.26
τ_{wave}	Average wage tax rate	0.214
τ_d	Dividend tax rate	0.163
τ_i	Interest income tax rate	0.152
τ_g	Composite good capital gains tax rate	0.05
τ_{gr}	Rental housing capital gains tax rate	0.05
τ_{go}	Owner-occupied housing capital gains tax rate	0
τ_s	Social security tax rate	0.107
τ_{sb}	Social security benefit tax rate	0.052
τ_b	Effective composite good business tax rate	0.288
τ_{rs}	Effective rental housing tax rate	0.21

SOURCE: Authors' model.

equal to 26 percent, and the average wage tax rate is 21.4 percent.[3] The tax rate on individual interest income is 15.2 percent, and the tax rate on dividends is 16.3 percent. Capital gains in the composite good and rental housing sectors are taxed at an effective annual accrual rate of 5 percent, and capital gains in the owner-occupied housing sector are untaxed.[4] The payroll tax is 10.7 percent; this is lower than the actual 15.3 percent rate because all wage income is subject to the payroll tax in the model. Social security benefits are taxed at 5.2 percent. The effective tax rate on investment in the composite good sector is 28.8 percent,[5] and the effective tax rate in the rental housing sector is 21 percent.[6] The model also includes deductions and credits in the calculation of taxable wage income. Deductions and credits are allowed only in the working period (the first forty-five years) of an individual's life; retired individuals do not receive deductions or credits.

Simulation Results

In this section we examine the macroeconomic and welfare effects of several alternative tax cuts under three different financing options. The magnitude of the tax reduction is determined so that the decrease in revenue over the ten-year period following enactment is $500 billion with no behavioral responses. The decrease in revenues is unanticipated and enacted immediately. For concreteness, we refer to the year of enactment as 2007, the year to which, as noted above, the initial steady state is calibrated. The tax cuts are permanent. There are three main financing methods: 1) government transfers (other than social security benefits) are reduced immediately to finance the tax cut; 2) government debt is used to finance the tax cut for ten years, and then government transfers (other than social security benefits) are reduced so that government debt grows at the steady-state rate of growth; and 3) government debt is used to finance the tax cut for ten years, and then all personal income tax rates (wage, interest, dividends, and capital gains) are increased proportionately so that government debt grows at the steady-state growth rate. The financing measures become known to agents when the tax cut is introduced.

Numerous other tax cuts and financing arrangements could be evaluated but are omitted due to space and other considerations. For two reasons, we do not consider a reduction in government purchases as a financing mechanism. First, we cannot model the intergenerational welfare effects, a key part of the analysis, without making arbitrary assumptions about the utility derived from the government purchases. Second, as an institutional matter, it is unclear whether government purchases, which are set in annual appropriation bills and which often respond to military developments and other volatile factors, could be reduced permanently as part of a fiscal reform.

For each financing mechanism, the discussion begins with a summary of the macroeconomic effects of enacting each of the tax cuts on prices, consumption, labor supply, investment, and output as well as the associated intergenerational welfare redistributions. We perform this analysis for cuts in the tax rates on wage, interest, dividend, and corporate income and for increases in tax credits.

Immediate Spending Offset. Table 7-6 shows the macroeconomic effects of a 3.9 percent reduction in the average and marginal wage tax rates, a 22.1 percent reduction in the effective tax rate on interest income, a 50.6 percent reduction in the effective tax rate on dividend income, a 12.3 percent reduction in the effective tax rate on corporate income, and a 41 percent increase in personal tax credits. In this set of simulations, transfer payments are immediately reduced to hold the amount of government debt constant.

Under the wage tax cut, the before-tax interest rate increases in the year of enactment by 23 basis points and then immediately returns to its approximate level in the initial steady state. Labor supply increases by 0.4 percent in every year after reform. The before-tax wage rate declines initially by 0.1 percent as labor supply increases immediately by 0.4 percent (note that the capital stock is initially fixed). Labor supply increases because the income-weighted after-tax wage rate increases by 1.6 percent in the year of reform (1.8 percent in the long run). Investment increases in all three production sectors, with investment in the housing sector increasing by twice as much as in the nonhousing sector in the years immediately following the reform. In the long run, investment in the nonhousing and housing sectors increases by 0.5 percent. Consumption increases by 0.2 percent in the year of enactment and by 0.4 percent in the long run. GDP increases by 0.3 percent in the year of reform and by 0.4 percent in the long run.

Under the interest income tax cut, the before-tax interest rate decreases in the year of enactment by five basis points and by thirty basis points in the long run. Labor supply increases by 0.1 percent in the year of enactment but then returns to its initial steady-state level. The before-tax wage rate is initially unchanged and increases by 0.1 percent in the long run as the capital stock increases by 0.4 percent. Investment increases in all three production sectors, with investment in the owner-occupied (rental) housing sector

TABLE 7-6

IMMEDIATE TRANSFER OFFSET

Year		2007	2008	2009	2012	2017	2027	2057	2107
Wage Tax Cut									
Δ	Before-tax interest rate	0.23	0.02	0.01	0.01	−0.01	−0.02	−0.02	−0.02
Δ%	Before-tax wage rate	−0.1	−0.1	−0.1	−0.1	0.0	0.0	0.0	0.0
Δ%	Labor supply	0.4	0.4	0.4	0.4	0.4	0.4	0.4	0.4
Δ%	Investment NH	0.4	0.4	0.4	0.4	0.5	0.5	0.5	0.5
Δ%	Investment RH	0.8	0.8	0.8	0.8	0.8	0.6	0.5	0.5
Δ%	Investment OH	0.8	0.9	0.8	0.8	0.8	0.6	0.5	0.5
Δ%	Consumption	0.2	0.2	0.3	0.3	0.3	0.3	0.4	0.4
Δ%	GDP	0.3	0.3	0.3	0.3	0.4	0.4	0.4	0.4
%	Debt to GDP	29.7	29.7	29.7	29.7	29.7	29.7	29.7	29.7
Interest Tax Cut									
Δ	Before-tax interest rate	−0.05	−0.27	−0.27	−0.28	−0.28	−0.29	−0.30	−0.30
Δ%	Before-tax wage rate	0.0	0.0	0.0	0.0	0.0	0.1	0.1	0.1
Δ%	Labor supply	0.1	0.0	0.0	0.0	0.0	0.0	0.0	0.0
Δ%	Investment NH	0.3	0.3	0.3	0.3	0.4	0.4	0.4	0.4
Δ%	Investment RH	0.6	0.6	0.6	0.6	0.6	0.5	0.4	0.4
Δ%	Investment OH	1.1	1.0	1.0	0.9	0.8	0.6	0.6	0.6
Δ%	Consumption	−0.1	−0.1	−0.1	−0.1	0.0	0.0	0.0	0.0
Δ%	GDP	0.0	0.0	0.0	0.0	0.1	0.1	0.1	0.1
%	Debt to GDP	29.8	29.8	29.8	29.8	29.8	29.8	29.8	29.8
Dividend Tax Cut									
Δ	Before-tax interest rate	0.24	0.17	0.15	0.14	0.11	0.08	0.05	0.04
Δ%	Before-tax wage rate	0.0	0.0	0.1	0.2	0.4	0.5	0.6	0.7
Δ%	Labor supply	0.1	0.1	0.1	0.1	0.1	0.1	0.1	0.1
Δ%	Investment NH	2.6	2.6	2.6	2.5	2.5	2.6	2.7	2.7
Δ%	Investment RH	−3.2	−2.6	−2.1	−1.4	−0.3	0.2	0.2	0.1
Δ%	Investment OH	−2.7	−2.2	−1.8	−1.2	−0.2	0.2	0.2	0.2
Δ%	Consumption	−0.2	−0.1	−0.1	0.0	0.2	0.3	0.4	0.4
Δ%	GDP	0.0	0.1	0.1	0.2	0.4	0.6	0.7	0.7
%	Debt to GDP	29.8	29.8	29.8	29.7	29.7	29.6	29.6	29.6

(*table 7-6 continued*)

Year		2007	2008	2009	2012	2017	2027	2057	2107
Corporate Tax Cut									
Δ	Before-tax interest rate	0.48	0.15	0.12	0.12	0.10	0.08	0.05	0.05
Δ%	Before-tax wage rate	0.0	0.0	0.1	0.1	0.3	0.4	0.5	0.5
Δ%	Labor supply	0.1	0.1	0.1	0.1	0.1	0.1	0.1	0.1
Δ%	Investment NH	1.9	1.9	1.9	1.9	1.9	1.9	2.1	2.1
Δ%	Investment RH	−2.8	−2.2	−1.9	−1.3	−0.4	0.0	0.0	0.0
Δ%	Investment OH	−2.3	−1.9	−1.6	−1.1	−0.3	0.0	0.1	0.0
Δ%	Consumption	−0.1	−0.1	−0.1	0.0	0.1	0.2	0.3	0.3
Δ%	GDP	0.0	0.1	0.1	0.2	0.3	0.5	0.5	0.5
%	Debt to GDP	29.8	29.8	29.8	29.7	29.7	29.7	29.6	29.6
Tax Credit Increase									
Δ	Before-tax interest rate	0.04	−0.01	−0.01	−0.01	−0.02	−0.02	−0.02	−0.02
Δ%	Before-tax wage rate	0.0	0.0	0.0	0.0	0.0	0.0	0.0	0.0
Δ%	Labor supply	0.0	0.0	0.0	0.0	0.0	0.0	0.0	0.0
Δ%	Investment NH	0.1	0.1	0.1	0.1	0.1	0.1	0.2	0.2
Δ%	Investment RH	0.1	0.2	0.2	0.2	0.2	0.1	0.1	0.1
Δ%	Investment OH	0.1	0.1	0.2	0.2	0.2	0.1	0.1	0.1
Δ%	Consumption	−0.1	−0.1	−0.1	−0.1	0.0	0.0	0.0	0.0
Δ%	GDP	0.0	0.0	0.0	0.0	0.0	0.0	0.0	0.0
%	Debt to GDP	29.8	29.8	29.8	29.8	29.8	29.8	29.8	29.8

SOURCE: Authors' calculations.
NOTES: NH = nonhousing, RH = rental housing, OH = owner-occupied housing.

increasing by 1.1 (0.6) percent in the year of reform. Nonhousing investment initially increases by 0.3 percent in the years immediately following the tax cut. In the long run, investment in the nonhousing and rental housing sectors increases by 0.4 percent, and investment in the owner-occupied housing sector increases by 0.6 percent. Consumption decreases by 0.1 percent in the year of enactment and then returns to its initial steady-state level after ten years. GDP increases by 0.1 percent in the long run.

The macroeconomic effects of reducing the dividend tax rates (recall that we are assuming the old view of dividend taxes) and corporate tax rates are similar to each other. The before-tax interest rate increases by twenty-four (forty-eight) basis points in the year the dividend (corporate) tax rate is cut and then gradually declines to a level that is four (five) basis points higher than in the initial steady state. Under the dividend and corporate rate cuts, labor supply increases by 0.1 percent in every year after enactment. Under the dividend (corporate) rate cut, the before-tax wage rate is initially unchanged and increases by 0.7 (0.5) percent in the long run as the capital stock increases by 2.7 (2.1) percent. Investment in the owner-occupied and rental housing sectors decreases 2.3 to 3.2 percent in the year of enactment. Nonhousing investment increases by 2.6 (1.9) percent in the year of enactment under the dividend (corporate) tax cut. In the long run, investment in the nonhousing sector increases by 2.7 (2.1) percent under the dividend (corporate) rate cut. Consumption decreases by 0.1 percent in the year of enactment and increases by 0.3 to 0.4 percent in the long run. Under the dividend (corporate) tax cut, GDP increases by 0.7 (0.5) percent in the long run.

One might think that corporate and dividend tax cuts of the same size should have identical quantitative effects, as well as similar qualitative effects, since they both reduce the effective tax rate on corporate investment. The two taxes differ, though, in a subtle but crucial respect. Due to accelerated depreciation, a corporate tax cut includes a windfall gain for existing capital, as some deferred tax liabilities are forgiven. In this old-view world, there is no similar windfall from the dividend tax cut. The dividend tax cut is therefore more powerful in promoting long-run growth because none of it is "wasted" on a lump-sum transfer to holders of existing assets. This is analytically similar, but quantitatively smaller, than the difference between adopting a wage tax and a consumption tax. We return to this key difference in our discussion of welfare effects.

An increase in personal tax credits offset by a reduction in transfers does not significantly affect the before-tax wage rate, labor supply, or GDP. The before-tax interest rate increases by four basis points in the year of enactment and then declines to a level two basis points lower than in the initial steady state. In the long run, investment in the owner-occupied and rental housing sectors increases by 0.1 percent, and nonhousing investment increases by 0.2 percent. Consumption decreases by 0.1 percent in the year of enactment and then returns to its initial steady-state level after ten years. Both the tax credits and the transfer payments are a lump sum, but the substitution of the former for the latter provides a slight boost to investment because the tax credits are distributed to younger cohorts.

Government Transfer Offset after Ten Years. Table 7-7 shows the macroeconomic effects of the various tax cuts if government debt is used to finance the tax cuts for ten years and transfer payments are then decreased to hold the growth rate of government debt constant at the steady-state rate of growth in the economy.

Under the wage tax cut with a reduction in government transfer payments after ten years, the before-tax interest rate increases by sixteen basis points in the year of enactment and by eight basis points in the long run. The before-tax wage rate declines by 0.1 percent as labor supply increases immediately by 0.4 percent (note, again, that the capital stock is initially fixed). Labor supply increases because the income-weighted after-tax wage rate increases by 1.6 percent in the year of reform (1.8 percent in the long run). In the years immediately following the tax cut, investment increases in all three production sectors, with investment in the housing sector increasing by twice as much as in the nonhousing sector. In the long run, investment in the nonhousing and housing sectors decreases by 0.1 to 0.2 percent. Consumption increases by 0.3 percent in the year of enactment and by 0.4 percent in the long run. GDP increases by 0.3 percent in the long run. The debt-to-GDP ratio increases from 29.7 percent in the initial steady state to 33.3 percent in the long run. In this case, the increase in government debt relative to GDP increases interest rates and crowds out private investment.

A reduction in the tax rate on interest income accompanied by a reduction in government transfers after ten years has very modest effects in the long run on the macroeconomic aggregates. The before-tax interest rate decreases in the year of enactment by eleven basis points and by twenty-two basis points in the long run. Labor supply, consumption, and GDP are essentially unchanged from the initial steady state. In the years immediately after the tax cut, investment increases in all three production sectors, with investment in the owner-occupied (rental) housing sector increasing by 0.8 (0.4) percent in the year of reform. Nonhousing investment increases by 0.1 percent in the year of the tax cut. In the long run, investment in the nonhousing and rental

TABLE 7-7

TRANSFER OFFSET AFTER TEN YEARS

Year		2007	2008	2009	2012	2017	2027	2057	2107
Wage Tax Cut									
Δ	Before-tax interest rate	0.16	0.03	0.03	0.02	0.03	0.04	0.08	0.08
Δ%	Before-tax wage rate	−0.1	−0.1	−0.1	−0.1	−0.1	−0.1	−0.1	−0.2
Δ%	Labor supply	0.4	0.4	0.4	0.4	0.4	0.4	0.4	0.4
Δ%	Investment NH	0.2	0.2	0.2	0.2	0.1	0.0	−0.2	−0.2
Δ%	Investment RH	0.5	0.5	0.5	0.4	0.2	0.0	−0.2	−0.2
Δ%	Investment OH	0.6	0.5	0.5	0.4	0.2	0.0	−0.2	−0.1
Δ%	Consumption	0.3	0.3	0.3	0.3	0.3	0.4	0.4	0.4
Δ%	GDP	0.3	0.3	0.3	0.3	0.3	0.3	0.3	0.3
%	Debt to GDP	29.7	30.0	30.3	30.9	32.8	33.3	33.3	33.3
Interest Tax Cut									
Δ	Before-tax interest rate	−0.11	−0.25	−0.26	−0.26	−0.26	−0.25	−0.22	−0.22
Δ%	Before-tax wage rate	0.0	0.0	0.0	0.0	0.0	0.0	0.0	−0.1
Δ%	Labor supply	0.0	0.0	0.0	0.0	0.0	0.0	0.0	0.0
Δ%	Investment NH	0.1	0.1	0.1	0.1	0.1	0.0	−0.2	−0.2
Δ%	Investment RH	0.4	0.4	0.4	0.3	0.1	0.0	−0.2	−0.1
Δ%	Investment OH	0.8	0.8	0.7	0.6	0.4	0.2	0.0	0.0
Δ%	Consumption	0.0	0.0	0.0	0.0	0.0	0.0	0.0	0.0
Δ%	GDP	0.0	0.0	0.0	0.0	0.0	0.0	0.0	0.0
%	Debt to GDP	29.8	30.1	30.3	30.8	32.3	32.7	32.7	32.7
Dividend Tax Cut									
Δ	Before-tax interest rate	0.17	0.17	0.17	0.16	0.16	0.15	0.17	0.17
Δ%	Before-tax wage rate	0.0	0.0	0.1	0.2	0.3	0.4	0.4	0.4
Δ%	Labor supply	0.1	0.1	0.1	0.1	0.1	0.1	0.1	0.1
Δ%	Investment NH	2.3	2.3	2.3	2.2	2.1	2.0	1.8	1.8
Δ%	Investment RH	−3.5	−3.0	−2.6	−2.0	−1.1	−0.6	−0.8	−0.7
Δ%	Investment OH	−3.1	−2.6	−2.3	−1.7	−1.0	−0.5	−0.7	−0.6
Δ%	Consumption	−0.1	−0.1	0.0	0.1	0.2	0.4	0.5	0.4
Δ%	GDP	0.0	0.1	0.1	0.2	0.4	0.5	0.5	0.5
%	Debt to GDP	29.8	30.1	30.5	31.3	33.6	34.1	34.1	34.1

(table 7-7 continued)

Year		2007	2008	2009	2012	2017	2027	2057	2107
Corporate Tax Cut									
Δ	Before-tax interest rate	0.41	0.15	0.14	0.14	0.14	0.14	0.17	0.17
Δ%	Before-tax wage rate	0.0	0.0	0.1	0.1	0.2	0.3	0.3	0.3
Δ%	Labor supply	0.1	0.1	0.1	0.1	0.1	0.1	0.1	0.1
Δ%	Investment NH	1.7	1.7	1.6	1.6	1.5	1.4	1.2	1.2
Δ%	Investment RH	−3.1	−2.6	−2.3	−1.8	−1.1	−0.7	−0.9	−0.8
Δ%	Investment OH	−2.7	−2.3	−2.0	−1.6	−1.0	−0.7	−0.8	−0.7
Δ%	Consumption	−0.1	0.0	0.0	0.1	0.2	0.3	0.4	0.3
Δ%	GDP	0.0	0.1	0.1	0.2	0.3	0.4	0.4	0.4
%	Debt to GDP	29.8	30.2	30.5	31.3	33.9	33.9	33.9	33.9
Tax Credit Increase									
Δ	Before-tax interest rate	−0.03	0.00	0.00	0.01	0.02	0.05	0.10	0.10
Δ%	Before-tax wage rate	0.0	0.0	0.0	0.0	0.0	−0.1	−0.2	−0.2
Δ%	Labor supply	0.0	0.0	0.0	0.0	0.0	0.0	0.0	0.0
Δ%	Investment NH	−0.1	−0.1	−0.1	−0.2	−0.3	−0.4	−0.7	−0.7
Δ%	Investment RH	−0.2	−0.2	−0.3	−0.3	−0.5	−0.6	−0.8	−0.7
Δ%	Investment OH	−0.2	−0.2	−0.3	−0.3	−0.5	−0.6	−0.7	−0.7
Δ%	Consumption	0.0	0.0	0.0	0.0	0.0	0.0	0.0	0.0
Δ%	GDP	0.0	0.0	0.0	0.0	0.0	0.0	−0.1	−0.1
%	Debt to GDP	29.8	30.1	30.5	31.2	34.1	34.1	34.1	34.1

SOURCE: Authors' calculations.
NOTES: NH = nonhousing, RH = rental housing, OH = owner-occupied housing.

housing sectors decreases by 0.1 to 0.2 percent as an increased debt-to-GDP ratio crowds out private investment. The debt-to-GDP ratio increases from 29.8 percent in the initial steady state to 32.7 percent in the long run. As a result of the lower interest rate, which reduces government spending, the debt-to-GDP ratio in this scenario increases by less than it does under the wage tax cut with the same financing assumption.

In this case, as under the immediate financing offset, the macroeconomic effects of reducing the dividend and corporate tax rates are similar to each other. Cutting the dividend tax rate causes the before-tax interest rate to increase by seventeen basis points in the year of enactment and in the long run. Cutting the corporate tax rate causes the before-tax interest rate to increase by forty-one basis points in the year of enactment and then gradually decline to a level that is seventeen basis points higher than in the initial steady state. Under the dividend and corporate rate cuts, labor supply increases by 0.1 percent in every year after enactment. Under the dividend (corporate) rate cut, the before-tax wage rate is initially unchanged and increases by 0.4 (0.3) percent in the long run as the capital stock increases by 2.7 (2.1) percent. Investment in the owner-occupied and rental housing sectors decreases 2.7 to 3.5 percent in the year of enactment. Nonhousing investment increases by 2.3 (1.7) percent in the year of enactment under the dividend (corporate) tax cut. In the long run, investment in the nonhousing sector increases by 1.8 (1.2) percent under the dividend (corporate) rate cut. Consumption decreases by 0.1 percent in the year of enactment and increases by 0.3 to 0.4 percent in the long run. Under the dividend (corporate) tax cut, GDP increases by 0.5 (0.4) percent in the long run.

An increase in personal tax credits offset by a reduction in transfers after ten years does not significantly affect the before-tax wage rate, labor supply, or consumption. The before-tax interest rate decreases by three basis points in the year of enactment and then increases to a level ten basis points higher than in the initial steady state. In the long run, investment in all three production sectors decreases by 0.7 percent. GDP decreases by 0.1 percent in the long run.

Across-the-Board Tax Increase after Ten Years. Table 7-8 shows the macroeconomic effects of the various tax cuts if government debt is used to finance the tax cuts for ten years, and an across-the-board tax increase is then implemented to hold the growth rate of government debt constant at the steady-state rate of growth in the economy. This tax rate increase is layered on top of the permanent tax cut.

In the case of a wage tax cut with an across-the-board increase in tax rates after ten years, the before-tax interest rate increases by thirteen basis points in the year of enactment and by fifteen basis points in the long run. The before-tax wage rate declines by 0.1 percent as labor supply increases immediately by 0.4 percent. Labor supply increases because the income-weighted after-tax wage rate increases by 1.6 percent in the ten years following enactment. After ten years, tax rates are increased to hold the growth of government debt constant. As a result, the increase in the after-tax wage rate declines from 1.6 percent to 0.6 percent in year 2017. In the long run, the after-tax wage rate increases by 0.04 percent as the net wage tax rate is reduced by 1 percent. Labor supply increases by 0.1 percent in the long run. In the year immediately following the tax cut, investment in the housing sector increases by 0.3 to 0.6 percent, while investment in the nonhousing sector is unchanged. In the long run, investment in the nonhousing sector decreases by 1.6 percent, and investment in housing decreases by 0.7 to 1.3 percent. Consumption increases by 0.3 percent in the year of enactment and decreases by 0.1 percent in the long run. GDP increases by 0.3 percent in the year of enactment and decreases by 0.3 percent in the long run. The debt-to-GDP ratio increases from 29.7 percent in the initial steady state to 33.6 percent in the long run. In this case, debt-financed tax cuts increase government debt relative to GDP and thus increase interest rates and crowd out private investment. Tax burdens on investment are also higher in the steady state, due to the tax increases.

Decreasing the tax rate on interest income with an across-the-board tax increase after ten years has very modest effects on the fundamental macroeconomic aggregates in the long run. The before-tax interest rate decreases in the year of enactment by thirteen basis points and by eighteen basis points in the long run. In the first ten years after enactment, the after-tax wage rate and labor supply are unchanged. After ten years, the increase in the marginal wage tax rate and the decline in the before-tax wage rate, which is related to slower growth in investment, lead to a 0.2 percent decrease in labor supply in the long run. In the year immediately after the tax cut, investment in owner-occupied housing increases by 0.9 percent, and investment in rental housing increases by 0.2 percent. Nonhousing investment is unchanged in the first few years following the tax cut. The across-the-board tax increase reduces investment beginning in 2017. In the long run, investment in the nonhousing sector decreases by 1.3 percent, and investment in the owner-occupied and rental housing sectors decreases by 0.5 and 1.1 percent, respectively. In this case, the debt-to-GDP ratio increases from 29.8 percent in the initial steady state to 32.9 percent in the long run. The debt-to-GDP ratio increases by less than it does under the

TABLE 7-8

TAX OFFSET AFTER TEN YEARS

Year		2007	2008	2009	2012	2017	2027	2057	2107
Wage Tax Cut									
Δ	Before-tax interest rate	0.13	0.03	0.03	0.03	0.04	0.06	0.13	0.15
Δ%	Before-tax wage rate	−0.1	−0.1	−0.1	−0.1	−0.1	−0.2	−0.4	−0.4
Δ%	Labor supply	0.4	0.4	0.4	0.4	0.4	0.1	0.1	0.1
Δ%	Investment NH	0.0	0.0	−0.1	−0.2	−0.7	−1.1	−1.5	−1.6
Δ%	Investment RH	0.3	0.3	0.2	0.1	−0.3	−1.3	−1.4	−1.3
Δ%	Investment OH	0.6	0.6	0.6	0.5	0.6	−0.6	−0.8	−0.7
Δ%	Consumption	0.3	0.3	0.3	0.4	0.4	0.1	0.0	−0.1
Δ%	GDP	0.3	0.3	0.3	0.3	0.3	−0.1	−0.2	−0.3
%	Debt to GDP	29.7	30.0	30.3	30.9	32.9	33.5	33.5	33.6
Interest Tax Cut									
Δ	Before-tax interest rate	−0.13	−0.25	−0.26	−0.26	−0.27	−0.24	−0.19	−0.18
Δ%	Before-tax wage rate	0.0	0.0	0.0	0.0	0.0	−0.1	−0.2	−0.3
Δ%	Labor supply	0.0	0.0	0.0	0.0	0.0	−0.2	−0.2	−0.2
Δ%	Investment NH	0.0	0.0	0.0	−0.1	−0.5	−0.9	−1.2	−1.3
Δ%	Investment RH	0.2	0.2	0.2	0.0	−0.3	−1.1	−1.2	−1.1
Δ%	Investment OH	0.9	0.9	0.8	0.7	0.8	−0.4	−0.5	−0.5
Δ%	Consumption	0.0	0.0	0.0	0.0	0.0	−0.2	−0.3	−0.4
Δ%	GDP	0.0	0.0	0.0	0.0	0.0	−0.3	−0.4	−0.5
%	Debt to GDP	29.8	30.1	30.3	30.8	32.4	32.9	32.9	32.9
Dividend Tax Cut									
Δ	Before-tax interest rate	0.14	0.17	0.17	0.17	0.16	0.19	0.24	0.25
Δ%	Before-tax wage rate	0.0	0.0	0.1	0.2	0.3	0.3	0.2	0.2
Δ%	Labor supply	0.1	0.1	0.1	0.1	0.0	−0.3	−0.3	−0.3
Δ%	Investment NH	2.2	2.1	2.0	1.9	1.2	0.8	0.5	0.4
Δ%	Investment RH	−3.8	−3.3	−2.9	−2.4	−1.8	−2.0	−2.0	−1.9
Δ%	Investment OH	−3.0	−2.6	−2.2	−1.6	−0.6	−1.3	−1.4	−1.3
Δ%	Consumption	−0.1	0.0	0.0	0.1	0.3	0.1	0.0	0.0
Δ%	GDP	0.0	0.1	0.1	0.2	0.3	0.1	0.0	0.0
%	Debt to GDP	29.8	30.1	30.5	31.3	33.7	34.4	34.4	34.4

(*table 7-8 continued*)

Year		2007	2008	2009	2012	2017	2027	2057	2107
Corporate Tax Cut									
Δ	Before-tax interest rate	0.37	0.15	0.14	0.15	0.15	0.18	0.24	0.25
Δ%	Before-tax wage rate	0.0	0.0	0.1	0.1	0.2	0.2	0.1	0.0
Δ%	Labor supply	0.0	0.0	0.0	0.0	0.0	−0.3	−0.3	−0.3
Δ%	Investment NH	1.5	1.5	1.4	1.3	0.7	0.2	−0.1	−0.2
Δ%	Investment RH	−3.3	−2.9	−2.6	−2.2	−1.7	−2.1	−2.1	−2.0
Δ%	Investment OH	−2.6	−2.2	−2.0	−1.5	−0.6	−1.4	−1.4	−1.4
Δ%	Consumption	0.0	0.0	0.0	0.1	0.2	0.0	−0.1	−0.1
Δ%	GDP	0.0	0.1	0.1	0.2	0.2	0.0	−0.1	−0.2
%	Debt to GDP	29.8	30.2	30.5	31.3	33.5	34.1	34.2	34.2
Tax Credit Increase									
Δ	Before-tax interest rate	−0.06	0.00	0.01	0.01	0.03	0.08	0.18	0.20
Δ%	Before-tax wage rate	0.0	0.0	0.0	0.0	−0.1	−0.2	−0.5	−0.5
Δ%	Labor supply	0.0	0.0	0.0	0.0	0.0	−0.4	−0.4	−0.4
Δ%	Investment NH	−0.3	−0.3	−0.4	−0.5	−1.1	−1.8	−2.4	−2.5
Δ%	Investment RH	−0.4	−0.5	−0.6	−0.7	−1.0	−2.4	−2.4	−2.2
Δ%	Investment OH	−0.1	−0.1	−0.1	−0.1	0.1	−1.5	−1.6	−1.5
Δ%	Consumption	0.0	0.0	0.0	0.0	0.0	−0.4	−0.6	−0.6
Δ%	GDP	0.0	0.0	0.0	0.0	−0.1	−0.5	−0.8	−0.8
%	Debt to GDP	29.8	30.1	30.5	31.2	33.6	34.4	34.4	34.5

SOURCE: Authors' calculations.
NOTES: NH = nonhousing, RH = rental housing, OH = owner-occupied housing.

wage tax cut with the same financing assumption, because the decrease in the interest rate reduces government spending on interest payments.

The macroeconomic effects of reducing the dividend and corporate tax rates are similar to each other in this case (an across-the-board tax increase), just as they were under the other two financing assumptions. Cutting the dividend tax rate causes the before-tax interest rate to increase by fourteen basis points in the year of enactment. After 2017, the before-tax interest rate increases steadily until it is twenty-five basis points higher in the long run. Cutting the corporate tax rate causes the before-tax interest rate to increase by thirty-seven basis points in the year of enactment and then to decline to a level that is fifteen basis points higher than in the initial steady state in the following year. After 2017, the before-tax interest rate gradually increases until it is twenty-five basis points higher than in the initial equilibrium. Under the dividend and corporate rate cuts, labor supply decreases by 0.3 percent in the long run. Under the dividend rate cut, the before-tax wage rate is initially unchanged and eventually increases by 0.2 percent; under the corporate rate cut, it remains largely unchanged. Under the dividend rate cut, investment in the owner-occupied and rental housing sectors decreases by 3.0 to 3.8 percent in the year of enactment. Nonhousing investment increases by 2.2 percent in the year of enactment. Under the corporate rate cut, investment in the owner-occupied and rental housing sectors decreases by 2.6 to 3.3 percent in the year of enactment. Nonhousing investment increases by 1.5 percent in the year of enactment. In the long run, investment in the nonhousing sector increases by 0.4 percent under the dividend rate cut and decreases by 0.2 percent under the corporate rate cut. Consumption changes by 0.0 to –0.1 percent in the year of enactment and by 0.0 to –0.2 percent in the long run. In the long run, a dividend tax cut does not change the level of GDP, while the corporate tax cut causes GDP to decrease by 0.2 percent.

An increase in personal tax credits with an across-the-board tax increase after ten years increases the before-tax interest rate by twenty basis points in the long run. The before-tax wage rate gradually decreases as government debt crowds out private capital and the tax increases depress investment. In the long run, the before-tax wage rate decreases by 0.5 percent, and labor supply decreases by 0.4 percent. Investment decreases in all three production sectors. In the long run, nonhousing investment decreases by 2.5 percent, and owner-occupied and rental housing investment decreases by 1.5 and 2.2 percent, respectively. Consumption decreases by 0.6 percent, and GDP decreases by 0.8 percent in the long run. The debt-to-GDP ratio increases to 34.5 percent.

Summary of Macroeconomic Effects. As one would expect, all four of the reductions in distortionary taxes increase long-run GDP when they are offset by an immediate reduction in transfer payments. The GDP boost is largest for reductions in dividend and corporate taxes, because those taxes are more distortionary. There is no GDP boost from the increase in personal tax credits.

When the reduction in transfer payments is delayed by ten years, however, the long-run effects are less beneficial. In each case, the GDP boost is diminished by 0.1 or 0.2 percentage points. This diminution brings the boost in the case of the interest tax cut to essentially zero, but a noticeable GDP gain still appears in the other three reductions of distortionary taxes. The long-run gains are smaller because the increase in debt crowds out private investment (there is virtually no change in labor supply). Notably, long-run nonhousing investment is increased by cuts in wage taxes and interest taxes when the transfer payment cut is immediate, but such investment is reduced in the presence of the ten-year lag. The dividend and corporate cuts, which are more directly targeted to investment, still boost long-run nonhousing investment even with the ten-year lag, but by significantly less than with an immediate transfer cut.

The macroeconomic effects are much worse when tax rates are increased to finance the deficit. Long-run GDP falls in every case, except for the dividend-tax cut, under which GDP is virtually unchanged. Nonhousing investment falls in every case, except the dividend tax cut. Long-run labor supply falls in every case, except for the wage tax reduction. With financing through tax increases, crowding out is reinforced by the distortionary effects of the increases.

Intergenerational Welfare Effects. As we indicated above, examining the macroeconomic effects of tax policy changes has become an important tool for tax policy analysts in the 2000s. No analysis to date, however, has provided policymakers with anything more than simple macroeconomic aggregates like the ones we just presented. This omission is unfortunate: macroeconomic aggregates are not always reliable indicators of whether certain policies make individuals better off, and they do not allow policymakers to examine the effects of policies across groups.

Figure 7-1 shows the intergenerational welfare effects (as a fraction of lifetime resources) of the five policies—cutting the tax rates on wage, interest, dividend, and corporate income and increasing tax credits—assuming that government transfers are cut immediately so that government debt grows at the steady-state rate of the economy. For generations alive at the time of reform (generations with an age between 0 and 54, on the left-hand side of the graph), the largest welfare gains occur under the corporate rate cut, the dividend rate cut, and the interest income tax cut.

FIGURE 7-1

EQUIVALENT VARIATION—IMMEDIATE TRANSFER OFFSET

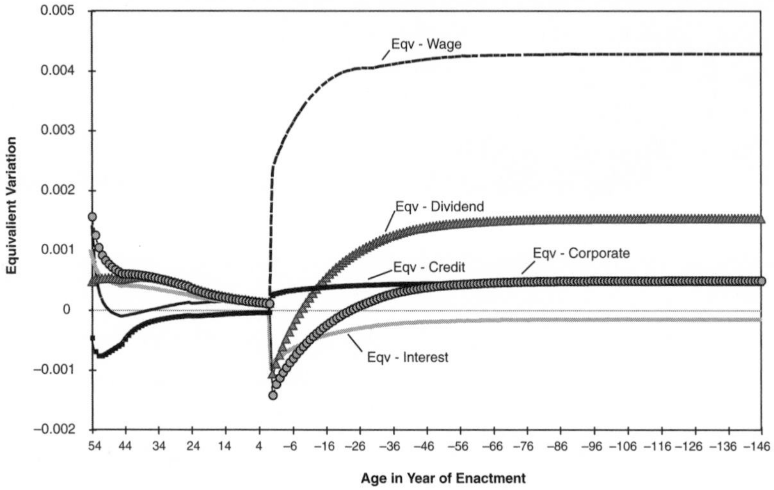

SOURCE: Authors' calculations.

The difference between the dividend and the corporate tax cuts again reflects the windfall gain to existing assets built into the latter, but not the former. The corporate tax cut is more beneficial to the early generations who hold those assets and is therefore less beneficial to later generations.

In the case of an increase in personal tax credits, all existing generations are worse off, while future generations are better off. This reflects the fact that the tax credits are distributed to younger cohorts, on average, than the transfer payments. As the generational accounting literature has long taught, a balanced-budget lump-sum redistribution from old to young harms current generations and helps future generations.

The deficit-financed tax cuts, shown in figures 7-2 and 7-3, uniformly reduce the well-being of future generations. This welfare loss occurs even when those generations are bequeathed a more efficient tax system (as is true in all cases where reductions in distortionary taxes are financed by delayed cuts in transfer payments). The reason for their welfare loss is the shift in net fiscal burdens; deficit financing moves such burdens away from current generations and onto future generations. As one would expect, the deficit-financed tax cuts almost uniformly benefit the generations alive at the time of the reform.

FIGURE 7-2

EQUIVALENT VARIATION—TRANSFER OFFSET AFTER TEN YEARS

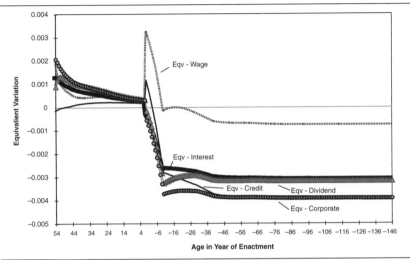

SOURCE: Authors' calculations.

FIGURE 7-3

EQUIVALENT VARIATION—TAX OFFSET AFTER TEN YEARS

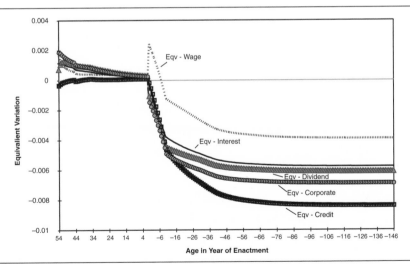

SOURCE: Authors' calculations.

Two of the cases feature an interesting set of effects. When wage taxes or dividend taxes are reduced and the revenue loss is offset by a reduction in transfer payments after ten years, steady-state utility declines although steady-state consumption increases. In the wage tax case, the utility decline reflects an increase in labor supply. In the dividend tax case, the explanation for the apparent paradox is more subtle. For a given value of aggregate steady-state consumption (holding labor supply fixed), steady-state utility is higher when the marginal rate of substitution between consumption at different ages, which is given by the after-tax interest rate, is closer to the growth rate of the economy. The dividend tax cut increases the after-tax interest rate further above the growth rate of the economy, thereby lowering steady-state utility as a function of aggregate steady-state consumption.[7]

Figure 7-4 shows the intergenerational welfare effects of reducing the wage and dividend tax rates assuming that government transfers are reduced twenty rather than ten years after the reform. In this case, the welfare losses are much larger for future generations. For the wage tax cut, the long-run welfare loss is 2 percent of lifetime resources instead of the 0.08 percent that pertains in the case of a ten-year deficit finance rule. For the dividend tax cut, the long-run welfare loss is 2.4 percent of lifetime resources instead of 0.32 percent. The welfare losses increase nonlinearly with the period of deficit finance; this finding is similar to that of Auerbach and Kotlikoff (1987).

A social planner concerned solely with the well-being of future generations would therefore want to pursue "fiscal responsibility" rather than "tax reform" if a choice had to be made. Recall, however, that the gains to future generations from fiscal restraint are accompanied by losses to earlier generations. A normative evaluation requires a social welfare function that specifies the weights to be given to the various generations.

How Are Deficit-Financed Tax Cuts Typically Paid For?

All the above results highlight the critical importance of the manner in which the deficit-financed tax cut is ultimately paid for. When a deficit-financed tax cut is passed, there is generally no consensus on how the resulting debt will ultimately be serviced. Yet that question should play a prominent role in an evaluation of the tax cut.

FIGURE 7-4

EQUIVALENT VARIATION—TRANSFER OFFSET AFTER TWENTY YEARS

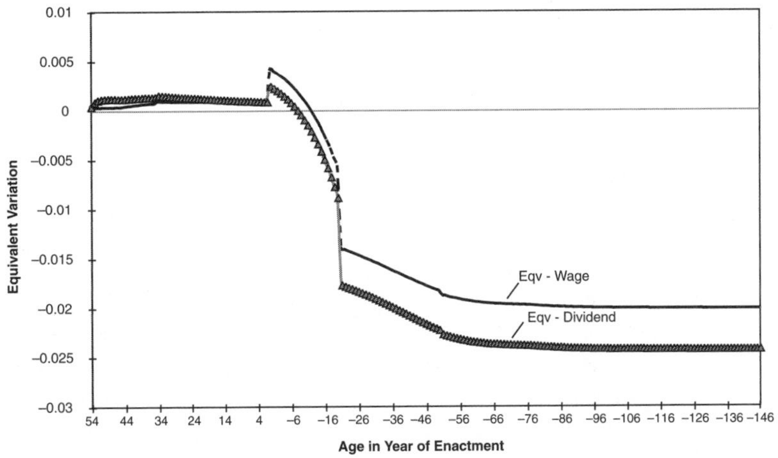

SOURCE: Authors' calculations.

It is generally impossible to conclusively determine how any tax cut was actually financed, because there is no way to determine how actual taxes and spending compare to those that would have existed in an alternative world without the tax cut. Econometric evidence can, however, shed light on the question if identifying assumptions are made.

Some early work by Bohn (1991) found that increases in debt are typically financed with a combination of revenue increases and spending cuts. Auerbach (2006), updating Auerbach (2003), takes a similar approach, regressing tax and spending "policy changes," as defined by CBO, on the lagged budget surplus and the GDP gap for the second quarter of 1984 through the first quarter of 2004. He finds that both revenue and expenditures respond to budgetary conditions, as measured by either the lagged surplus or projected future surpluses. Revenue and spending are about equally responsive. Most of the spending response comes from nondefense discretionary spending.

Chung and Leeper (2007) find that vector autoregressions (VARs) for taxes and spending are noninvertible when government debt is not included, i.e., that estimated innovations in the no-debt VARs are predictable from past values of debt and are therefore not true innovations. They therefore construct a VAR that includes government debt and interest rates, on which they impose the transversality condition requiring that a change in debt be offset by changes in the present value of future surpluses, discounted at the interest rate on government debt. They emphasize that the change in the present value of future surpluses reflects a combination of changes in future surpluses and changes in the interest rate on government debt. They estimate this VAR using data from National Income and Product Accounts (NIPA) on taxes, government purchases, and transfer payments (for the federal government only) from the second quarter of 1947 through the second quarter of 2006. They find that tax cuts tend to be followed by large tax increases, partly offset by increases in transfer payments (and possibly government purchases), with relatively little change in real interest rates. The confidence intervals on the estimates, however, are quite wide, making most of their estimates statistically insignificant.

Romer and Romer (2007) use a narrative approach to distinguish between various types of tax cuts. They discard tax changes that are motivated by countercyclical considerations and those that are enacted to finance contemporaneous changes in government spending, as well as tax increases adopted to finance inherited deficits. They instead focus their analysis on long-run tax changes, those that are adopted to promote economic growth or efficiency or to reduce the size of government. The largest such changes were the tax cuts enacted in 1948, 1964, 1981, 2001, and 2003.

They regress the growth of real (noninterest) government expenditures on current and lagged values of the revenue impacts from these long-run tax changes. Somewhat surprisingly, they find that expenditures actually rise in response to these tax cuts, beginning about one year after the revenue loss occurs. The point estimates indicate that, eventually (three to five years out), spending rises by roughly the same amount as the tax cut, although the estimates have sizable standard errors.[8]

The Romer and Romer estimates are not completely robust. A variety of estimation changes tends to weaken or eliminate the evidence that tax cuts increase spending, although they do not generate evidence that tax cuts reduce spending. Deleting the Korean War period, for example, renders the estimated spending increases statistically insignificant. Similarly, the cumulative impact on spending at a ten-year horizon is statistically insignificant. Looking only at nondefense spending yields point estimates that imply a spending-reduction effect, but the estimates are statistically insignificant.

Studies finding evidence that tax cuts drive spending down may be biased, Romer and Romer suggest, by the inclusion of tax changes that are adopted to finance contemporaneous spending. They find that after two years, the revenue impact of a long-run tax cut is not statistically different from zero, implying that the initial tax cut was reversed by subsequent increases in receipts. Further analysis reveals that the increase in receipts is largely due to the subsequent enactment of deficit-driven tax increases and spending-driven tax increases. For example, the 1964 tax cut was partially reversed by the tax surcharge adopted in 1968, and the 1981 tax cut was partially reversed by tax increases adopted in 1982 and later years.

Davig and Leeper (2006) estimate a regime-switching model in which fiscal policy alternates between an active regime and a passive regime. The active policy increases annual taxes net of transfer payments by about five cents in response to an additional dollar of outstanding government debt, while the passive policy lowers annual net taxes by more than three cents for each additional dollar of debt. In the period from 1948 through 2004, Davig and Leeper estimate that twelve fiscal regime changes occurred, with fiscal policy being active 55 percent of the time. The authors do not break down the fiscal policy response between taxes and transfer payments. Their results suggest that a single policy rule cannot accurately describe government responses under all circumstances.

Models of Infinite-Lived Agents

Another strand of the literature has examined models of infinite-lived agents, which generally are variants of the original Ramsey (1928) model.

Early work was done by Judd (1985). He examined a policy that cuts labor and capital income taxes today and later reduces government spending, under the assumption that labor supply is inelastic. If the spending cuts are in the form of transfer payments (or government purchases that are perfectly substitutable for private consumption), then the capital stock and output grow steadily from the beginning. With an infinite horizon and Ricardian equivalence, the timing of the transfer payment cuts is irrelevant. If the spending cuts are in the form of government purchases that are separable from private consumption, then capital is likely to decline in the short run, as consumption rises.

The work done in the 2000s has largely elaborated on the earlier findings without any profound changes. Yang (2007) studies an economy with infinite-horizon agents, some of whom intertemporally optimize and some of whom simply consume current disposable income. The government provides a consumption good (each unit of which is perfectly substitutable for 0.2 unit of private consumption) and investment in government capital that is complementary to private capital, and it also makes transfer payments to the nonsavers. Yang considers a deficit-financed permanent reduction in the capital tax rate from 39 to 35.1 percent. She considers three fiscal reaction functions, each of which features a different fiscal instrument responding to the debt level: government consumption (–0.64 elasticity with respect to debt), government investment (–2.83 elasticity), or transfer payments (–5.32 elasticity). In each case, the capital income tax cut causes the debt-output ratio to rise from 0.43 to 0.46 in the new steady state.

When the debt is financed by reductions in government consumption, the capital income tax cut has the expected effect on savers; they reduce current consumption and current leisure and enjoy greater future consumption and future leisure. Nonsavers also enjoy higher consumption due to higher wages; the substitution effect of the higher wages also prompts higher labor supply. Output rises at all dates. Both groups experience a lifetime welfare gain from the tax cut, which is unsurprising given the limited utility from government consumption in the model.

When transfers to nonsavers are reduced to finance debt, savers are affected by the tax cut in roughly the same manner as when government consumption is the financing tool. But the capital tax cut then has adverse effects for nonsavers, whose loss of transfers outweighs the increase in their wages. As a result, nonsavers consume less and work harder. Output rises at all dates. Savers experience a welfare gain and nonsavers a welfare loss.

Quite different results arise when debt is financed by reductions in government investment. Savers face lower consumption at most dates as the smaller government capital stock drives down rates of return on private capital. Nonsavers also experience lower consumption at most dates due to declining wage rates. Output falls at all dates, except the first few years. Both groups experience a welfare loss from the tax cut.

Yang notes that, if the government responds less aggressively to debt, it must ultimately make a larger response because more debt accumulates. When it is government investment that responds, the less aggressive policy therefore magnifies the harmful effects.

Leeper and Yang (2008) study a similar economy, except that government consumption is separable (or, alternatively, worthless) and there is no government investment. They consider reductions in both labor and capital tax rates. When tax cuts of either type are financed by reductions in transfer payments, capital and labor both expand. When a capital tax cut is financed by labor tax increases, however, steady-state output falls, an initially surprising outcome. Although investment rises, labor supply falls in the steady state, which could be due to intertemporal substitution. When a labor tax cut is financed by reducing government consumption, private output falls in the steady state due to wealth effects. There is also a fall in the tax base when capital taxes finance the labor tax cut.

CBO (2008) also uses an infinite-horizon model to study the president's tax and budget proposals. When the revenue losses are offset by reductions in government spending, CBO finds that the proposals increase 2009–2013 GNP by 0.2 percent and 2014–2018 GNP by 0.3 percent. With the tax rate adjustment, the increases are 0.2 percent in both periods. Long-run results are not presented.

Conclusion and Extensions

Our results and those of other studies indicate that deficit-financed tax cuts can increase long-run output if the financing mechanism is less distortionary than the tax that is initially reduced, and if the financing begins relatively soon after the tax cut is adopted. Even then, however, the shift in fiscal burdens generally reduces the well-being of later generations while increasing that of earlier generations.

Our research could be extended in a variety of ways. One possible improvement over our approach would be to alter the baseline path. Due to the long-term fiscal imbalance, future tax rates are likely to be higher than current ones, increasing the marginal deadweight loss from boosting future tax rates. This alteration would reinforce the harmful effects of deficit-financed tax cuts, except when the debt is fully serviced on the spending side, because the marginal deadweight loss from the future tax increases would then exceed the marginal deadweight loss avoided by the current tax cut.

The model assumes that government debt carries an interest rate equal to the marginal product of capital. In reality, the interest rate on safe government debt is lower than the expected value of the stochastic marginal product of capital. If the difference is solely due to risk aversion, treating the interest rate as equal to the marginal product is probably the best approach. (Of course, it would be desirable to explicitly incorporate uncertainty, but that is a very difficult undertaking.) If the rate is lower due to other advantages of government debt, such as liquidity services, then it is appropriate to model the interest rate as lower than the marginal product. It might be useful to present results under that alternative assumption, because doing so would ameliorate the harmful consequences of deficit-financed tax cuts.

We also think that an extension to an open-economy framework would be desirable, although it would significantly complicate the model. The extension could make the greatest difference for analysis of changes in the corporate income tax, because a change in the corporate income tax rate could trigger significant international capital flows in an open economy. The impact on capital flows would be muted, however, if a change in the U.S. corporate tax rate caused other countries to change their tax rates in the same direction.

Finally, the proper modeling of bequests is a difficult question on which further work is necessary. Certainly the joy-of-giving framework we adopt is not entirely satisfactory. When one generation leaves a private bequest to its children, the transfer is assumed to yield utility to both generations. If the same transfer is implemented through government fiscal policy, however, only the children's utility is assumed to be affected. Arguably, the different treatment accurately reflects the different attitudes that people have toward the two types of transactions. Still, it results in different utility effects from otherwise identical transactions, which is a departure from standard economic assumptions.

Alternatives to the joy-of-giving framework could be considered. For example, bequests could be modeled as accidental, resulting from individual lifespan uncertainty and the lack of perfect annuity markets. Of course, that approach would add complexity. Also, while some bequests undoubtedly arise by accident, it seems clear that the large bequests left by wealthy households must reflect other factors.

It should be noted that the joy-of-giving framework we use produces a best-case scenario for future generations affected by deficit-financed tax cuts, since current generations offset part of future generations' losses through increased bequests. In any case, changing the modeling of bequests would probably have little impact on macroeconomic effects, such as the effect on saving, for the policies that we consider in this chapter.

Appendix

This appendix provides a more detailed description of the model utilized above (in the sections above entitled "Model Structure and Calibration" and "Simulation Results"). A complete description is provided in Diamond and Zodrow (2005).

The Nonresidential Production Sector. In each period s, firms in the composite good production sector produce output (X_s) using capital K_s^X and labor L_s^X using a CES production function with an elasticity of substitution in production σ_X and a capital share parameter a_X. Firms are assumed to choose the time path of investment to maximize the present value of firm profits or, equivalently, maximize firm value V_X, net of all taxes. Total taxes in the composite good production sector in period s are

$$T_s^X = \tau_{bs}^X \; [p_s^X X_s - w_s L_s^X - \Phi_s^X I_s^X - i_s B_s^X - \delta_\tau^X K_{\tau s}^X] + (1 - \tau_{bs}^X) \, \tau_{ps}^X K_s^X,$$

where τ_{bs}^X is the tax rate on business income in the composite good sector, p_s^X is the price of the composite good, w_s is the wage rate, I_s^X is gross investment, Φ_s^X are (deductible) adjustment costs per unit of investment, i_s is the before-tax interest rate, B_s^X is total indebtedness, $\delta_{\tau s}^X$ is depreciation for tax purposes, $K_{\tau s}^X$ is the remaining tax basis of the capital stock, τ_{ps}^X is the property tax rate on both the composite good sector and nonresidential capital, with property taxes assumed to be fully deductible against the business income tax.[9]

Following Goulder and Summers (1989) and Cummins, Hassett, and Hubbard (1994), the adjustment cost function per unit of investment is assumed to be a quadratic function of gross investment per unit of capital

$$\Phi_s \left(\frac{I_s^X}{K_s^X} \right) = \frac{p_s^X (\beta^X / 2)(I_s^X / K_s^X - \mu^X)^2}{I_s^X / K_s^X},$$

where β^X is the parameter that determines the level of adjustment costs, and μ^X is set so that adjustment costs are zero in the steady state.

Assuming firms do not make any financial investments, then total net cash receipts, including net new bonds issued BN_s^X and net new shares issued

VN_s^X, must either be used to finance new investments (including adjustment costs) or be distributed to shareholders

$$[P_s^X X_s - w_s L_s^X - i_s B_s^X] - T_s^X + BN_s^X + VN_s^X = I_s^X(1+\Phi_s^X) + DIV_s^X ,$$

where DIV_s^X is the dividend payout in the composite good sector. Each firm is assumed to maintain a fixed debt-asset ratio b^X and pay out a constant fraction of earnings after taxes and depreciation in each period. This implies that new investments are financed with debt and new share issues if retained earnings do not supply enough equity to finance the desired level of investment.

The model assumes individual-level arbitrage, which implies that the after-tax return to bonds must equal the after-tax return received by the shareholders of the firm, or

$$(1-\tau_{is})i_s = \frac{(1-\tau_{ds})DIV_s^X + (1-\tau_{gs})(V_{s+1}^X - V_s^X - VN_s^X)}{V_s^X} ,$$

where τ_{is} is the average marginal personal income tax rate on interest income, τ_{ds} is the average marginal tax rate on dividends, and τ_{gs} is the average effective annual accrual tax rate on capital gains $[V_{s+1}^X - V_s^X - VN_s^X]$. Solving this expression for V_s^X, subject to the transversality condition requiring a finite value of the firm, yields

$$V_s^X = \sum_{u=s}^{\infty} \frac{[(1-\tau_{du})/(1-\tau_{gu})]DIV_u^X - VN_u^X}{\prod_{v=s}^{u} [1 + (1-\tau_{iv})i_v/(1-\tau_{gv})]} .$$

That is, the value of the firm in the composite good sector equals the present value of all future net distributions to the owners of the firm. The time path of investment that maximizes this expression in the presence of adjustment costs is

$$\frac{I_s^X}{K_s^X} = \frac{q_{s+1}^X - 1 + b^X + Z_{s+1}^X}{p_s^X \beta^X (1-\tau_{bs}^X \Omega_s^X)} ,$$

where q_{s+1}^X is shadow price of additional capital (commonly referred to as "marginal q," which equals the ratio of the market value of a marginal unit of capital to its replacement cost), Ω_s^X is a weighted average of the dividend and capital gains tax rates divided by 1 minus the capital gains tax rate, and Z_{s+1}^X is the tax savings from accelerated depreciation allowances on future investments.

The relationship between "marginal q" and "average q" (denoted as Q_s^X) is

$$q_s^X = \frac{V_s^X - X_s^X}{K_s^X} = Q_s^X - \frac{X_s^X}{K_s^X},$$

where X_s^X is the value of future accelerated depreciation deductions on the existing stock of capital used in the production of the composite good.

The Owner-Occupied and Rental Housing Production Sectors. Housing is produced in the owner-occupied and rental housing production sectors. As in Goulder and Summers (1989) and Goulder (1989), rental housing is produced by noncorporate landlords, and owner-occupied housing is produced by the owners. The technology used in the production of rental housing (R_s) and owner-occupied housing (O_s) is assumed to be identical—capital and labor combined in a CES production function with an elasticity of substitution in production of σ_H and a capital share parameter of a_H.[10] Landlords and owner-occupiers are also assumed to choose time paths of investment to maximize the equivalent of firm value, net of total taxes.

In the case of the rental housing sector, the firm is modeled as a noncorporate firm. This implies that landlords are taxed at the individual level, so total taxes paid are

$$T_s^R = \tau_{bs}^R \, [p_s^R R_s - w L_s^R - \Phi_s^R I_s^R - i_s B_s^R - m K_s^R - \delta_\tau^R K_{\tau s}^R] + (1 - \tau_{bs}^R) \tau_{ps}^R K_s^R,$$

where τ_{bs}^R is the average marginal tax rate applied to rental housing income, m is annual maintenance expenditures per unit of rental housing capital, and the definitions of all other variables are analogous to those in the composite good production sector. Solving the cash flow equation in the rental housing sector for after-tax rents received by landlords S_s^R yields

$$S_s^R = p_s^R R_s - w L_s^R - i_s B_s^R - m K_s^R - T_s^R + B N_s^R + E_s^R - I_s^R (1 + \Phi_s^R),$$

where E_s^R is net new equity invested by landlords in the rental housing sector. Individual arbitrage in this case implies

$$(1- \tau_{is})i_s = \frac{S_s^R + (1 - \tau_{gs})(V_{s+1}^R - V_s^R - E_s^R)}{V_s^R},$$

which can be solved for the value of the rental housing firm thus:

$$V_s^R = \sum_{u=s}^{\infty} \frac{[1/(1- \tau_{gu})] \, S_s^R - E_s^R}{\prod_{v=s}^{u} [1 + (1- \tau_{iv})i_v/(1- \tau_{gv})]}.$$

The time path of investment that maximizes this expression in the presence of adjustment costs is

$$\frac{I_s^R}{K_s^R} = \frac{q_{s+1}^R - \Omega_s^R + b^R\Omega_s^R + Z_{s+1}^R}{p_s\Omega_s^R\beta^R(1 -\tau_{bs}^R)}.$$

The expression for the relationship between "marginal q" and "average q" in the rental housing sector is analogous to that in the composite good sector.

By comparison, in the owner-occupied housing sector, imputed rents are untaxed and maintenance expenditures are not deductible, while mortgage interest and property taxes are deductible; thus total taxes are

$$T_s^O = -z \tau_{is} i_s B_s^O + (1- z\tau_{is}) \, \tau_{ps}^O K_s^O,$$

where z_s is the fraction of individuals who are itemizers. The flow of (untaxed) imputed rents to owner-occupiers is

$$S_s^O = P_s^O F_s^O - w_s L_s^O - i_s B_s^O - T_s^O - mK_s^O + BN_s^O + E_s^O - I_s^O(1 + \Phi_s^O).$$

The expressions for individual-level arbitrage and firm value are analogous to those in the rental housing sector, and investment in the owner-occupied sector is

$$\frac{I_s^O}{K_s^O} = \frac{q_{s+1}^O - \Omega_s^O + b^O\Omega_s^O}{p_s\Omega_s^O\beta^O}.$$

The expression for the relationship between "marginal q" and "average q" in the owner-occupied housing sector is analogous to that in the composite good sector.

Individual Behavior. On the individual side, the model has a dynamic overlapping-generations framework with fifty-five generations alive at each point in time. There is a representative individual for each generation, who has an economic life span (which begins upon entry into the workforce) of fifty-five years, with the first forty-five of those years spent working, and the last ten spent in retirement. Individual tastes are identical so that differences in behavior across generations are due solely to differences in lifetime budget constraints. An individual accumulates assets from the time of "economic birth" that are used to finance both consumption over the life cycle, especially during the retirement period, and the making of bequests. The model includes a joy-of-giving bequest motive. Inheritances are assumed to be received at the economic age of twenty-five.

At any point in time s, the consumer maximizes rest-of-life utility LU_s subject to a lifetime budget constraint that requires the present value of lifetime wealth, including inheritances, to equal the present value of lifetime consumption, including bequests. In particular, an individual of age a at time $s = t$ chooses the time path of consumption of an aggregate consumption good and leisure in each period s to maximize rest-of-life utility

$$LU_s = \frac{\sigma}{\sigma - 1} \sum_{s=t}^{t+54-a} \frac{U_s(a)^{\left(\frac{\sigma-1}{\sigma}\right)}}{(1+\rho)^{s-t}},$$

where σ is the intertemporal elasticity of substitution, ρ is the pure rate of time preference, and $U_s(a)$ is assumed to be a CES function of consumption of the aggregate consumption good and leisure in period s with an intratemporal elasticity of ε and a leisure share parameter of a_E. The aggregate consumption good is modeled as a CES function of the composite good and aggregate housing services (including a minimum purchase requirement for both goods), with aggregate housing services in turn modeled as CES function of owner-occupied and rental housing services. In addition, as described in detail in Diamond and Zodrow (2005), the model includes exogenous population and technology growth rates, a simple social security system, government purchases of the composite good, transfer payments, a humpbacked wage profile over the life cycle, a progressive tax on wage income, and constant effective marginal tax rates applied to interest income, dividends, and capital gains.

Notes

1. This implies that the aggregate uncompensated labor supply elasticity is approximately 0.24, which is within the range of empirical estimates. This value is significantly lower than the value assumed in Altig et al. (2001) and Auerbach and Kotlikoff (1987), but yields an aggregate labor supply elasticity that is consistent with most of the empirical literature. It is, however, inconsistent with the relatively large labor supply elasticities found in the work of Prescott (2005) and Davis and Henrekson (2004).

2. Estimates of housing demand elasticities span a wide range. DiPasquale and Wheaton (1994) report an estimated housing demand elasticity equal to –0.15, while Riddel (2004) reports an estimated elasticity equal to –1.5.

3. The value of marginal and average tax rates is based on data from the Department of the Treasury, Office of Tax Analysis.

4. The effective annual accrual tax rate on capital gains in the owner-occupied housing sector is assumed to equal 0, since the Taxpayer Relief Act of 1997 exempted gains up to $250,000 on the sale of a house for single taxpayers and up to $500,000 for married taxpayers filing a joint return.

5. The corporate tax rate is assumed to be 35 percent, with accelerated depreciation allowed for the purpose of calculating taxable income. The amount of remaining basis for tax purposes is explicitly calculated in each period and used in the calculations of depreciation allowances. The corporate share of the composite-goods sector is 62 percent. This is used to calculate a weighted-average tax rate in each production sector. Note that the non-housing production sector is treated as a corporate firm in the model.

6. For the purpose of calculating the weighted average tax rate in the rental housing sector, the corporate share of the rental-housing sector is assumed to be 10 percent. Note that the rental housing firm is treated as a noncorporate firm in the model.

7. Despite its adverse effect on steady-state utility for a given level of aggregate steady-state consumption, increasing the after-tax interest rate above the economy's growth rate may be desirable once the impact on transitional generations is considered. A planner who cares about both transitional and steady-state generations and has unrestricted access to lump-sum taxes should adopt intergenerational transfers that drive the capital stock to the modified golden rule level, with a before-tax interest rate greater than the growth rate of the economy, and should eschew capital taxation so that the after-tax interest rate also exceeds the growth rate.

8. The estimated spending impacts from the other types of tax cuts generally accorded with a priori expectations, although the estimates were usually statistically insignificant. Tax increases to reduce the deficit were associated with reduced spending (although only for a short time), countercyclical tax cuts were

associated with increased spending, and tax increases adopted to finance contemporaneous new spending were indeed associated with increased spending.

9. The property tax on businesses is treated as a tax on capital rather than a benefit tax (Muthitacharoen and Zodrow 2006).

10. Thus the producer prices of rental and owner-occupied housing services are identical. However, rental and owner-occupied housing services are not perfect substitutes, so the mix of rental and owner-occupied housing services changes along the transition path to a new equilibrium.

References

Altig, David, Alan J. Auerbach, Laurence J. Kotlikoff, Kent A. Smetters, and Jan Walliser. 2001. Simulating fundamental tax reform in the United States. *American Economic Review* 91, no. 3: 574–95.

Auerbach, Alan J. 1996. Tax reform, capital allocation, efficiency, and growth. In *Economic effects of fundamental tax reform*, ed. Henry J. Aaron and William G. Gale, 29–82. Washington, DC: Brookings Institution.

_____. 2002. The Bush tax cut and national saving. *National Tax Journal* 55, no. 3: 387–407.

_____. 2003. Fiscal policy, past and present. *Brookings Papers on Economic Activity* 1: 75–122.

_____. 2006. American fiscal policy in the post-war era: An interpretive history. In *The macroeconomics of fiscal policy*, ed. Richard Kopcke, Geoffrey M. B. Tootell, and Robert K. Triest, 77–100. Cambridge, MA: MIT Press.

_____, and Laurence J. Kotlikoff. 1987. *Dynamic fiscal policy*. Cambridge: Cambridge University Press.

Bohn, Henning. 1991. Budget balance through revenue or spending adjustments? Some historical evidence for the United States. *Journal of Monetary Economics* 27, no. 3: 333–59.

Chung, Hess, and Eric M. Leeper. 2007. What has financed government debt? NBER Working Paper No. 13425, Cambridge, MA.

Congressional Budget Office. 2008. An analysis of the president's budgetary proposals for fiscal year 2009. Washington, DC: CBO.

Cummins, Jason, Kevin Hassett, and R. Glenn Hubbard. 1994. A reconsideration of investment behavior using tax reforms as natural experiments. *Brookings Papers on Economic Activity* 2: 1–74.

Davig, T., and Eric M. Leeper. 2006. Fluctuating macro policies and the fiscal theory. In *NBER Macroeconomics Annual*, ed. D. Acemoglu, Kenneth Rogoff, and Michael Woodford, 247–316. Cambridge, MA: MIT Press.

Davis, Steven J., and Magnus Henrekson. 2004. Tax effects on work activity, industry mix and shadow economy size: Evidence from rich country comparisons. NBER Working Paper No. 10509, Cambridge, MA.

Dennis, Robert, Douglas Hamilton, Robert Arnold, Ufuk Demiroglu, Tracy Foertsch, Mark Lasky, Shinichi Nishiyama, Larry Ozanne, John Peterson, Frank Russek, John Sturrock, and David Weiner. 2004. *Macroeconomic Analysis of a 10 Percent Cut in Income Tax Rates*, Congressional Budget Office Technical Paper 2004-07.

Diamond, John W. 2005. Dynamic effects of extending the 2001 and 2003 income tax cuts. *International Tax and Public Finance* 12, no. 2: 165–92.

Diamond, John W., Timothy Gunning, and George R. Zodrow. Forthcoming. Selecting parameter values for general equilibrium model simulations. *Proceedings of the one hundredth annual conference on taxation*. Washington, DC: National Tax Association.

Diamond, John W., and George R. Zodrow. 2005. Description of the Tax Policy Advisers general equilibrium model. Manuscript, Rice University, Houston, TX.

————. 2006. Reflections on the use of life-cycle computable general equilibrium models in analyzing the effects of tax reform. *NTA Network* (April): 3–4.

————. 2008. Consumption tax reform: Changes in business equity and housing prices. In *Fundamental tax reform: Issues, choices and implications*, ed. John W. Diamond and George R. Zodrow, 227–60. Cambridge, MA: MIT Press.

DiPasquale, Denise, and William C. Wheaton. 1994. Housing market dynamics and the future of housing prices. *Journal of Urban Economics* 35, no. 1: 1–27.

Fullerton, Don, and Diane Lim Rogers. 1993. *Who bears the lifetime tax burden?* Washington, DC: Brookings Institution.

Goulder, Lawrence H. 1989. Tax policy, housing prices, and housing investment. NBER Working Paper No. 2814, Cambridge, MA.

————, and Lawrence H. Summers. 1989. Tax policy, asset prices, and growth. *Journal of Public Economics* 38, no. 3: 265–96.

Hayashi, Fumio. 1982. Tobin's marginal q and average q: A neoclassical interpretation. *Econometrica* 50, no. 1: 213–24.

Jorgenson, Dale W., and Kun-Young Yun. 2001. *Investment*. Vol. 3. Cambridge, MA: MIT Press.

Judd, Kenneth L. 1985. Short-run analysis of fiscal policy in a perfect foresight model. *Journal of Political Economy* 93, no. 2: 298–319.

Keuschnigg, Christian. 1990. Corporate taxation and growth: Dynamic general equilibrium simulation study. In *Simulation models in tax and transfer policy*, ed. Johann Brunner and Hans-Georg Petersen, 245–77. Frankfurt/Main and New York: Campus Verlag.

Leeper, Eric M., and Shu-Chun Susan Yang. 2008. Dynamic scoring: Alternative financing schemes. *Journal of Public Economics* 92, no. 1-2: 159–82.

Muthitacharoen, Athiphat, and George R. Zodrow. 2006. State and local taxation of business property: A small open economy perspective. *Proceedings of the ninety-eighth annual conference on taxation*. Washington, DC: National Tax Association.

Prescott, Edward C. 2005. The elasticity of labor supply and the consequences for tax policy. In *Toward fundamental tax reform*, ed. Alan J. Auerbach and Kevin A. Hassett, 123–34. Washington, DC: AEI Press.

Ramsey, Frank P. 1928. A mathematical theory of saving. *Economic Journal* 38, no. 152: 543–59.

Riddel, Mary. 2004 Housing-market disequilibrium: An examination of housing-market price and stock dynamics 1967–1998. *Journal of Housing Economics* 13, no. 2: 120–35.

Romer, Christina D., and David H. Romer. 2007. Do tax cuts starve the beast? The effect of tax changes on government spending. NBER Working Paper No. 13548, Cambridge, MA.

Rosen, Harvey S. 1985. Housing subsidies: Effects on housing decisions, efficiency, and equity. In *Handbook of Public Economics*. Vol. 1, ed. Alan J. Auerbach and Martin Feldstein, 375–420. Amsterdam: Elsevier Science.

Shapiro, Matthew D. 1986. The dynamic demand for capital and labor. *Quarterly Journal of Economics* 101, no. 3: 513–42.

Summers, Lawrence H. 1981. Capital taxation and accumulation in a life cycle growth model. *American Economic Review* 71, no. 4: 533–44.

U.S. Bureau of Economic Analysis. 2007. National income and product accounts. *Survey of Current Business* 87, no. 11 (November).

U.S. Congress. Joint Committee on Taxation. 2006. *Macroeconomic analysis of a proposal to broaden the individual income tax base and lower individual income tax rates*. JCX-53-06. http://www.house.gov/jct/x-53-06.pdf.

U.S. Department of the Treasury. 2006. Office of Tax Analysis. *A dynamic analysis of permanent extension of the president's tax relief*. Washington, DC.

Yang, Shu-Chun Susan. 2007. Do capital income tax cuts trickle down? *National Tax Journal* 60, no. 3: 551–68.

Ziliak, James P., and Thomas J. Kniesner. 1999. Estimating life cycle labor supply effects. *Journal of Political Economy* 107, no. 2: 326–59.

8

A Response to John W. Diamond and Alan D. Viard

Laurence J. Kotlikoff

As the previous chapter so usefully reminds us, fiscal policy has a long half-life, and its ultimate impact can be the opposite of its short-run impact. Transferring resources to current generations from future generations may temporarily provide current generations with better work and saving incentives, but it leaves future generations with worse work and saving incentives; it may lead to more labor supply, investment, and output in the short run, but at the price of less labor supply, investment, and (consequently) consumption in the long run.

Note that I am describing policy in terms of the budget constraints facing different generations because such descriptions are *label free*, i.e., they are invariant to our choice of how to label government receipts and payments. As demonstrated in Green and Kotlikoff (2006), neoclassical economic theory does not pin down the government's cash flows. It doesn't tell us whether the government should call current receipts a) "taxes" or b) "borrowing plus future repayment and future taxes." Nor does it pin down whether the government should call current payments "transfers" or "repayment of past borrowing." There is a degree of freedom in the choice of labels that makes the description of a policy in terms of the time path of "deficits" entirely arbitrary.

The implication of this point for Diamond and Viard's chapter is this: what the authors describe as "deficit-financed short-term tax cuts" could equally be labeled "surplus-financed short-term improvements in work incentives." To give a simple example, suppose that the government has in place what some would label a proportional wage tax, and that the government at time *t* engages in real policy that could be labeled a temporary cut in the wage tax rate. This same policy change could alternatively be described as a major increase in the current tax rate on current labor supply, plus an even larger future transfer payment that depends on *current* labor supply. Under both sets of labels, the agent has the same lifetime budget constraint and the same work incentives now and in the future. But the second set of words permits the government to report a surplus.

The linkage, at the margin, of future "transfers" to current labor supply is not, by the way, merely a linguistic construct. The payment of Social Security benefits to the elderly based on their past covered earnings (i.e., based, in part, on their past labor supply) is an example of this linkage in the real world.

Language is extremely flexible. We can discuss economics in French, German, or Russian. And the choice of fiscal labels is no different from the choice of national tongue. This general relativity of fiscal language—the fact that fiscal language is always and everywhere arbitrary—means that one can't make anything per se of any statements that rely on the terms "deficits," "taxes," or "transfer payments." Nor, for that matter, can one make anything of statements that invoke "private saving." This criticism applies, of course, to some of my own work (individually authored and coauthored), especially my past work with Alan Auerbach on computable general equilibrium models (Auerbach and Kotlikoff 1987).

This is not to denigrate the economic lessons of the chapter by Diamond and Viard (or of my own work). Those lessons are valid and important. But they are really about the co-workings of intergenerational redistribution and generation-specific changes in marginal incentives—they aren't lessons about deficit policy, because deficit policy is not well defined.

If we are native speakers of French and can speak only a few words of English, we're naturally going to use French to discuss economics; i.e., we're going to use the language which is convenient. In economics, discussing policy in terms of changes in lifetime budget constraints is like using a foreign language. But I think we economists all need to start using that foreign language if we are going to avoid treating mere linguistic changes as true changes in policy.

The simulations in the previous chapter entail generation-specific changes in lifetime budget constraints (changes in generational accounts assuming no change in behavior) and incentives. If the authors were to show these changes, they would help us to understand how these policies are alike and how they are different. This would be particularly helpful in clarifying differences across alternative policies that are generating ten-year $500 billion increases in deficits. As just indicated, each of the policies being considered could just as easily be labeled in a way that would entail completely different ten-year deficits. And a plethora (indeed an infinity) of policies not simulated by the authors, with dramatically different real short- and long-term effects, could be also labeled in a way that would increase federal debt by $500 billion over the next ten years.

If readers of the previous chapter can't make economic sense of its reported government cash flows, they can see through the particular policies to what is really going on—they know government redistribution and an ultimate worsening in labor supply and saving incentives when they see them. They can also get the main point, particularly by looking at the chapter's simulated welfare effects: namely, that government redistribution is a zero-sum game, and that short-run reductions in marginal tax rates (which are well-defined concepts) at the cost of long-run increases in marginal tax rates are a losing proposition from the perspective of economic efficiency. This point reflects the fact that the economy's excess burden has a present value (see Kotlikoff 2003) and that distortions are nonlinear increasing functions of effective tax rates.

The bottom line, then, is that I like the chapter's message if not its packaging. There are, however, a number of ways in which the modeling might be improved to make the findings more realistic. First, as in Fehr, Jokisch, and Kotlikoff (2008), one could incorporate uncertain lifespan and "bequests" arising from incomplete annuitization. I put "bequests" in quotation marks because what we measure as a bequest is also a function of our language. This is why positing a joy-of-giving bequests utility function, as the authors do, implicitly assumes irrationality on the part of the model's agents. Were one to relabel bequests as taxes levied on parents coupled with transfers made to children, there would be no change in the actual resource position of any agents, but there would be a reduction in utility, because the relabeling has someone besides the agent himself, namely the government, take money and give it to the children. To put this a different way, I think the authors should assume either that children's utility doesn't enter their parents' utility functions, or that it does.

I also think the authors could model demographics more accurately by permitting agents to give birth to fractions of children at different ages. They could open up the economy as well. Treating it as a small open economy would be a good alternative to treating it as closed. Finally, they could usefully include policy changes that entail cuts in government consumption or spending. I don't see why the authors take government spending as essentially immutable. Federal discretionary spending has certainly changed over time as a share of GDP.

In closing, let me stress the chapter's most important point, namely that the longer one waits to pay for redistribution toward current generations—the more generations one lets off the hook with respect to paying for the redistribution to those now alive—the larger will be the burden on those who ultimately must pay. And this burden will come not just in the form of higher lifetime net taxes (a well-defined concept), but also in the form of reduced lifetime labor income, thanks to general equilibrium factor-price effects that also serve to redistribute across generations in a zero-sum fashion (see Kotlikoff 2003).

References

Auerbach, Alan J., and Laurence J. Kotlikoff. 1987. *Dynamic fiscal policy.* Cambridge, MA: Cambridge University Press.

Fehr, Hans, Sabine Jokisch, and Laurence J. Kotlikoff. 2008. Will China eat our lunch or take us to dinner? Simulating the transition paths of the U.S., EU, Japan, and China. In *Fiscal policy and management in East Asia*, ed. Takatoshi Ito and Andrew K. Rose, 133–93. University of Chicago Press, 2008.

Green, Jerry, and Laurence J. Kotlikoff. 2006. On the general relativity of fiscal language. NBER Working Paper No. 12344, Cambridge, MA.

Kotlikoff, Laurence J. 2003. *Generational policy.* Cambridge, MA: MIT Press

9

The Impact of Taxes on Dividends and Corporate Financial Policy: Lessons from the 2000s

Dhammika Dharmapala

The impact of taxes on dividends and corporate financial policy has been debated by scholars for decades. The current decade has provided an unusual opportunity to test the various theories that have been proposed, and to draw empirical lessons for tax policy.[1] In 2003, the taxation of dividend income was transformed when Congress passed the Jobs and Growth Tax Relief Reconciliation Act (JGTRRA). This reform reduced the dividend tax rate from a maximum of 38.6 percent (for taxpayers in the highest bracket before 2003) to a maximum of 15 percent. The tax relief provided by JGTRRA applied to dividends paid by all U.S. firms and to dividends from most—but, importantly, not all—foreign corporations. This chapter reviews some of the major lessons that scholars have drawn from studying the impact of the 2003 tax reform. The focus is on both dividend policy and financial policy (with the latter interpreted broadly to encompass U.S. investors' preference for holding equity versus debt). The framework used here emphasizes the integrated nature of global financial markets in the 2000s, and envisages JGTRRA as a reform that

The author would like to thank Doug Shackelford, as well as Alan Auerbach, Mihir Desai, Mike Devereux, Kevin Hassett, and participants at the American Enterprise Institute's conference on tax policy lessons from the 2000s for helpful comments. Any remaining errors are the author's. Dr. Dharmapala also thanks the Oxford University Centre for Business Taxation for its hospitality during the writing of part of this chapter.

changed the personal tax regime facing a subset of the world's investors—namely, those investors resident in the United States.

This chapter explores two types of consequences of JGTRRA. The first has to do with the effect of JGTRRA on dividends and stock prices. We would expect U.S. stockholders to have become more inclined to receive equity returns in the form of dividends after JGTRRA. This would be true of Americans holding stock in both U.S. and foreign firms, but only in the former are U.S. shareholders likely to be a large and influential constituency in determining payout policy. Thus, the empirical literature has focused on the dividend behavior of U.S. firms in the aftermath of JGTRRA (e.g., Blouin, Raedy, and Shackelford 2004, 2007; Chetty and Saez 2005; Brown, Liang, and Weisbenner 2007). The main conclusion is that there was a large and immediate positive response of dividends paid by U.S. firms, especially in the form of new dividend initiations, after JGTRRA. While there are many potential alternative explanations, Chetty and Saez (2005) argue strongly for a causal impact of the tax reform. Moreover, the increase in dividends was concentrated among firms in which an influential constituency benefited from the tax cut, highlighting possible agency influences in determining firms' responses to the tax reform (Chetty and Saez 2007). In addition, the literature has examined the impact of JGTRRA on stock prices and firm value, using a variety of approaches (Auerbach and Hassett 2006, 2007; Dhaliwal, Krull, and Li 2007; Amromin, Harrison, and Sharpe 2006). The main lesson drawn is that stock prices rose for high-dividend firms relative to low-dividend firms, while the value of non-dividend-paying firms also rose.

The second type of consequence concerns the effect of reductions in the taxation of equity returns brought about by JGTRRA. These reductions would be expected to increase U.S. investors' preference for holding equity rather than debt. This conclusion is illustrated within a simple framework that extends Miller's (1977) theory of financial equilibrium to an international setting. In this model, JGTRRA induces U.S. investors to hold more equity, but has no systematic effect on U.S. firms' propensity to issue equity rather than debt. While it is difficult to test for these portfolio effects, Desai and Dharmapala (2007) exploit a relatively obscure feature of JGTRRA—its restriction of the favorable tax rate on foreign dividends to those countries that have signed tax treaties with the United States—to find evidence consistent with an increase in U.S. investors' equity holdings in foreign countries that enjoyed favorable dividend tax treatment under the act.

The overall findings of this literature appear to be most consistent with the new view of dividend taxation (described in the section below). However, they also leave some unresolved issues for future inquiry. For instance, the temporary nature of JGTRRA (the tax cuts are scheduled to expire in 2010) and the fact that the tax cut was deficit financed complicate the analysis of the long-term consequences. However, there can be little doubt that it has had a substantial effect on the policies of U.S. firms and on the behavior of U.S. investors at home and abroad, underscoring the important role of taxation in determining choices by firms and investors.

JGTRRA was intended by its proponents as an important step forward in the integration of corporate and personal taxes. Scholars have long argued for corporate tax integration as a means of reducing the distortions—to organizational form, payout policy, and financing decisions—created by the "double taxation" of corporate income (e.g., Hubbard 1993, 2005). The chapter ends with some reflections on two related questions: whether the dividend tax regime created by JGTRRA should be extended, and how corporate tax integration may best be pursued in the future. It argues that the increasing degree of international financial integration that has characterized the 2000s tends to reduce the effectiveness of JGTRRA's shareholder-level (partial) dividend exclusion mechanism as a means of achieving corporate tax integration. Instead, alternative approaches that are specifically directed at U.S. firms may be more effective in this environment in influencing firm policies on payout and capital structure. Reductions in the corporate tax rate may also be desirable in this new context.

The chapter is structured as follows. It first discusses the lessons of JGTRRA regarding dividends, payout policy, and firm value. It then develops a simple model of international financial equilibrium, discusses the evidence on U.S. investors' portfolio responses to JGTRRA, and draws out some implications of the experience with JGTRRA for policies designed to achieve corporate tax integration.

Lessons about Dividends, Payout Policy, and Firm Value

The primary questions addressed by the literature on JGTRRA center on how the reform affected the propensity of U.S. firms to pay dividends, how the change in this propensity affected total levels of payout, and how the reform influenced firm valuation. The discussion of these findings below begins with a simple equilibrium condition that serves as a framework for characterizing the various theories that have guided researchers in this area. It also provides some insights into how the relevant variables would respond to a reform such as JGTRRA. It then discusses the empirical literature on payout and valuation, and summarizes the lessons that flow from this research.

A Simple Equilibrium Condition. Consider a taxable investor who faces a dividend tax rate of $t_d \varepsilon$ (0, 1) and holds stock in a firm while also holding another asset such as a bond.[2] Let the (fixed) after-tax return to the investor from the bond be r^+. Suppose that the firm's pretax rate of return is r, and assume that both the corporate and the capital gains tax rates are zero.[3] The firm pays out a fraction $d \varepsilon(0, 1)$ of the returns to the shareholder as dividends, with the remaining fraction $(1 - d)$ being received in the form of (tax-exempt) capital gains. Let $u(dr)$ be an increasing, concave function of the dividend returns paid by the firm, and let γ and α be nonnegative parameters. Then, assuming that both the stock and the alternative asset are riskless, the following condition must be satisfied if the investor holds the firm's stock:

$$\gamma u(dr) + r(1 - \alpha dt_d) = r^+. \quad (1)$$

The tax penalty usually imposed on dividends relative to capital gains (triggered whenever the firm sets $d > 0$) is offset here by $u(dr)$, which represents in reduced form any of a variety of benefits that have been hypothesized to be derived by shareholders from the payment of cash dividends.

Equation (1) nests several of the major theoretical approaches that have been used in the analysis of dividend taxation. Most straightforwardly, Miller and Scholes (1978) argue that the marginal investor will generally be tax exempt. This can be represented by imposing the restrictions $\gamma = \alpha = 0$, so that $r = r^+$. In this view, the firm's pretax return (and hence its share price) as well as its dividend policy are independent of t_d; JGTRRA would thus affect neither the firm's dividend policy nor its valuation. As discussed below, perhaps the clearest and least contentious conclusion to emerge from the analysis of the effects of JGTRRA is that this tax irrelevance theory is contradicted by the evidence.

The new view of dividend taxation (Auerbach 1979; Bradford 1981; King 1977), on the other hand, is premised on the assumption that shareholders are burdened by the existence of dividend taxes. Moreover, this burden is assumed to be inescapable, as all payout must take the form of dividends at some point in time.[4] Even when the firm retains current earnings for reinvestment, dividend taxes are not avoided; rather, the returns generated by that investment are haunted by the specter of future dividend taxes. As is well known, these assumptions imply that when retained earnings are the marginal source of funds for investment, firms' investment decisions are unaffected by dividend taxes. In terms of equation (1), the new view can be represented by setting $\gamma = 0$ and $\alpha = (1/d)$, so that a firm issuing new equity must offer a pretax return:

$$r = \frac{r^+}{1 - t_d} . \quad (2)$$

The dividend tax is capitalized into the firm's value, regardless of whether *this particular firm* pays dividends or not. Under the new view, a reduction in t_d would lead to a reduction in the firm's required pretax return r (i.e., to an increase in the firm's share price). However, as d is determined as a residual after the firm has exhausted its investment opportunities, which are independent of t_d, there should be no change in d. As discussed below, however, this result applies only to a permanent change in t_d; a temporary reduction makes dividend payout today less costly in tax terms than future payout, and would be expected to lead to an increase in d.

The new view is often contrasted with what is termed the "traditional view" of dividend taxation (implicit in Feldstein 1970 and described in Poterba and Summers 1985). The traditional view imposes fewer restrictions on equation (1), and can be represented by setting $\gamma > 0$ and $\alpha = 1$. It assumes that firms have the option of paying returns to shareholders in the form of dividends or capital gains, but that there exists some reason why the firm must pay dividends despite the tax penalty. Under this assumption, the firm's *own* dividend yield d becomes relevant to its valuation (unlike in the new view): the pretax return the firm must pay its shareholders is increasing in d (holding fixed the benefits from dividends). It follows that a reduction in t_d would reduce the firm's cost of capital and so induce it to increase its level of investment (again in contrast to the new view).

The traditional view per se does not provide a theory of why dividend payments are necessary or desirable from the point of view of shareholders. However, financial economists have developed a variety of theories to explain what Black (1976) terms the "dividend puzzle"—i.e., why firms pay dividends despite the tax penalty.[5] One influential theory (originating with Bhattacharya 1979) is that managers can use dividends to signal private information about future firm performance to investors. In some formulations of the signaling theory, it is precisely the tax penalty associated with dividends that enables them to serve as a credible signal: firms with better future prospects are able to "burn money" through dividends to an extent that firms with less rosy prospects cannot. Another widely discussed theory (Jensen 1986) is premised on the idea that the retention of earnings creates the temptation for managers to use this free cash flow for purposes (such as unprofitable investments) that do not enhance shareholder value. The payment of dividends can thus avert these agency problems by returning cash to shareholders. The monitoring theory (Allen, Bernardo, and Welch 2000) starts with the observation that much investment in the stock market occurs through institutions (such as pension funds) that are tax exempt or tax favored, and that institutions also generally have greater capacity to monitor managers than do individual shareholders. Thus, the payment of dividends can drive away individual investors and attract a clientele of institutions which provide "monitoring services" that raise the value of the firm.

These theories are not entirely compelling. For instance, even if managers have private information about future performance, the signaling theory gives rise to another puzzle—namely, why a less costly method of signaling has not been devised. Similarly, the free cash flow theory per se does not explain why firms cannot disgorge cash to shareholders through repurchases rather than dividends. In other words, Black's (1976) "dividend puzzle" continues to elude any simple solution. In equation (1), any or all of the theories described above are represented in reduced form by $u(dr)$; it should be stressed, though, that this is merely a "black box" approach that reflects our ignorance of the precise factors at work.

Without necessarily imposing any of the restrictions discussed above, equation (1) can be used to straightforwardly derive some likely consequences of JGTRRA. The tax reform disturbed the initial equilibrium by reducing t_d. Equation (1) suggests two possible channels through which equilibrium could be restored: an increase in d and a decrease in r (in the short run, the latter would be manifested in the form of an increase in the firm's share price).[6] The rest of this section discusses the empirical evidence on both these questions.

The Effects of JGTRRA on Dividends. Evidence that JGTRRA was followed by a large increase in dividend payout began to emerge soon after the legislation was passed. Blouin, Raedy, and Shackelford (2004) compare the payout policies of a sample of firms that declared dividends in the six months following the enactment of JGTRRA with those of a control group that declared dividends during the corresponding six-month period in 2002. They find that firms substantially increased both their regular and special dividend payments following JGTRRA. They do not, however, find that this effect is stronger for firms that have more individual ownership. Consequently, they are cautious about inferring a causal connection between the tax reform and the increase in dividend payments.

Chetty and Saez (2005) also analyze this question, using a large sample of firms over the period from 1980 to the second quarter of 2004. They, too, find a large increase in dividends following JGTRRA, but distinguish between increases along the intensive margin (i.e., increases in the amount paid by firms that previously paid dividends) and the extensive margins (i.e., dividend initiations by firms that were previously nonpayers). They find a particularly large effect in the latter case, with a substantial increase in initiations after the reform. To address the issue of causality, they develop an identification strategy that involves using a control group of firms with nontaxable institutions as the largest shareholders.[7] The idea is that if the surge in dividends was caused by the tax cut, it should only be observed among firms with taxable shareholders. On the other hand, other possible explanations, such as changes in the corporate governance environment or the general economic climate, would arguably apply to all firms, including those with large nontaxable ownership. Chetty and Saez (2005) find that there is indeed no increase in dividends for the control group. They argue that, notwithstanding potentially confounding factors such as contemporaneous corporate governance scandals, this result suggests a causal role for JGTRRA in increasing dividends.

The dividend increase after JGTRRA was large in magnitude—amounting to a 20 percent increase in payments (Chetty and Saez 2005)—but its efficiency consequences depend, in large measure, on whether total payout increased as well. For instance, under the agency theory (Jensen 1986) JGTRRA would have beneficial consequences only to the extent that it encouraged managers to disgorge more cash to shareholders. If the observed growth in dividends merely represented a substitution from share repurchases to dividends—a change in the *form* of payout—then more cash in aggregate would not be paid out.

Researchers have vigorously debated the question of whether total payout increased as a result of JGTRRA. Brown, Liang, and Weisbenner (2007) find that among those firms that initiated dividends following JGTRRA, about one-third did not increase total payout. As this is a substantially larger fraction than was true for firms initiating dividends in years prior to 2003, they view this as evidence of substitution among those firms that initiated dividends in the wake of JGTRRA. Blouin, Raedy, and Shackelford (2007) point out that dividend initiators in 2003 paid only a small fraction of aggregate dividends. They find evidence of substitution between dividends and repurchases—in particular, an increase in the fraction of payout in the form of dividends after JGTRRA—in a broader sample of firms. Moreover, the extent of this substitution increases with the fraction of individual ownership in the firm; the authors interpret this as evidence that the change was caused by the reform rather than reflecting a general trend toward dividend payment over time. On the other hand, Chetty and Saez (2005, 2006) argue that the time-series pattern of share repurchases is too volatile to support any robust inference about substitution. However, they do find that for the subsample of firms that initiated dividends after JGTRRA, share repurchases increased as well, casting some doubt on the substitution hypothesis.

Equation (1) suggests that the magnitude of the increase in d in response to JGTRRA should be larger the smaller is γ. A small γ would be expected, for instance, when there is more shareholder monitoring of management or better alignment of managerial incentives (so that, for example, the disgorgement of free cash flow is less important to shareholders). Indeed, Chetty and Saez (2005) find that the increase in dividends was concentrated among firms where managers owned substantial amounts of stock, among firms where taxable institutions were large shareholders, and among those where a large independent shareholder served on the board of directors. However, an incentive-alignment story cannot necessarily account for all of the evidence. For instance, Brown, Liang, and Weisbenner (2007) find that dividend increases were concentrated among firms whose managers had relatively large stock holdings. In contrast, managers with large amounts of unexercised stock options (which are typically not dividend protected) did not change their behavior in response to JGTRRA. This suggests that in addition to the strength of incentive alignment, self-interest played a role in how managers responded to JGTRRA. This evidence has led Chetty and Saez (2007) to develop an agency theory of managers' responses to the tax reform, which is discussed below.

The Effects of JGTRRA on Firm Value. Equation (1) suggests that equilibrium can be restored following JGTRRA through a decrease in the firm's pretax return r (as well as by increases in d). In other words, the reduction of the tax penalty for dividends implies that shareholders can now be compensated less for holding stock in a dividend-paying firm. This would be manifested in the short term by an increase in the share price. Equation (1) also predicts that the valuation response to JGTRRA is increasing in the firm's initial dividend yield d. The empirical literature has found results broadly consistent with both these predictions.[8]

Auerbach and Hassett (2007) identify significant event dates during the period from December 2002 to May 2003 as the president's initial proposal was announced and made its way through Congress. The vicissitudes undergone by the proposal provide an abundance of opportunities to use an event-study approach to measure market reactions to changes in the probability of JGTRRA's enactment. Auerbach and Hassett (2007) analyze abnormal returns for subsets of firms expected to be differentially affected by the reform. They find that news events indicating a higher probability of enactment were associated with higher abnormal returns (relative to the market) for firms with higher dividend yields. Dhaliwal, Krull, and Li (2007) find a similar result using an alternative approach that uses analysts' earnings forecasts—obtained from the Institutional Brokers' Estimate System (I/B/E/S) database—to construct a measure of the *ex ante* rate of return demanded by equity investors. They find that following JGTRRA the implied cost of equity capital for high-dividend-yield firms decreased relative to that for low-dividend-yield firms. For non-dividend-paying firms, Auerbach and Hassett (2007) and Dhaliwal, Krull, and Li (2007) find a positive reaction (using the different approaches outlined above) that is even larger than the effect for dividend-paying firms. Auerbach and Hassett (2007) also report a similar finding for firms that are predicted to issue new shares in the future.[9]

The event-study approach of Auerbach and Hassett (2007) does not address the overall market reaction to JGTRRA, as the market return is used as the control. Dhaliwal, Krull, and Li (2007) find an overall decrease in the implied cost of equity capital for U.S. firms. Their approach, however, requires that there was no change in investors' risk preferences over the period studied. Amromin, Harrison, and Sharpe (2006) use European stock markets (and real estate investment trusts, which are subject to distinctive tax treatment) as controls, and find no aggregate impact of JGTRRA on the U.S. stock market. However, Auerbach and Hassett (2006) point out that this approach is not sufficiently precise to detect a positive reaction of the magnitude that might be expected, such as the 6 percent increase in market value predicted by Poterba (2004).

Interpreting the Evidence. The scholarly literature suggests that JGTRRA led to a substantial and rapid increase in dividends. There is evidence of an increase in the value of firms with higher dividend yields, but also of an even larger increase in the value of non-dividend-paying firms. This picture, in its entirety, may seem difficult to reconcile with any of the existing theories outlined above. However, it is possible to explain these apparently divergent findings using the interpretation of the new view presented by Auerbach and Hassett (2007).

Consider three representative firms H, L and Y, where H is a dividend-paying firm with a high dividend yield, L is a dividend-paying firm with a low dividend yield, and Y is a young firm that has yet to pay dividends.

Under the new view, a dividend tax cut that is expected to be permanent would increase the value of Y more than that of L (because Y is likely to issue additional equity, the dividends on which will also benefit from the lower tax rate), and it would increase the value of L more than that of H (as L is more likely to issue shares than H). For concreteness, assume that Y's value would increase by 10 percent, L's by 5 percent, and H's by 4 percent. On the other hand, if the tax cut were expected to be temporary and of short duration, then H would enjoy the largest increase in value (as it would pay the most dividends during the brief period of lower rates), followed by L and then by Y: assume that H's value would rise by 3 percent, L's would rise by 1 percent, and Y's would be unaffected. Auerbach and Hassett (2007) construct a test based on the 2004 presidential elections that provides some evidence consistent with this assumed pattern, suggesting that increases in the probability of the tax cuts being made permanent were associated with a decrease in the valuation premium for H relative to L.

Suppose that investors, aware of the political and budgetary uncertainty about the duration of the tax cut, believe that there is a probability of one-half that the cut will be permanent. Then the observed valuation increases would be 3.5 percent for H, 3 percent for L, and 5 percent for Y; in relative terms, this pattern is consistent with the empirical evidence. The probability of one-half that the tax cut will be temporary will (under the new view) also induce higher dividend payments, as found in the literature discussed above. However, under the new view, these dividend increases are inefficient, in the sense that firms eschew profitable investment projects in order to pay dividends during the temporary period of low tax rates (Bank 2007; Dharmapala 2007; see also Korinek and Stiglitz 2008).

On the other hand, the evidence appears less favorable to the traditional view. Of course, the traditional view per se does not explain dividend payment, so it is difficult to determine whether the dividend response is consistent with this theory. However, a central contention of the traditional view is that a reduction in dividend taxes leads to higher investment. This will eventually be reflected in higher dividends, but not with the immediacy of the observed response to JGTRRA (Chetty and Saez 2007). Moreover, the test described above using the 2004 presidential election tends to support the new view over the traditional view (Auerbach and Hassett 2007).

Overall, the evidence consistent with the new view suggests that JGTRRA may not have had any positive impact on investment.[10]

As discussed earlier, the increase in dividends was concentrated among firms where managers or influential shareholders were directly affected by the reform. The importance of agency issues in firms' responses to JGTRRA lies beyond the scope of both the new and traditional views. Chetty and Saez (2007) construct a model in which managers can invest in a "pet project" that does not generate benefits for shareholders; they can also pay dividends or invest in profitable projects. When managers pursue the pet project, and there is imperfect alignment of interests between managers and shareholders, managers will pay lower dividends than shareholders would wish. A dividend tax cut raises the cost to managers of investing in their pet project—or more precisely reduces the tax penalty associated with paying out dividends—and so induces an immediate increase in dividend payments. This model provides a unified explanation for many of the responses to JGTRRA that researchers have found.[11]

Consistent with this model, Chetty and Saez (2006) find some evidence that JGTRRA led to a reallocation of funds from firms with lower growth prospects (measured using analysts' forecasts, as reported in the I/B/E/S database) to those with greater investment opportunities. If there was any positive efficiency impact of JGTRRA, it is most likely to have occurred through this reshuffling of funds: the increase in dividend payments would have enabled investors to reinvest in firms that issue new shares to finance profitable investment opportunities. This process is likely to enhance efficiency to the extent that the retained earnings in more mature firms would have been used for lower-value projects or consumed as managerial rents.

Lessons about Corporate Financial Policy and Portfolio Choices

The aim of this section is to analyze the consequences of JGTRRA for corporate financial policy and the portfolio choices of U.S. investors (with a particular focus on their preference for debt versus equity). These consequences are illustrated using a simple framework that extends the model of financial equilibrium introduced by Miller (1977), although the formulation below is closer to the version in Auerbach (2002) and Desai,

Dharmapala, and Fung (2007).[12] As will be obvious, this model presents a highly simplified view of the world.[13] Nonetheless, it provides some important insights, which are used to derive predictions about the effects of JGTRRA. The section then discusses some relevant empirical evidence.

International Financial Equilibrium. As is well known, the corporate tax system creates a preference for debt financing, as interest payments are tax deductible to the corporation, while returns paid to equity holders are not. In a setting where firms endogenously issue both equity and bonds, Miller (1977) argues that this tax advantage of debt is offset for some investors by a personal tax preference for equity returns because of the lower personal tax rate on the latter. Miller uses this insight to characterize an equilibrium in which each firm is indifferent about its debt-equity ratio; investors sort into clienteles for stocks and bonds according to their personal tax characteristics. The Miller model assumes a closed economy, but it has been extended to the international context by Hodder and Senbet (1990), some of whose central insights are used in the model below.

Assume that there are two countries: the United States (denoted US) and a foreign country (denoted F). Firms in this model are assumed to have an exogenously fixed country of residence (although they may operate abroad through a subsidiary, as discussed below). They face a residence-based corporate tax on their worldwide income of $\tau^{US}\epsilon(0, 1)$ if resident in US and $\tau^F\epsilon(0, 1)$ if resident in F; their foreign operations face a source-based tax imposed by the host country, with a (limited) foreign tax credit allowed by their home country. Without loss of generality (and in deference to current realities) it is assumed that $\tau^{US} > \tau^F$.[14] Firms can issue two kinds of assets: bonds and stock. Firms pay interest on the bonds they issue, and pay equity returns in the form of dividends and/or capital gains (the distinction does not matter for the purposes of this model). There is no risk associated with the returns from either bonds or equity.

There exists a continuum of investors in each country. These investors are distinguished by their personal tax rate t. US investors face tax rates in the interval $[0, t^{USmax}]$ and investors resident in F face tax rates in the interval $[0, t^{Fmax}]$. For concreteness, it is assumed that $t^{Fmax} > t^{USmax}$; this is not, however, crucial to any of the results. Both tFmax and tUSmax are assumed to be sufficiently large that some investors in each country wish to hold equity.[15] Investors are assumed to face only residence-based personal taxes. They are also restricted to holding nonnegative amounts of the two kinds of assets—corporate bonds and equity—issued by firms. The returns from these assets differ in their tax treatment at the personal level, with equity returns being taxed more lightly. Specifically, it is assumed that a US investor with personal tax rate t faces a tax rate of t on interest income and a tax rate of $e^{US}t$ on equity returns, while an investor with personal tax rate t resident in F faces a tax rate of t on interest income and a tax rate of $e^F t$ on equity returns; e^{US} and e^F are country-specific parameters in the interval $[0, 1]$. For concreteness, it is assumed that $e^F > e^{US}$; this is not, however, crucial to any of the results.

In Miller's (1977) equilibrium, the pretax returns on bonds and stock adjust to equate the return to equity and the net-of-tax interest rate (see also Auerbach 2002). It is therefore possible to define a parameter $\theta(t)$ that captures the degree of preference of investors for bonds relative to equity. Specifically, $\theta(t)$ is the ratio of the after-personal-tax value of $1 of interest income to the after-personal-tax value of $1 of equity income. For US investors:

$$\theta^{US}(t) \equiv \frac{1 - t}{1 - e^{US}t} \quad (3)$$

and for investors in F:

$$\theta^F(t) \equiv \frac{1 - t}{1 - e^F t} \quad (4)$$

The smaller is θ, the greater is the investor's tax preference for equity. As $\theta^{US\prime}(t) < 0$ and $\theta^{F\prime}(t) < 0$, the personal tax preference for bonds decreases with the investor's tax rate.

A firm's corporate tax preference for debt depends on the corporate tax rate at which it is able to deduct interest payments. For US firms, this rate will always be τ^{US} regardless of whether the interest payments are made by the parent or by a subsidiary in F. For firms resident in F, however, there is an incentive to deduct interest payments in US rather than in F (see Hodder and Senbet 1990). These firms can arrange to deduct payments in US through a variety of strategies that involve transferring interest deductions

FIGURE 9-1

INTERNATIONAL FINANCIAL EQUILIBRIUM

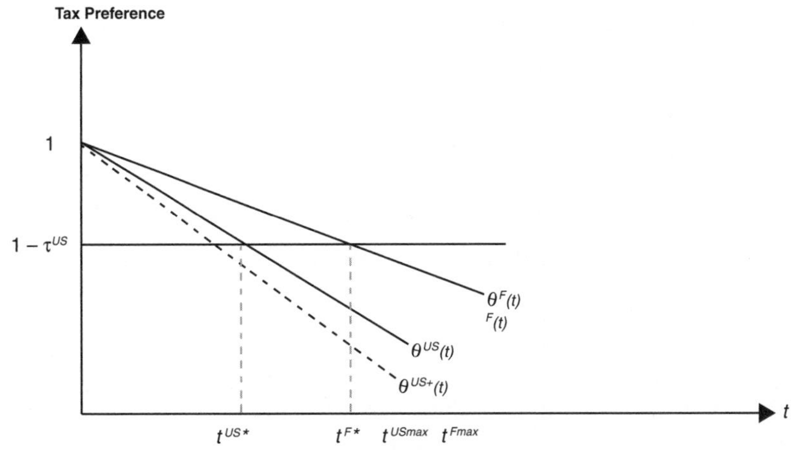

SOURCE: Author's diagram.

to a US subsidiary.[16] Thus all firms will have a corporate tax preference for debt that is given by $(1 - \tau^{US})$.

The corporate tax preference for debt and investors' personal tax preference for equity are depicted in figure 9-1. To characterize the financial equilibrium shown in figure 9-1, attention is restricted to cases where each country's investors hold assets issued in both countries. Let r^{US} be the pretax return to equity issued by US firms, and let r^F be the pretax return to equity issued by F firms. Similarly, let i^{US} be the pretax return to debt issued by US firms, and let i^F be the pretax return to debt issued by F firms. If US investors facing some sufficiently high personal tax rate t hold both US and F equities,[17] then it must be the case that

$$r^F(1 - \tau^F)(1 - e^{US}t) = r^{US} (1 - \tau^{US})(1 - e^{US}t) \quad (5)$$

and hence that

$$r^F(1 - \tau^F) = r^{US} (1 - \tau^{US}) = r^* \quad (6)$$

where $r*$ is the world after-corporate-tax return to equity. That is, returns after corporate taxes are equated across US and F firms.[18] If US investors with sufficiently low t hold both US and F bonds, then $i^F(1 - t) = i^{US}(1 - t)$, and hence $i^F = i^{US} = i*$ (i.e., the interest rates offered by US and F firms are equated at $i*$).

In figure 9-1, equilibrium requires that the personal tax preference for equity—given by θ^{US} and θ^F—equal the corporate tax preference for debt—given by $(1 - t^{US})$. US investors facing the personal tax rate $t^{US}*$ are indifferent between holding bonds issued in either country and equity issued by firms in either country; thus

$$i*(1 - t^{US}*) = r*(1 - e^{US}t^{US}*) \quad (7)$$

(and an analogous condition holds for F investors facing the personal tax rate t^F*). Hence

$$\frac{r*}{i*} = \frac{1 - t^{US}*}{1 - e^{US}t^{US}*} = \theta^{US}(t^{US}*) = \frac{1 - t^F*}{1 - e^F t^F*} = \theta^F(t^F*) = 1 - r^{US}, \quad (8)$$

so that

$$i*(1 - \tau^{US}) = r*. \quad (9)$$

The left-hand side represents the cost of borrowing to a firm (whether located in US or F), taking into account the subsidy provided by the (US) corporate tax, while the right-hand side represents the rate of return demanded by equity holders. Thus each firm is indifferent about its debt-equity ratio in this international financial equilibrium. All US investors with personal tax rates above $t^{US}*$ and all F investors with personal tax rates above t^F* hold stock. All US investors with personal tax rates below $t^{US}*$ and all F investors with personal tax rates below t^F* hold bonds. In each case, the national origin of the assets owned by each investor is indeterminate. Firms issue a sufficient number of bonds to satisfy the demand of investors who prefer bonds and a sufficient amount of equity to satisfy the demand of investors who prefer equity. Thus, there is a determinate debt-equity ratio at the *global* level; however, as each firm is indifferent about its capital structure, the aggregate debt-equity ratio at the *national* level is indeterminate.

The Effect of JGTRRA on U.S. Investors' Equity Holdings. JGTRRA can be viewed as having disturbed the international financial equilibrium characterized above by reducing the parameter e^{US}, thereby increasing the tax preference for equity among U.S. investors. This is depicted in figure 9-1 as a shift of $\theta^{US}(t)$ to $\theta^{US+}(t)$; clearly, the new equilibrium involves a larger fraction of U.S. investors wishing to hold stock. This change entails that firms issue more equity and that the *global* debt-equity ratio falls. However, there is no necessary presumption in this model that the firms issuing the additional equity are U.S. firms: the increased demand for equity by U.S. investors could be satisfied (in theory, entirely) by foreign firms. The capital structure of U.S. firms is indeterminate in both the old and the new equilibria, and so within this framework there is no basis for predicting that JGTRRA would reduce U.S. firms' use of debt, as was suggested by some proponents of the reform.

Obviously, if U.S. investors are highly home-biased, then the reduction in the global debt-equity ratio will surely be concentrated among U.S. firms. There is indeed considerable evidence of home bias in U.S. equity holdings. Figure 9-2 depicts the location of U.S. equity holdings in 2004, computed from the Treasury International Capital (TIC) system dataset.[19] The TIC system reports the portfolio holdings of foreign securities by U.S. investors and the portfolio holdings of U.S. securities by foreign residents. It is based on periodic surveys of banks, other financial institutions, securities brokers, and dealers. The holdings are divided into equity foreign portfolio investment (FPI) and debt FPI, with the latter category further subdivided into long-term and short-term debt. While there are some limitations of the TIC data, they nonetheless represent the best available source of information on inbound and outbound U.S. FPI. As shown in figure 9-2, the TIC data indicate that most portfolio equity investment by U.S. investors—88 percent—is located in the U.S.

However, this is not necessarily the most relevant information in this context. JGTRRA induced U.S. investors to hold more equity, so what matters more is whether these *incremental* holdings of equity are in U.S. or foreign stocks; it is the location of these incremental holdings that determines how much less debt U.S. firms issue. The home bias of U.S. investors has clearly eroded over time. Figure 9-3 depicts the location of the *increase* in equity holdings by U.S. investors from 2004 to 2005 (in each case, the data

FIGURE 9-2

HOLDINGS OF DOMESTIC AND FOREIGN EQUITY BY
U.S. PORTFOLIO INVESTORS, 2004

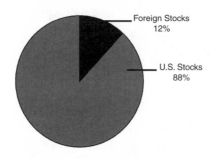

SOURCE: Author's calculations, based on data from the U.S. Department of the Treasury, Treasury International Capital System.
NOTE: U.S. investors' aggregate holdings are computed as U.S. market capitalization minus foreigners' holdings of U.S. equities plus U.S. investors' foreign equity holdings.

FIGURE 9-3

INCREASES IN HOLDINGS OF DOMESTIC AND FOREIGN EQUITY BY
U.S. PORTFOLIO INVESTORS, 2004–5

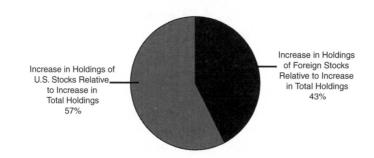

SOURCE: Author's calculations, based on data from U.S. Department of the Treasury, Treasury International Capital System.
NOTE: U.S. investors' aggregate holdings in each year are computed as U.S. market capitalization minus foreigners' holdings of U.S. equities plus U.S. investors' foreign equity holdings.

are for December 31 of the relevant year). Specifically, what figure 9-3 reports is the percentage of this increase—43 percent—that was accounted for by increased holdings of foreign equity. This suggests that any increase in U.S. investors' desire for equity as a result of JGTRRA would have been met in substantial measure by the acquisition of stock in foreign rather than U.S. corporations.

Thus, it seems reasonable to conclude that the main discernible effect of JGTRRA is likely to be on U.S. investors' portfolio choices. To be sure, there is likely to be some impact on the global debt-equity ratio, but any observed change in this variable would potentially be confounded with changes (other than JGTRRA) that occurred in 2003. Thus the main focus here is on changes in U.S. investors' portfolios. However, it is difficult to test this prediction using domestic (U.S.) holdings, due to possible supply-side responses by U.S. firms (in terms of the types of assets that they issue). In addition, the very existence of a home bias suggests that U.S. investment in U.S. firms may reflect different forces than U.S. investment in foreign firms. There is of course no other "home" country for U.S. investors that can be used to control for these potential differences.

These considerations suggest that a more promising approach would be to compare U.S. investment across different foreign countries. Indeed, a relatively obscure provision of JGTRRA relating to the treatment of foreign dividends provides a source of identification for just such an approach (Desai and Dharmapala 2007). The lower tax rate for dividends under JGTRRA applies only to dividends paid by "qualified" foreign corporations. A foreign corporation is deemed to be qualified if it satisfies at least one of three tests established by the legislation. Of these, the most relevant is the "treaty test," which establishes that a corporation resident in a country with which the United States has a tax treaty meeting certain criteria qualifies for the lower dividend tax rate.[20] In October 2003, the IRS released a list of fifty-two countries that were deemed to satisfy the treaty test;[21] these countries (listed in table 9-1) are referred to below as "treaty" countries, while all those excluded from the list are referred to as "nontreaty" countries.

Qualification provides the U.S. shareholders of foreign corporations with a substantially lower tax rate—for a top-bracket U.S. shareholder, dividends from a British firm are taxed at 15 percent, while dividends from an Argentine firm are taxed at 35 percent. Desai and Dharmapala (2007) use

TABLE 9-1
LIST OF TREATY COUNTRIES UNDER JGTRRA

Australia	Greece	Lithuania	Slovak Republic
Austria	Hungary	Luxembourg	Slovenia
Belgium	Iceland	Mexico	South Africa
Canada	India	Morocco	Spain
China	Indonesia	Netherlands	Sweden
Cyprus	Ireland	New Zealand	Switzerland
Czech Republic	Israel	Norway	Thailand
Denmark	Italy	Pakistan	Trinidad and Tobago
Egypt	Jamaica	Philippines	Tunisia
Estonia	Japan	Poland	Turkey
Finland	Kazakhstan	Portugal	Ukraine
France	Korea	Romania	United Kingdom
Germany	Latvia	Russian Federation	Venezuela

SOURCE: Internal Revenue Service.

this difference in tax rates to analyze the sensitivity of portfolio choices to dividend taxation, and they find a substantial effect. This same source of variation can be used to shed some light on the predictions of the simple model presented above. In particular, if a foreign country is a treaty country, then the reduced dividend tax applies, and U.S. investors will wish to increase their equity holdings in both U.S. firms and the foreign country's firms, relative to holdings of debt. On the other hand, if a foreign country is a nontreaty country, then there is no reduction in dividend taxes for its firms, and so while U.S. investors will want to increase equity holdings in U.S. firms, there is no incentive to do so in the other country's firms.[22] Thus if U.S. investors responded to JGTRRA's incentives to switch from debt to equity holdings, then this effect should appear only in treaty countries. It might be expected, therefore, that the equity-to-debt ratio for U.S. investment in treaty countries would rise, relative to the corresponding ratio for nontreaty countries.

Figure 9-4 shows how the ratio of equity to debt in U.S. portfolio holdings changed after JGTRRA in treaty and nontreaty countries. The equity-

FIGURE 9-4

HOLDINGS OF FOREIGN EQUITY RELATIVE TO FOREIGN
DEBT BY U.S. PORTFOLIO INVESTORS

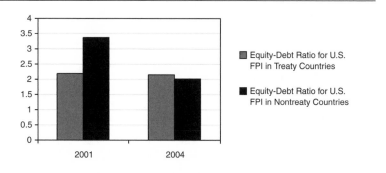

SOURCE: Author's calculations, based on data from U.S. Department of the Treasury, Treasury International Capital System.
NOTES: The equity-to-debt ratio for treaty countries is computed by aggregating equity FPI across treaty countries and dividing by the sum of debt FPI holdings (also aggregated across treaty countries). The equity-to-debt ratio for nontreaty countries is computed in an analogous manner. The ratios are shown on the vertical axis; the horizontal axis represents the years 2001 and 2004.

to-debt ratio for treaty countries is computed by aggregating U.S. investors' equity holdings across treaty countries, and dividing by U.S. investors' debt holdings in the same group of countries. An analogous procedure is used for the equity-to-debt ratio in nontreaty countries.[23] The comparison is between 2001 (the last year prior to the reform for which TIC data are available) and 2004. The equity-to-debt ratio in treaty countries remained essentially unchanged over this period, apparently contradicting the theoretical prediction. However, using nontreaty countries as a control group suggests a different picture: the equity-to-debt ratio for nontreaty countries fell sharply over this period, so that (as expected) the equity-to-debt ratio for U.S. investment in treaty countries rose, relative to the corresponding ratio for nontreaty countries.[24]

A more rigorous test along these lines is presented by Desai and Dharmapala (2007), although the primary emphasis of their paper is the location of equity FPI across countries, rather than the mix of equity and debt. Desai and Dharmapala (2007) undertake a difference-in-difference analysis using panel data on U.S. equity FPI, comparing investment in treaty and nontreaty countries before and after JGTRRA. Column 5 of table 3 in Desai and Dharmapala (2007) reports results controlling for debt FPI (and so essentially captures the effect on the equity-to-debt ratio); this also controls for other relevant factors such as changes in GDP, changes in market capitalization, and changes in a stock market returns index. U.S. equity FPI in treaty countries (relative to nontreaty countries) rose after JGTRRA, implying that the equity-to-debt ratio would also have risen correspondingly.

The overall lesson is that JGTRRA appears to have induced U.S. investors to hold more equity. On the other hand, the effects of JGTRRA on the capital structure of U.S. firms are not clear on theoretical grounds. Moreover, there does not appear to be any empirical evidence on this issue. Possibly, this is because dividends from all U.S. firms were subject to JGTRRA, and it is therefore difficult to find a valid control group.

Lessons about Corporate Tax Integration

JGTRRA was intended by its proponents as an important step forward in the integration of corporate and personal taxes. Scholars have long argued for corporate tax integration (CTI) as a means of reducing the distortions—to organizational form, payout policy, and financing decisions—created by the "double taxation" of corporate income (e.g., Hubbard 1993, 2005). This section begins by clarifying the efficiency consequences of these distortions. It then discusses some international dimensions of CTI. The section ends with some reflections on two related questions: whether the dividend tax regime created by JGTRRA should be extended, and how further advances toward CTI may best be pursued in the future.

The Efficiency Costs of Corporate Financial Distortions. The undesirability of distortions to corporate financial decisions is generally presumed by economists. However, conceptualizing—not to mention quantifying—the social costs of these distortions is not entirely straightforward (in contrast, it is easier to understand the efficiency costs of distortions to firms' investment decisions due to corporate taxes). Consider the case where firms use more debt than they otherwise would because of the tax deductibility of interest payments. This practice can potentially give rise to more bank-ruptcies than would otherwise occur, along with the associated transaction costs of reorganization. Suppose that these transaction costs are manifested in the form of fees paid to lawyers. The fees are of course simply a transfer, but may give rise to a social cost via labor market incentives. Specifically, the returns to entering the legal profession would rise, drawing in some individuals at the margin who would (absent the tax incentive for firms to use too much debt) have been more productive in some other occupation. In this account, the efficiency cost of distortions to firms' capital structure is a reduction in society's output due to a misallocation of labor.

Similar examples can be given for distortions to firms' payout decisions. If the tax penalty on dividends causes firms to retain earnings that they would otherwise have paid out, then managers may use these retained earnings for negative-value projects or consume them as rents. Inefficient projects entail an obvious social cost, but there may also be distortions to the labor market. As shareholders reduce managerial compensation to take account of the private benefits enjoyed by managers, the managerial profession will tend to attract those individuals who value private benefits over standard forms of compensation, even if such individuals would be more productive in some other occupation (absent the tax incentive for firms to retain too much of their earnings).

These types of social costs are generally not borne by shareholders as such, but rather are dispersed across society in the form of lower output. Even in the case of excessive retention of earnings, the expected agency costs are presumably capitalized into the share price. Thus, the efficiency gains from eliminating these distortions are conceptually separate from any redistribution toward shareholders that may be entailed by the actual implementation of CTI. In addition, although these social costs are inher-ently very difficult to quantify, that does not imply that they are necessarily small in magnitude.

Corporate Tax Integration and International Financial Integration. Historically, the dominant approach to CTI has involved dividend imputa-tion credits. Under an imputation system, shareholders receive a credit for corporate taxes paid at the firm level; this credit can be used to offset share-holders' personal tax liability on their dividend income. Imputation credits, however, are typically restricted to corporate taxes paid by domestic firms, resulting in a lower tax rate on domestic equity returns than on foreign equity returns. This creates a tax incentive to invest in domestic rather than foreign corporations, potentially causing inefficient underdiversification among domestic investors (see e.g. Fuest and Huber 2001; Avi-Yonah 2005). From an individual investor's point of view, it may be rational to accept a higher level of risk by concentrating on domestic equities in order to obtain the higher expected after-tax return on those domestic securities. However, from society's point of view, the tax payments are (to a first approximation) simply a transfer. Thus, society as a whole ends up with a welfare loss by bearing more risk than necessary for the expected returns obtained. This implies that while CTI ameliorates domestic distortions, it creates new inefficiencies in international portfolio choices. Comparing U.S. FPI in treaty and nontreaty countries after JGTRRA, Desai and Dharmapala (2007) find a large elasticity of equity FPI with respect to dividend taxes. Thus, an important lesson from investors' response to JGTRRA is that tax-induced international portfolio distortions may be substantial.

In the 2000s, international diversification issues have become more important than ever. At the same time, the dividend imputation systems of Europe have encountered legal problems, running afoul of the European Union's nondiscrimination principles (see, e.g., Graetz and Warren 2007). As a result, there has been a movement away from dividend imputation toward shareholder-level dividend exclusion.[25] JGTRRA's partial shareholder-level dividend exclusion can be viewed as part of this worldwide trend. As a mechanism for CTI in a globalized economy, JGTRRA's approach appears to be superior to a dividend imputation system. Most importantly, it does not restrict its partial dividend exclusion to dividends paid by U.S. firms. However, as discussed above, JGTRRA does not treat all foreign countries identically. Admittedly, most U.S. equity FPI is subject to the favorable tax regime under JGTRRA. Nonetheless, dividends from firms located in some significant destinations for U.S. investment—such as Argentina, Brazil, Hong Kong, Malaysia, Singapore, and Taiwan—do not qualify for this favorable treatment.

The various justifications offered for JGTRRA's distinction between treaty and nontreaty countries are not entirely persuasive. In the legislative discussion surrounding the act, concern was expressed about extending the benefits of JGTRRA to income on which no corporate tax had ever been paid (Sheppard 2004). However, the distinction that JGTRRA draws between treaty and nontreaty countries does not have any necessary relationship to countries' corporate tax rates. The focus on information exchange in defining which treaties are eligible for "qualification" may reflect fears about tax avoidance strategies or about tax evasion, but these concerns have never been described in detail.[26] Moreover, concerns about the exchange of information are perhaps best addressed through the tax information exchange agreements (TIEAs) that the United States has signed with many countries, including some with which it does not have tax treaties. Yet JGTRRA uses treaty status rather than the presence of TIEAs as the basis for its applicability. Thus while JGTRRA's treatment of foreign dividends is clearly preferable to that of most dividend imputation systems, it nonetheless distorts the location of FPI.

While the effects of CTI on international portfolio diversification are widely appreciated, the model used in the section above suggests another dimension to the interaction between global financial integration and CTI. In particular, it suggests a growing disjuncture between two different effects of CTI: influencing the portfolio choices of investors resident in the United States, and influencing the behavior of firms resident in the United States. In a closed economy, these two effects are intrinsically linked, as the number and types of securities issued by domestic firms must meet the demands of domestic investors. However, this link is severed in an open economy, as illustrated by the model used above. Thus while JGTRRA was apparently able to induce U.S. firms to pay more dividends, its efficacy in achieving this aim was reduced by the fact that a typical U.S. shareholder benefiting from the tax cut held about a tenth of her portfolio overseas. The revenue loss from the lower tax rate on foreign (treaty country) dividends is of course not compensated for by any payout policy changes by U.S. firms. This dissipation is much larger in the case of the impact of JGTRRA on U.S. firms' capital structure. As figure 9-3 suggests, we would expect nearly half of the increase in demand for equities by U.S. investors to be satisfied by foreign firms. Thus the impact on U.S. firms' capital structure is likely to be only about half what it would be in a closed economy.[27] This is not, of course, to argue that the tax cut should not have been extended to foreign dividends. Rather, the point is that in a globalized economy, there are constraints on what governments can accomplish, and the achievement of CTI is no exception to this rule.

Future Directions for Dividend Tax Policy. The higher costs of achieving CTI raise several questions about future policy. Most obvious is the impending issue of whether the dividend tax cuts (scheduled to expire in 2010) should be extended. If they are not, then it is unlikely that the increases in dividends in the wake of JGTRRA would be reversed; firms, after all, are loath to reduce regular dividend payments.[28] However, there would be reduced pressure on managers of firms that do not currently pay dividends to do so in the future. This might in turn slow down the reallocation of investment funds that Chetty and Saez (2006, 2007) argue was spurred by JGTRRA. In any event, as JGTRRA achieved only a partial implementation of CTI, there is scope for further progress toward this goal, regardless of whether the tax cuts are extended or allowed to lapse.

One policy option that goes beyond merely extending the tax cuts would be to further reduce dividend taxes, perhaps moving to full dividend exclusion. There are of course many budgetary and distributional concerns that are relevant to this decision. One issue that has not attracted much attention, however, is the impact on international portfolio choices. A dividend tax rate below 15 percent would be less than the withholding tax rates imposed by foreign countries on dividends paid to U.S. shareholders (typically, this rate is 15 percent for treaty countries).[29] For example, consider a U.S. investor who owns stock in the United States and France. If the United States dividend tax rate were lowered to zero, the dividends she receives from her U.S. stock would be tax exempt, but she would pay a 15 percent withholding tax to France on her French dividends. Moreover, she would not have a U.S. tax liability on the French dividends against which to claim a foreign tax credit.[30] This outcome would obviously discourage international diversification.

Of course, tax treaties could be renegotiated, perhaps to eliminate withholding taxes altogether. However, as treaty provisions are typically reciprocal, this would entail an additional revenue cost to the United States (from eliminating withholding taxes imposed by the United States on dividends paid by U.S. firms to foreign shareholders), in addition to the direct revenue loss from reducing dividend taxes on U.S. residents. It therefore seems inadvisable to pursue further dividend tax cuts without taking account of these international ramifications.

Firm-Level Approaches to Corporate Tax Integration. The previous arguments suggest that if the aim of policymakers is to influence corporate financial policy, then they should perhaps use measures directed more specifically at U.S. firms. One such approach is a firm-level deduction for dividends paid (Hubbard 1993, 2005). This would create neutrality between debt and equity financing if firms pay out all their profits as dividends. A more general way to achieve neutrality is an allowance for corporate equity (ACE) systems (e.g., see Devereux and Freeman 1991; Klemm 2007). An ACE system allows firms to deduct a normal rate of return on their equity. As this rate of return is, to a first approximation, equal to the return the firm must pay on its bonds, an ACE system eliminates the incentive under the current tax system to issue excessive amounts of debt. In addition, it is possible to eliminate distortions to corporate financial policy by disallowing interest deductions, as in the Comprehensive Business Income Tax (CBIT) model developed by the Treasury in the 1990s (Kleinbard 2007).

Beyond its effects on financial policy, an ACE system has other significant advantages, for instance eliminating distortions to investment at the margin. Moreover, it is not merely a theoretical curiosity: a variant of an ACE has been used in Brazil since 1996,[31] and an ACE system was introduced in Belgium in 2006. Nonetheless, none of the firm-level approaches to CTI has been widely adopted. One major reason is the substantial revenue cost involved (Hubbard 1993, 2005).[32] An ACE system taxes only the economic rents generated in the corporate sector, and so necessarily narrows the corporate tax base. Moreover, much of the revenue loss is associated with inframarginal equity—i.e., equity that was (or would have been) issued despite the current tax preference for debt. In theory, it is possible to limit the revenue loss by distinguishing between old and new equity, and ensuring neutrality with debt only for the latter. However, this is difficult to achieve in practice for an ACE because firms have an incentive to repurchase existing stock and issue new equity.[33] Thus policymakers must decide whether the efficiency gains discussed at the beginning of this section warrant incurring the significant revenue losses involved.

Finally, another firm-level policy that can ameliorate distortions to corporate financial policy (and to the choice of organizational form) is a reduction in the corporate tax rate. This would not only reduce the tax advantage of debt, but would likely have a variety of other potential benefits as well. For instance, the U.S. corporate tax rate is widely viewed as being out of step with foreign rates, and there is growing evidence that the burden of the tax falls to a substantial degree on workers (see, e.g., Viard 2008). Reducing the corporate tax rate would lessen both these problems.

Conclusion

The 2003 tax reform provided scholars with an unusual opportunity to analyze the impact of a large reduction in dividend taxes. A number of important lessons for tax policy can be distilled from this episode. The fall in dividend taxes led to a substantial and immediate increase in dividend payments by U.S. firms, especially in the form of dividend initiations. These dividend increases were concentrated among firms with influential shareholders or managers who benefited from the reform. JGTRRA also increased the value of firms with high dividend yields relative to firms with lower yields, while also raising the value of firms that had yet to pay any dividends. These findings are most consistent with the new view of dividend taxation, but leave some unresolved issues for future inquiry. The reform also appears to have changed U.S. investors' preference for equity over debt. However, in an ever more financially integrated world, there is no clear basis for expecting significant changes in U.S. firms' capital structure. Finally, JGTRRA offers important lessons for policies relating to the integration of corporate and personal taxes. In particular, it appears that JGTRRA's shareholder-level approach may be less effective in a financially integrated world economy than measures directed specifically at U.S. firms. However, many of the longer-term consequences of the reform are still unclear, especially given the ostensibly temporary nature of the tax cut.

Notes

1. JGTRRA is not, however, entirely unique in providing the opportunity to study the impact of dividend taxation. See Bond, Devereux, and Klemm (2007a, 2007b) for an analysis of a 1997 reform to the tax treatment of dividends in the UK.

2. In the Miller (1977) model discussed below, for example, t_d would be the dividend tax rate faced by the marginal investor who is indifferent between equity and bonds. However, this type of restriction is not imposed at this stage. The discussion here and below relies on the "marginal investor" approach to market equilibrium. An alternative approach would be to use a framework such as the after-tax capital asset pricing model (CAPM) developed by Brennan (1970). In this approach, the market equilibrium is influenced by all investors, with each investor's influence being weighted by her wealth and risk tolerance; see also Auerbach and King (1983) and Bond, Devereux, and Klemm (2007a, 2007b).

3. Equivalently, r could be interpreted as the after-corporate-tax (but before-personal-tax) rate of return.

4. For this reason, the new view is also sometimes referred to as the "trapped equity" view. The argument that dividend taxes are unavoidable is supported, for example, by the existence of U.S. tax rules (e.g., Section 302) that potentially subject share repurchases to the higher dividend tax rate if repurchases are undertaken with sufficient regularity. However, repurchases by U.S. firms have grown substantially in recent decades without triggering these tax provisions.

5. The new view does not address this puzzle, as it assumes that dividend taxes are unavoidable in the long run.

6. Implicit differentiation of equation (1) suggests that reducing t_d results in an increase in d, as long as the initial t_d is sufficiently large relative to the marginal utility of dividend returns. A reduction in t_d also leads to a decrease in the required pre-tax return r; in the short run, this would be manifested in the form of an increase in the firm's share price. Moreover, the valuation response to JGTRRA is predicted to be increasing in the firm's initial dividend yield d (subject to the same condition that the initial t_d is "sufficiently large").

7. Empirically identifying nontaxable institutions in itself poses a considerable challenge, as the standard data source (Thomson Financial's database, which reports institutional ownership based on 13-F filings) does not classify institutions by tax status. Chetty and Saez (2005) thus hand-classify institutions (based on their names) into categories subject to different tax treatment.

8. Another aspect of valuation that has been examined by researchers is the impact of JGTRRA on ex-dividend day price behavior. This term refers to the change in the price of a stock at the time a dividend is paid. This price change reveals how much investors value the dividend, and in particular provides evidence on whether dividend taxes are incorporated into their valuation. Elton and Gruber (1970) find that the price falls by less than the amount of the dividend, suggesting the capitalization

of dividend taxes. Chetty, Rosenberg, and Saez (2007) find that the magnitude of this phenomenon changed in 2003 in a manner consistent with JGTRRA's reduction of dividend taxes. However, they also show that this inference is not robust because of the long-run time-series volatility in ex-dividend-day price behavior.

9. Amromin, Harrison, and Sharpe (2006) argue that the positive abnormal returns for non-dividend-paying stock were unrelated to the tax reform, and were also found among non-dividend-paying UK stocks over this period. However, Auerbach and Hassett (2006) find that the magnitude of the abnormal returns for nonpayers was positively related to the predicted probability of issuing new shares, suggesting that the effect was indeed related to JGTRRA.

10. A direct test of the impact of JGTRRA on corporate investment would be very difficult, given the long-run time-series volatility of investment (see, for example, Chetty and Saez 2005).

11. However, there are certain possibilities this model does not encompass, such as a signaling value for dividends, or circumstances in which managers are so intent on enjoying leisure that they forgo profitable investment opportunities and pay excessively high dividends. The study by Chetty and Saez (2007) is also an example of a growing literature analyzing the linkages between taxation and corporate governance, as are studies by Desai and Dharmapala (2006, 2008); for a survey of this literature, see Desai and Dharmapala (forthcoming). Bank (2007), however, cautions against using the tax code to achieve corporate governance objectives.

12. The relevant pages in Auerbach (2002) are 1271–73 and in Desai, Dharmapala, and Fung (2007) are 351–54.

13. See Auerbach and King (1983) for a model of financial equilibrium that incorporates uncertainty about asset returns.

14. In practice, these assumptions mean that a firm resident in F faces a tax rate of τ^F on its domestic operations and a tax rate of τ^{US} on its US operations, while a firm resident in US faces a tax rate of τ^{US} on both its domestic and foreign operations. Note that these corporate taxes are assumed to offer full deductibility of losses, as in Miller (1977).

15. A minimal necessary condition for the Miller equilibrium is that the maximum personal tax rate exceeds the corporate rate. It is much less clear that this is the case today in the United States than when Miller (1977) proposed his theory. However, even today (when the maximum federal tax rate of 35 percent equals the corporate rate), incorporating state taxes into the analysis may result in some investors facing a personal tax rate on interest income that exceeds the corporate rate. Also, nontax considerations are ignored here, but subtracting the nontax cost of debt (e.g., a bankruptcy cost) from the expression for the tax advantage of debt will also result in some investors preferring equity.

16. For example, suppose that an F corporation needs $100 of loans to finance a new factory in F; assume the factory will generate a return of $15 and that the interest rate demanded by lenders is 10 percent. Instead of issuing bonds itself, the F

corporation could set up a subsidiary in US, which would then borrow $100 and use the proceeds to repurchase stock owned by the parent. The parent then invests in the factory and generates the $15 return; it uses $10 of that return to infuse new equity into the US subsidiary, which the latter uses to pay interest on the bonds. These interest payments are thus deducted at the higher US tax rate τ^{US} (recall that the corporate tax is assumed to treat losses symmetrically). In practice, such strategies are restricted by "thin capitalization" rules, such as Section 162(j) of the United States tax code. However, Desai, Foley, and Hines (2004) find evidence consistent with multinational corporations locating debt in higher-tax countries.

17. Given the existence of source-based corporate taxation, it might be thought that firms resident in F would face a corporate tax rate that is some weighted average of τ^F and τ^{US} (as they face the US tax rate on their US operations). It is implicitly assumed in equation (5) that F firms are able to source their (positive) income solely in F, just as they were earlier assumed to be able to source all interest deductions in US. The basic conclusions are unaffected, however, if F firms face a weighted average of τ^F and τ^{US}.

18. This condition is similar, for example, to that in Devereux (2000). Note that the pre-tax return does not reflect shareholder-level taxes. This situation is thus a little different from that assumed in some of the theories of dividend taxation discussed earlier; however, this difference does not matter for the questions addressed in this section.

19. The TIC data are available at www.treas.gov/tic/ and are described in more detail in Bertaut, Griever, and Tryon (2006) and Desai and Dharmapala (2007). Following Cai and Warnock (2006), the approach here is to compute U.S. investors' aggregate holdings as U.S. market capitalization minus foreigners' holdings of U.S. equities plus U.S. investors' foreign equity holdings (all of which are obtained from TIC).

20. In addition, under the "possessions test," corporations resident in a U.S. possession (such as Puerto Rico), or certain former U.S. territories that are treated as possessions for tax purposes, automatically qualify. Under the "market test," dividends from corporations whose shares are traded in the United States are also eligible for the favorable dividend tax treatment.

21. IRS 2003. Desai and Dharmapala (2007) calculate that these fifty-two countries together hosted 82 percent of U.S. outbound equity FPI holdings in 2001. Thus, most U.S. portfolio investment is subject to the favorable tax regime under JGTRRA. Nonetheless, firms located in some significant destinations for U.S. investment—such as Argentina, Brazil, Hong Kong, Malaysia, Singapore, and Taiwan—do not qualify for this favorable treatment.

22. JGTRRA reduced the top marginal rate on ordinary income from 38.6 percent to 35 percent, but this affects interest income and dividends from nontreaty countries symmetrically.

23. In particular, note that these ratios are *not* obtained by averaging equity-to-debt ratios across countries. Thus the weight placed on countries where there is little U.S. investment is very small.

24. This could represent a reallocation of equity investment from nontreaty to treaty countries. Up to a point, that would be consistent with the story being told here, but this reallocation may have occurred without any net increase in foreign equity holdings. This seems unlikely, given the trend toward higher levels of investment abroad over this period (see figure 9-3), but is difficult to test as there is no good control for the overall level of U.S. equity FPI.

25. For example, the German tax reform of 2001 abandoned dividend imputation in favor of partial dividend exclusion (Fuest and Huber 2001).

26. Another possible reason for this distinction—that Congress wished to provide researchers with a "natural experiment"—can safely be dismissed.

27. On the other hand, if policymakers are primarily interested in influencing the portfolio holdings of U.S. investors rather than the behavior of U.S. firms, then shareholder-level dividend exclusion involves no such dissipation. For instance, if stock market participation is viewed as being inefficiently low, then there may be some potential justification for government policy to promote equity holdings (see Desai, Dharmapala, and Fung 2007 for a discussion). However, the political rhetoric surrounding JGTRRA did not focus on these types of issues.

28. Given the ostensibly temporary nature of the tax cut, it is perhaps somewhat surprising that firms did not rely more on increases in special dividends.

29. Wacker (2004, table 1) details the withholding tax rates specified in the tax treaties to which the United States is a signatory.

30. This problem would be mitigated, at least in part, if the taxpayer had other foreign-source income (such as interest) that was subject to U.S. taxation, or could gain exposure to French stocks through derivative instruments such as equity swaps.

31. Klemm (2007) analyzes the consequences of the Brazilian system and finds a substantial increase in dividend payments but only a limited impact on capital structure.

32. Another reason is that these forms of CTI appear to benefit foreign shareholders (see, e.g., Avi-Yonah 2005). However, as discussed above, the efficiency gains from eliminating distortions to corporate financial policy primarily take the form of increases in domestic output.

33. However, it may be possible to implement a rough form of grandfathering with a firm-level dividend deduction by restricting deductibility to dividends above some prereform baseline level (or above a baseline ratio relative to earnings).

References

Allen, F., A. Bernardo, and I. Welch. 2000. A theory of dividends based on tax clienteles. *Journal of Finance* 55, no. 6: 2499–2536.

Amromin, G., P. Harrison, and S. Sharpe. 2006. How did the 2003 dividend tax cut affect stock prices? Federal Reserve Bank of Chicago Working Paper 2006-17.

Auerbach, A. J. 1979. Wealth maximization and the cost of capital. *Quarterly Journal of Economics* 93, no. 3: 433–46.

———. 2002. Taxation and corporate financial policy. In *Handbook of public economics*. Vol. 3, ed. A. J. Auerbach and M. Feldstein, 1251–92. Amsterdam: Elsevier Science.

Auerbach, A. J., and K. A. Hassett. 2006. Dividend taxes and firm valuation: New evidence. *American Economic Review Papers and Proceedings* 96, no. 2: 119–23.

———. 2007. The 2003 dividend tax cut and the value of the firm: An event study. In *Taxing corporate income in the 21st century*, ed. A. J. Auerbach, J. R. Hines Jr., and J. Slemrod, 93–126. Cambridge: Cambridge University Press.

Auerbach, A. J., and M. A. King. 1983. Taxation, portfolio choice, and debt-equity ratios: A general equilibrium model. *Quarterly Journal of Economics* 98, no. 4: 587–609.

Avi-Yonah, R. S. 2005. The pitfalls of international integration: A comment on the Bush proposal and its aftermath. *International Tax and Public Finance* 12, no. 1: 87–95.

Bank, S. A. 2007. Dividends and tax policy in the long run. *University of Illinois Law Review* 2007, no. 2: 533–74.

Bertaut, C., W. L. Griever, and R. W. Tryon. 2006. Understanding U.S. cross-border securities data. *Federal Reserve Bulletin* 92: A59–A75.

Bhattacharya, S. 1979. Imperfect information, dividend policy, and "the bird in the hand" fallacy. *Bell Journal of Economics* 10, no. 1: 259–70.

Black, F. 1976. The dividend puzzle. *Journal of Portfolio Management* 2, no. 2: 5–8.

Blouin, J. L., J. S. Raedy, and D. A. Shackelford. 2004. Did dividends increase immediately after the 2003 reduction in tax rates? NBER Working Paper No. 10301, Cambridge, MA.

———. 2007. Did firms substitute dividends for share repurchases after the 2003 reductions in shareholder tax rates? NBER Working Paper No. 13601, Cambridge, MA.

Bond, S. R., M. P. Devereux, and A. Klemm. 2007a. Dissecting dividend decisions: Some clues about the effects of dividend taxation from recent UK reforms. In *Taxing corporate income in the 21st century*, ed. A. J. Auerbach, J. R. Hines Jr., and J. Slemrod, 41–75. Cambridge: Cambridge University Press.

———. 2007b. The effects of dividend taxes on equity prices: A re-examination of the 1997 UK tax reform. Oxford University Centre for Business Taxation Working Paper 0701.

Bradford, D. F. 1981. The incidence and allocation effects of a tax on corporate distributions. *Journal of Public Economics* 15, no. 1: 1–22.

Brennan, M. J. 1970. Taxes, market valuation and corporate financial policy. *National Tax Journal*, 23, no. 4: 417–27.

Brown, J. R., N. Liang, and S. Weisbenner. 2007. Executive financial incentives and payout policy: Firm responses to the 2003 dividend tax cut. *Journal of Finance* 62, no. 4: 1935–65.

Cai, F. and F. E. Warnock. 2006. International diversification at home and abroad. NBER Working Paper No. 12220, Cambridge, MA.

Chetty, R., J. Rosenberg, and E. Saez. 2007. The effects of taxes on market responses to dividend announcements and payments: What can we learn from the 2003 dividend tax cut? In *Taxing corporate income in the 21st century*, ed. A. J. Auerbach, J. R. Hines Jr., and J. Slemrod, 1–32. Cambridge: Cambridge University Press.

Chetty, R., and E. Saez. 2005. Dividend taxes and corporate behavior: Evidence from the 2003 dividend tax cut. *Quarterly Journal of Economics* 120, no. 3: 791–834.

———. 2006. The effects of the 2003 dividend tax cut on corporate behavior: Interpreting the evidence. *American Economic Review Papers and Proceedings* 96, no. 2: 124–29.

———. 2007. An agency theory of dividend taxation. NBER Working Paper No.13538, Cambridge, MA.

Desai, M. A., and D. Dharmapala. 2006. Corporate tax avoidance and high powered incentives. *Journal of Financial Economics* 79, no. 1: 145–79.

———. 2007. Taxes and portfolio choice: Evidence from JGTRRA's treatment of international dividends. NBER Working Paper No. 13281, Cambridge, MA.

———. 2008. Tax and corporate governance: An economic approach. In *Tax and corporate governance*, ed. W. Schön, 13–30. Berlin and Heidelberg: Springer Verlag.

———. Forthcoming. Corporate tax avoidance and firm value. *Review of Economics and Statistics*.

———, and W. Fung. 2007. Taxation and the evolution of aggregate corporate ownership concentration. In *Taxing corporate income in the 21st century*, ed. A. J. Auerbach, J. R. Hines Jr., and J. Slemrod, 345–83. Cambridge: Cambridge University Press.

Desai, M. A., C. F. Foley, and J. R. Hines Jr. 2004. A multinational perspective on capital structure choice and internal capital markets. *Journal of Finance* 59, no. 6: 2451–87.

Devereux, M. P. 2000. Issues in the taxation of income from foreign portfolio and direct investment. In *Taxing capital income in the European Union: Issues and options for reform*, ed. S. Cnossen, 110–34. Oxford: Oxford University Press.

———, and H. Freeman. 1991. A general neutral profits tax. *Fiscal Studies* 12, no. 3: 1–15.

Dhaliwal, D. S., L. Krull, and O. Z. Li. 2007. Did the 2003 tax act reduce the cost of equity capital? *Journal of Accounting and Economics* 43, no. 1: 121–50.

Dharmapala, D. 2007. Dividends and tax policy in the long run: Discussion. *University of Illinois Law Forum* 2007:1–5.

Elton, E., and M. Gruber. 1970. Marginal stockholder tax rates and the clientele effect. *Review of Economics and Statistics* 52, no. 1: 68–74.

Feldstein, M. S. 1970. Corporate taxation and dividend behavior. *Review of Economic Studies* 37, no. 1: 57–72.

Fuest, C., and B. Huber. 2001. Can corporate-personal tax integration survive in open economies? Lessons from the German tax reform. *Finanzarchiv* 57, no. 4: 514 –24.

Graetz, M. J., and A. C. Warren Jr. 2007. Dividend taxation in Europe: When the ECJ makes tax policy. Harvard Public Law Working Paper No. 07/18 Cambridge, MA.

Hodder, J. E., and L. W. Senbet. 1990. International capital structure equilibrium. *Journal of Finance* 45, no. 5: 1495–1516.

Hubbard, R. G. 1993. Corporate tax integration: A view from the Treasury Department. *Journal of Economic Perspectives* 7, no. 1: 115–32.

_____. G. 2005. Economic effects of the 2003 partial integration proposal in the United States. *International Tax and Public Finance* 12, no. 1: 97–108.

Internal Revenue Service. 2003. Notice 2003-69. United States income tax treaties that meet the requirements of Section 1(h)(11)(C)(i)(II). http://www.irs.gov/irb/2003-42_IRB/ar09.html.

Jensen, M. C. 1986. Agency costs of free cash flow, corporate finance, and takeovers. *American Economic Review Papers and Proceedings* 76: 323–29.

King, M. A. 1977. *Public policy and the corporation*. London: Chapman and Hall.

Kleinbard, E. D. 2007. Designing an income tax on capital. In *Taxing capital income*, ed. H. J. Aaron, L. E. Burman, and C. E. Steuerle, 165–210. Washington, DC: Urban Institute Press.

Klemm, A. 2007. Allowances for corporate equity in practice. *CESifo Economic Studies* 53, no. 2: 229–62.

Korinek, A., and J. E. Stiglitz. 2008. Dividend taxation and intertemporal tax arbitrage. NBER Working Paper No.13858, Cambridge, MA.

Miller, M. H. 1977. Debt and taxes. *Journal of Finance* 32, no. 2: 261–75.

_____, and M. S. Scholes. 1978. Dividends and taxes. *Journal of Financial Economics* 6, no. 4: 333–64.

Poterba, J. M. 2004. Taxation and corporate payout policy. *American Economic Review Papers and Proceedings* 94, no. 2: 171–75.

_____, and L. H. Summers. 1985. The economic effects of dividend taxation. In *Recent advances in corporate finance*, ed. E. Altman and M. Subrahmanyam, 227–84. Homewood, IL: Richard D. Irwin.

Sheppard, H. E. 2004. Reduced tax rates on foreign dividends under JGTRRA: Ambiguities and opportunities. *Journal of International Taxation* 15, no. 7: 14–27, 62.

U.S. Department of the Treasury. Treasury International Capital (TIC) System. www.treas.gov/tic/.

Viard, A. D. 2008. Three cheers for the decline of the corporate income tax. *Tax policy outlook* 2. American Enterprise Institute. Washington, DC. April.

Wacker, R. F. 2004. U.S. taxation of international dividends under JGTRRA. *International Tax Journal* 30, no. 1: 19–34.

10

A Response to Dhammika Dharmapala

Douglas A. Shackelford

The 2003 Jobs and Growth Tax Relief Reconciliation Act (JGTRRA) reduced the maximum individual tax rate on dividend income from 38.1 percent to 15 percent. This dramatic reduction in the dividend tax rate has prompted several studies of how dividend policy, the capital market, and portfolios responded to the rate reduction.

Dharmapala provides an excellent review of this research. He summarizes the findings, evaluates them in light of extant theories, and posits directions for future work. I strongly recommend his chapter to anyone interested in this area of inquiry. My comments here will offer some further perspective on the issues Dharmapala addresses and critique the inferences being drawn from the studies in this field.

I conclude that, although we have documented many facts about the impact of JGTRRA, we may not completely understand what these facts mean or what their broader implications are for dividend taxation. Our current theories are inadequate to explain the findings, some of which are puzzling and in conflict with each other. Indeed, understanding the findings may be difficult unless and until the dividend rate reduction expires (as it is scheduled to do at the end of 2010).

Why JGTRRA Might Have Had No Effect on Dividend Policy

We now know, among other things, that the number of companies paying dividends and the amounts they paid increased substantially following the

The author appreciates helpful discussions with Jennifer Blouin and Kevin Markle.

May 2003 enactment of JGTRRA. However, to appreciate the research find-ings, we need to consider the prevailing thought at the time of JGTRRA's passage, when there were many reasons to doubt that JGTRRA would sub-stantially increase regular quarterly dividend issuances.

Blouin, Raedy, and Shackelford (2004) detail several reasons why JGTRRA might be expected to have no effect on dividend policy. I summa-rize their reasons here and refer the interested reader to their paper for more details. In essence, each of their reasons questions whether dividend taxa-tion for U.S. individuals is a binding constraint on dividend issuances.

Shareholders Not Benefiting from JGTRRA Influence Dividend Policy. The JGTRRA dividend tax rate reduction directly benefited individuals who held shares in taxable accounts and indirectly benefited individuals who held shares in flow-through entities (for example, mutual funds, partner-ships, trusts, S corporations, and limited liability corporations) in which the dividend income was passed through to personal U.S. tax returns. For the reduced rates to apply, individual shareholders must have held shares for at least 60 days in the 120-day period beginning 60 days before the ex-dividend date. The legislation, then, did not affect the taxation of individu-als with shorter trading horizons or of tax-exempt organizations, tax-deferred accounts (e.g., pensions, IRAs, and 401(k)s), corporations, and foreigners. Thus, if unaffected shareholders controlled or substantially influenced a firm's dividend policy (and in many companies they may have done so, since they held majority interests), the firm likely would not have significantly altered its distribution policy following JGTRRA.[1]

Repurchases Remained More Tax-Efficient than Dividends. Even after the JGTRRA dividend tax rate cut, repurchases remained the tax-efficient means of distributing profits to shareholders. Although the maximum statutory tax rate on dividends now equals the top rate on long-term capi-tal gains (which JGTRRA reduced from 20 percent to 15 percent), divi-dends continue to be taxed disadvantageously compared with capital gains for at least four reasons: 1) Dividends accelerate the tax payment that can be deferred until the stock is sold (or fully avoided if held until the share-holder dies). 2) Shareholders are able to time the realization of capital gains so that the capital gains tax is paid when the shareholder's marginal tax rate is low. Shareholders are unable to similarly time the realization of dividend income. 3) With capital gains, a portion of the proceeds is treated as a return of basis and thus goes untaxed. Conversely, basis cannot offset dividend income. 4) Since only $3,000 of capital losses (net of capital gains) can be deducted each year, capital gains, unlike dividends, enable individuals to accelerate utilization of their pool of capital losses, an important consideration for many individuals following the downturn in the equity markets in the early 2000s.

Dividends Were Unpopular. In 2003, dividends were unpopular. Fama and French (2001) documented that the number of publicly traded companies paying dividends fell from 67 percent in 1978 to 21 percent in 1999. Only 70 percent of the Standard & Poor's 500 were paying dividends at the end of 2001, down from 94 percent in 1980 (Teitelbaum 2002). DeAngelo, DeAngelo, and Skinner (2004) found that just twenty-five companies accounted for over half of the total dollar amount of dividends in the United States in 2000. Regardless of the dividend tax rate, unprofitable and cash-constrained firms (of which there were many following the economic downturn in the early part of the decade) were in no position to increase dividends (consistent with work dating back to Lintner 1956). In addition, growth firms, a large sector of the economy, typically enjoyed investment opportunities with higher expected returns than shareholders could expect from investing increased dividend payments. Moreover, even many highly profitable firms with substantial cash balances were paying no dividends (e.g., Intel, Dell, Cisco, and—until 2003—Microsoft).

Rate Reductions Were Temporary. The JGTRRA dividend tax rate reductions were scheduled to expire at the end of 2008 (now deferred to the end of 2010). If a firm increased its regular quarterly dividends in 2003 in response to the tax cut and then reduced its dividends when the lower rates expired, it could have difficulty convincing the capital markets that the cut in dividends was a response to the tax change rather than an indication of economic setbacks. To the extent that the market (mis)attributed the reduction in dividends to factors unrelated to taxes, the firm could face a drop in share prices, because share prices typically decline following cutbacks in dividend payments. (Imagine if the tax rates had expired in 2008, as originally scheduled, and firms were trying to convince the market today that they were cutting their dividends for tax reasons, rather than in response to the current economic downturn.) Furthermore, it was unclear in 2003 whether the dividend tax rate reductions would remain in place until 2008, because the 2004 Democratic presidential candidate, John Kerry, had promised to restore the higher dividend tax rate for individuals in the two highest tax brackets. In short, the costs of rescinding their regular quarterly dividend payments may have discouraged firms from increasing their dividends following JGTRRA. An alternative dividend distribution might have been a one-time special dividend, which would have avoided a (perceived) long-term commitment to a higher level of payout.

Adjustments Distort Dividend Signaling. Scholars have long debated the reasons that firms pay dividends, given the tax costs to shareholders. Among the asserted benefits of regular quarterly dividends is that they alleviate asymmetric information costs by conveying (costly) information about future earnings to the market (see Bhattacharya 1979, Miller and Rock 1985, and John and Williams 1985, among others). If so, tax-motivated adjustments in the quarterly dividends could distort the intended signal. Again, special dividends could enable firms to distribute cash at the lower dividend tax rate without losing any of the signaling or other benefits of regular quarterly dividends.

Increased Dividends Have Adverse Implications for Stock Options. Because stock options are not dividend protected, increasing dividends in response to JGTRRA could have forced firms to grant additional stock options to employees or shift to other forms of compensation. For some firms, the costs of restructuring existing compensation arrangements and undermining the incentives provided by stock options may have exceeded the benefits of lower dividend taxes for their individual investors. Microsoft, for instance, had to get shareholder approval to amend its stock option plans before it could issue its $32 billion special dividend in 2004.

Alternative Minimum Tax Dulls Benefit. For individual shareholders paying the alternative minimum tax (AMT), the maximum dividend tax rate before the rate reduction was 28 percent. Since many individual shareholders in dividend-paying firms likely faced the AMT in 2003 (or could reasonably expect to face it in the future), they benefited less from the dividend tax rate reduction than did investors not facing the AMT. Specifically, their tax cut was a less dramatic reduction from 28 percent to 15 percent, rather than the 38.1 percent to 15 percent enjoyed by individual investors in the top regular tax bracket. Thus, while still substantial, the tax benefit for some individual shareholders was diminished by the AMT.

Summary. Given the increase in dividends since 2003, it is easy to forget that there were many reasons in 2003 to expect little, if any, response to a reduction in dividend tax rates. However, the increase in dividends after 2003 does not exclude the possibility that the increase was caused (at least in part) by nontax factors.

Nontax Explanations for the Increase in Dividends

There are at least four explanations for the dividend increase following JGTTRA that are not related to taxes. Given that these explanations are plausible and cannot be ruled out, a causal link between the dividend tax rate cut and the dividend increase cannot be definitively established.

One alternative explanation for the dividend increase is that the economy was strengthening rapidly in 2003.[2] Since dividends typically increase as the economy expands, macroeconomic effects may have driven the dividend increase following enactment of JGTRRA more than the dividend tax rate cuts did. Julio and Ikenberry (2004) even claim that dividends had already begun to rise before 2003. Federal Express, Maxim Integrated Products, and Outback Steakhouse, for example, initiated quarterly dividends in 2002.

A second explanation is that following the collapse of Enron, WorldCom, and other companies that had reported high profits but little cash, the capital markets began to look increasingly to cash flow rather than accounting earnings to assess a firm's financial strength. If capital markets did indeed put greater emphasis on cash flow, then while the dividend tax rate was falling, dividends were becoming a more important instrument for signaling quality.

A third explanation is that many companies had large cash balances in 2003. To the extent that these funds reflected a lack of investment opportunities, companies might have increased shareholder distributions without any dividend tax rate reduction. Consistent with a need to distribute excess cash, the total amount of repurchases actually increased more than the total amount of dividends in the two years following JGTRRA's passage (Blouin, Raedy, and Shackelford 2007).

Finally, the most highly publicized dividend initiation in 2003 provides compelling evidence that JGTRRA was not the driving force behind every dividend initiation. Some observers—for example, Aboody and Kasznik (2008), Brown, Liang, and Weisbenner (2007), and Chetty and Saez (2005)—point to Microsoft's January 17, 2003, announcement that it would begin to distribute dividends as evidence of JGTRRA's impact on dividend initiations; but Brav et al. (2007) and Blouin, Raedy, and Shackelford (2007) stress how unlikely it was that JGTRRA drove Microsoft's decision. The Microsoft announcement preceded JGTRRA's passage by over five months (JGTRRA was a controversial bill that passed only after Vice President Cheney cast the tie-breaking vote) and followed President Bush's initial announcement of his plan for dividend tax relief by only ten days.[3] Although Microsoft's decision was driven principally by its holding over $43 billion in cash, the factors that caused Microsoft to initiate dividends likely mattered in the dividend initiations of at least some other companies in 2003. (That said, it should be noted that JGTRRA may have played a role in Microsoft's subsequent decisions to increase its quarterly dividends and issue a very large special dividend.)

What We Have Learned from the Extant Studies

This section lists the principal findings from extant research on why JGTRRA might not have exerted much influence on dividend increases. First, managers themselves claim that JGTRRA had little impact on their dividend payouts. Brav et al. (2005) surveyed managers before passage of the dividend tax rate cut and found that they expected it to have little effect on their dividend policy. In a follow-up survey after passage, managers reported that it had indeed had little impact on their dividends, leading Brav et al. (2007) to conclude that JGTRRA affected the dividend payments only for a few firms at the margin.

These survey responses are consistent with individuals who hold stock through taxable accounts having relatively little influence over dividend policy. Nonetheless, dividends did increase substantially following JGTRRA. These increases are consistent with (a) managers not being forthright about the reasons for their dividend increases, (b) nontax factors being an important consideration (though largely ignored in the literature), and (c) dividends regaining popularity (for whatever reason) around the time of legislation.

Second, dividend initiations increased in 2003 (Chetty and Saez 2005), an important development because dividends are sticky, partly because the market penalizes firms for cutting or omitting dividends. Thus if JGTRRA increased dividend initiations, it likely had a long-term effect on firms' distributions. However, Brown, Liang, and Weisbenner (2007) claim that the 2003 dividend initiations coincided with reductions in repurchases for companies held mostly by officers and directors. Blouin, Raedy, and Shackelford (2007) add that this substitution pattern for insider-controlled firms held for a much larger set of dividend-paying firms, the noninitiators, which accounted for 97 percent of the total dividends paid in 2003. Thus, while JGTRRA may have increased dividend initiations, total corporate distributions may not have increased if reductions in repurchases offset the dividend increases.

Third, repurchases increased even more than dividends (Blouin, Raedy, and Shackelford 2007). The finding that both these forms of shareholder distributions increased is consistent with distributions being affected by both the dividend and capital gains tax rate reductions in JGTRRA. However, given the greater reduction in the dividend tax rate, it is surprising (and somewhat disturbing) that repurchases increased more than dividends. Nonetheless, this finding is consistent with repurchases continuing to be more tax-efficient than dividends, even after JGTRRA.

Fourth, Blouin, Raedy, and Shackelford (2004) document that some firms paid special dividends soon after passage of JGTRRA, but special dividends (despite the advantages noted above) were not widespread and were far less common and smaller in amount than the increases in regular quarterly dividends. The one (very large) exception was Microsoft's $32 billion special dividend in 2004. However, it is unclear to what extent taxes, as opposed to an exorbitant cash balance, drove this special dividend.[4] Microsoft notwithstanding, the data suggest that special dividends did not become an important and widespread vehicle for distributing cash after JGTRRA (see discussions in Blouin, Raedy, and Shackelford 2004, and

Korinek and Stiglitz 2008). They also imply that firms neither expected the rate reductions to expire nor were particularly concerned about deleterious effects on signaling and other purported benefits of dividends.

Fifth, Desai and Dharmapala (2007) claim that some extraordinary shifts in foreign equity holdings occurred after JGTRRA. Exploiting the fact that the dividend tax rate reduction applies to dividends from companies in some countries, but not all countries, Desai and Dharmapala (2007) report that more equity flowed to those countries where the dividend tax cut applied than to those countries where it did not. Their estimates imply seemingly unrealistic elasticities and remarkably quick responses by individual investors. However, assuming that their findings hold and that foreign portfolio holdings are indeed highly responsive to taxes, then we must ask whether individual investors in domestic companies also dramatically shifted their holdings to companies whose returns were most advantaged by the rate reduction (e.g., companies with large dividend payouts) and, if not, why foreign and domestic portfolio responses differed.

Sixth, during this period when the tax costs of paying dividends to individual investors decreased significantly (and thus equity became more attractive to individual investors), proportional holdings by individual investors fell dramatically. Blouin, Raedy, and Shackelford (2007) report that average holdings in dividend-paying stocks by individuals who were not insiders fell from 36 percent in 2001–2002 to 27 percent in 2003–2004. Individual equity investments through taxable accounts have been falling as a percentage of total shareholdings for many years, but surprisingly JGTRRA appears to have done little to reverse that trend. If JGTRRA did slow the decline, then imagine how large the decline would have been if the dividend tax rate had not been cut.

Seventh, changes in share prices varied across stocks according to their dividend policy (Auerbach and Hassett 2007; Dhaliwal, Krull, and Li 2007). As expected, the share prices for companies that paid large dividends rose more than the share prices for companies that paid small dividends. Surprisingly, however, the share prices of companies that did not pay any dividends outperformed the high-dividend-paying stocks. This finding is consistent with an expectation by the market that the dividend tax cuts would continue until the non-dividend-paying stocks were paying large dividends, a time far beyond the original 2008 sunset.

Enough time has elapsed and enough studies have been conducted for us to conclude that these facts are accurate. Taken together, however, these facts are difficult, if not impossible, to reconcile. In short, we know what happened following JGTRRA, but we do not know why. I hope that new emerging models, such as Korinek and Stiglitz (2008), Chetty and Saez (2007), and Gordon and Dietz (2006), will provide the theoretical structure needed to reconcile the facts that have been documented. I am pessimistic about our ability to really understand what happened after JGTRRA until theory catches up with the empirical work and makes sense of the findings we have.

Great Paper, circa 2013

Perhaps further understanding of JGTRRA is a few years away. If the JGTRRA tax rates expire, are repealed, or are substantially altered, scholars will have an excellent opportunity to revisit the JGTRRA studies. This round-trip experience with dividend tax changes would aid in our ability to separate the changes that were tax related from those that were not.

For example, suppose the dividend and capital gains tax rate cuts expire at the end of 2010, as scheduled. Based on the extant studies, we would expect 1) managers to deny that the expirations will affect their pay-outs, 2) dividend initiations to slow, particularly among insider-dominated companies, 3) repurchases to crowd out dividends in insider-dominated companies, 4) little change to occur in special dividends, 5) large and immediate rebalancing to take place among foreign portfolio holdings, and 6) share price declines to fall most heavily on non-dividend-paying firms, less heavily on high-dividend–paying firms, and least heavily on low-dividend–paying firms. To the extent that these reversals occur, they will inspire confidence that the original JGTRRA links were not spurious, i.e., the changes attributed to JGTRRA were indeed caused by it. However, if they do not occur, doubts will be raised about the extent to which JGTRRA actually caused the changes that have been attributed to it.

It is difficult to know what to expect about two puzzling findings: the relative change in repurchases and dividends (recall that repurchases increased more rapidly than dividends following JGTRRA) and the percentage of shares held in taxable accounts by individual investors, which, contrary to expectations, fell sharply following JGTRRA.

The Forgotten Capital Gains Tax Cut

To my knowledge, no one has studied the effects of JGTRRA's reduction in the capital gains tax rate from 20 percent to 15 percent. This is particularly surprising, given the sizable increases in capital gains realizations in 1986 in advance of an increase in the capital gains tax rate from 20 percent to 28 percent (Burman, Clausing, and O'Hare 1994), and given capital markets responses (price, volume, and volatility) following the 1997 reduction in the capital gains tax rate from 28 percent to 20 percent (Dai, Maydew, et al. 2008; Dai, Shackelford, and Zhang 2008). The rare opportunity to study an even more substantial cut in the dividend tax rate is the reason that the capital gains tax rate change has been ignored. However, if the sole change in JGTRRA had been a five percentage point reduction in the capital gains tax rate, many scholars would have studied its impact. Moreover, given some of the surprising JGTRRA findings (e.g., repurchases, which are taxed at the capital gains tax rate, increased more rapidly than dividends, and non-dividend–paying firms outperformed dividend-paying firms), research is warranted to identify the effects of the 2003 capital gains tax rate reduction on corporate distributions. Segregating the dividend tax effects from the capital gains tax effects could greatly aid our understanding of the full effects of JGTRRA.

Conclusion

Not surprisingly, the extraordinary dividend tax rate reductions in JGTRRA have generated considerable research. Dharmapala provides an excellent review and analysis of the scholarly work, and I strongly recommend his chapter.

My comments here provide further context for understanding the impact of JGTRRA. To summarize: A priori, it was not clear that the rate reductions in JGTRRA would substantially affect corporate payouts. Even the finding that dividends increased after its enactment does not rule out the possibility that some nontax factors played an important role in the dividend increases. Nevertheless, the evidence clearly points to some predictable reactions to the dividend tax rate cut, namely, an increase in dividends, dividend initiations, substitution of dividends for repurchases, and shifts toward (at least foreign) portfolio holdings that qualify for the lower tax rate. That said, there are several puzzling findings: repurchases increased more than dividends, few special dividends were paid, individual holdings of dividend-paying stocks decreased dramatically, and non-dividend–paying shares showed a stronger market response than dividend-paying shares. It is difficult to reconcile these findings with prior findings about corporate and capital market responses to dividend taxes. We know much about the effects of JGTRRA, but I do not think that we can explain why they happened. We need a new theory to help reconcile the empirical findings, research into the effects of the forgotten capital gains tax cuts, and a new round of studies should the JGTRRA rate cuts expire.

Notes

1. In 2003, the literature was mixed about whether the tax status of shareholders affected dividend policy. See Barclay, Holderness, and Sheehan (forthcoming), Pérez-González (2003), and Lie and Lie (1999), among others.

2. For example, gross domestic product grew more in the four quarters following passage of JGTRRA (7.2 percent) than it had in the previous nine quarters combined (6.9 percent).

3. On December 25, 2002, the *New York Times* reported that the Bush administration was considering some form of dividend tax relief (see Lohr 2002). To my knowledge, that was the first such public report. However, no plan was rolled out until January 7, 2003.

4. When Microsoft announced its special dividend and made a simultaneous boost to its quarterly dividend, it made no mention of dividend taxes affecting either decision. See Microsoft 2004.

References

Aboody, David, and Ron Kasznik. 2008. Executive stock-based compensation and firms' cash payout: The role of shareholders' tax-related payout preferences. *Review of Accounting Studies* 13 (2-3): 216–51.

Auerbach, Alan J., and Kevin A. Hassett. 2007. The 2003 dividend tax cuts and the value of the firm: An event study. In *Taxing corporate income in the 21st century*, ed. Alan J. Auerbach, James R. Hines Jr., and Joel Slemrod, 93–126. Cambridge: Cambridge University Press.

Barclay, Michael, Clifford Holderness, and Dennis Sheehan. Forthcoming. Dividends and corporate shareholders. *Review of Financial Studies*.

Bhattacharya, Sudipto. 1979. Imperfect information, dividend policy, and "the bird in the hand" fallacy. *Bell Journal of Economics* 10 (1): 259–70.

Blouin, Jennifer L., Jana Smith Raedy, and Douglas A. Shackelford. 2004. Did dividends increase immediately after the 2003 reduction in tax rates? NBER Working Paper No. 10301, Cambridge, MA.

_____. 2007. Did firms substitute dividends for share repurchases after the 2003 reductions in shareholder tax rates? Working Paper, University of North Carolina.

Brav, Alon, John Graham, Campbell Harvey, and Roni Michaely. 2005. Payout policy in the 21st century. *Journal of Financial Economics* 77: 483–527.

_____. 2007. Managerial response to the May 2003 dividend tax cut. Working Paper, Duke University, Durham, NC.

Brown, Jeffrey, Nellie Liang, and Scott Weisbenner. 2007. Executive financial incentives and payout policy: Firm responses to the 2003 dividend tax cut. *Journal of Finance* 62 (4): 1935–65.

Burman, Leonard E., Kimberly A. Clausing, and John F. O'Hare. 1994. Tax reform and realizations of capital gains in 1986. *National Tax Journal* 47(1): 1–18.

Chetty, Raj, and Emmanuel Saez. 2005. Dividend taxes and corporate behavior: Evidence from the 2003 dividend tax cut. *Quarterly Journal of Economics* 120 (3): 791–833.

_____. 2007. An agency theory of dividend taxation. NBER Working Paper No. 13538, Cambridge, MA.

Dai, Zhonglan, Edward Maydew, Douglas A. Shackelford, and Harold Zhang. 2008. Capital gains taxes and asset prices: Capitalization or lock-in? *Journal of Finance* 63 (2): 709–42.

Dai, Zhonglan, Douglas A. Shackelford, and Harold Zhang. 2008. Capital gains taxes and stock return volatility: Evidence from the taxpayer relief act of 1997. Working Paper, University of North Carolina.

DeAngelo, Harry, Linda DeAngelo, and Doug Skinner. 2004. Are dividends disappearing? Dividend concentration and the consolidation of earnings. *Journal of Financial Economics* 72 (3): 425–56.

Desai, Mihir, and Dhammika Dharmapala. 2007. Taxes and portfolio choice: Evidence from JGTRRA's treatment of international dividends. NBER Working Paper No. 13281, Cambridge, MA.

Dhaliwal, Dan, Linda Krull, and Oliver Li. 2007. Did the 2003 tax act reduce the cost of equity capital? *Journal of Accounting and Economics* 43:121–50.

Fama, Eugene, and Kenneth French. 2001. Disappearing dividends: Changing firm characteristics or lower propensity to pay. *Journal of Financial Economics* 60: 3–43.

Gordon, Roger, and Martin Dietz. 2006. Dividends and taxes. NBER Working Paper No. 12292, Cambridge, MA.

John, Kose, and Joseph Williams. 1985. Dividends, dilution, and taxes: A signalling equilibrium. *Journal of Finance* 40 (4): 1053–70.

Julio, Brandon, and David Ikenberry. 2004. Reappearing dividends. *Journal of Applied Corporate Finance* 16 (4): 89–100.

Korinek, Anton, and Joseph E. Stiglitz. 2008. Dividend taxation and intertemporal tax arbitrage. NBER Working Paper No. 13858, Cambridge, MA.

Lie, Erik, and Heidi Lie. 1999. The role of personal taxes in corporate decisions: An empirical analysis of share repurchases and dividends. *Journal of Financial and Quantitative Analysis* 34: 533–52.

Lintner, John. 1956. Distribution of incomes of corporations among dividends, retained earnings, and taxes. *American Economic Review* 46: 97–113.

Lohr, Steve. 2002. White House aides push for 50% cut in dividend taxes. *New York Times*, December 25.

Microsoft. 2004. Microsoft outlines quarterly dividend, four-year stock buyback plan, and special dividend to shareholders. Press release. http://www.microsoft.com/presspass/press/2004/jul04/07-20boardPR.mspx.

Miller, Merton H., and Kevin Rock. 1985. Dividend policy under asymmetric information. *Journal of Finance* 40 (4): 1031–51.

Pérez-González, Francisco. 2003. Large shareholders and dividends: Evidence from U.S. tax reforms. Working paper, Stanford University, Palo Alto, CA.

Teitelbaum, Richard. 2002. Playing the dividend market with income stocks, you don't just get the chicken, you get the eggs too. The trick is to pick 'em right. *Fortune*, December 9.

11

Taxes and Business Investment: Lessons from the Past Decade

Alan J. Auerbach and Kevin A. Hassett

When President Bush took office in January 2001, research into the impact of fiscal policy on investment was experiencing a resurgence. As the 1990s began, the conventional wisdom—based on a large literature utilizing time-series data—was that tax policy had little or no effect on business fixed investment, which was best explained by models such as the traditional accelerator or the financial accelerator.[1] But by the end of that decade, a large literature drawing on panel data and natural experiments had converged to a view that tax policy could indeed influence investment significantly. At the same time, the results based on models that appealed to accelerator effects or financial frictions became more hotly disputed.[2]

The literature documenting tax effects generally employed versions of the standard Hall-Jorgenson user cost model, which maps changes in investment tax credits, statutory tax rates, and depreciation rules to a user cost measure of the marginal incentive to invest (see Hassett and Newmark 2008). The literature thus provided an ambitious policy entrepreneur with a fairly detailed road map to an economic model. A canonical model existed with well-specified and easy-to-adjust policy parameters. These tax variables fed into a user cost formula that had an established link to investment.

Whether this evidence that tax policy could influence investment played a role or not, U.S. investment policy began to change. Responding to a recession that (according to the National Bureau of Economic Research) began in March

The authors thank Dhammika Dharmapala, Matthew Shapiro, and other conference participants for comments on a previous draft.

2001 and to a sharp drop in business fixed investment, Congress passed legislation introducing "bonus depreciation" for qualifying investment, generally investment with a depreciation lifetime no greater than twenty years. Under the provisions of the 2002 legislation, investors could forgo regular depreciation schedules and immediately write off 30 percent of investment expenditures for any investment made during a three-year period starting on September 11, 2001. In 2003, the program was amended to increase this bonus depreciation or "partial expensing" to 50 percent of each qualifying purchase, and to cover investment through the end of 2004. Although there were some attempts to extend bonus depreciation even longer, the 2003 changes to the program were the last made, and the provisions expired at the end of 2004. The February 2008 stimulus package did, however, provide 50 percent partial expensing for investments made in 2008.

This partial expensing was the first major change to investment policy in the United States in sixteen years. The change was accompanied in 2003 by a reduction in the maximum tax rates on capital gains and dividends; the capital gains rate went from 20 to 15 percent, and the dividends rate for taxpayers in the highest tax bracket went from 35 to 15 percent. While this is not the first time dividend tax rates have changed, previous changes, such as those included in the Tax Reform Act of 1986, have been associated with other changes in tax rates on individual investors, which affected investment through other channels as well. The 2003 change in dividend taxation is thus unique in providing an opportunity to isolate the effects of changes in the taxation of dividends.

Combined, these two policies provided economists with important challenges and significant research opportunities, and a new literature has subsequently exploded. Scholarship has proceeded in two main stages. First, before data were available to allow researchers to study the impact of the new policies, several papers explored the theoretical impact of these changes. Implicit in their analysis was the maintained hypothesis that understanding the user cost impact of a given set of policies would help us understand the policies' likely impact overall, because the link between the user cost and investment was so well understood. Then, in a second wave of scholarship (which particularly in the area of dividends could be classified as a tidal wave), economists have explored the actual empirical effects of these policies.

For perspective on these matters, consider figure 11-1, which details the tax changes that are the focus of this chapter. On October 10, 2001, 30 percent par-

FIGURE 11–1

MANUFACTURERS' NEW ORDERS: NONDEFENSE CAPITAL GOODS EXCLUDING AIRCRAFT

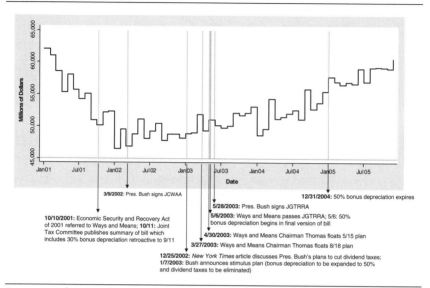

SOURCE: Manufacturer's Shipments, Inventories, and Orders (M3) Survey.

tial expensing first passed the House, but it did not formally become law until March 9, 2002 (at which time it was made to apply retroactively to September 11, 2001). On Christmas Day of 2003, the *New York Times* reported that President Bush would seek to lower the dividend tax in 2003. On May 28, 2003, the maximum tax on dividends and capital gains was lowered to 15 percent, and partial expensing was increased to 50 percent. The partial expensing expired on the last day of 2004. Figure 11-1 also includes data for Manufacturers' New Orders of Nondefense Capital Goods Excluding Aircraft over the same period. The aggregate data confirm that partial expensing was introduced after an enormous decline in investment activity and that the steady increase of aggregate investment continued until partial expensing was repealed at the end of 2004. These changes, of course, suggest only a possible influence of tax policy, as many other factors changed as well over this time period.

The purpose of this chapter is to review the findings of the new research brought about by these policy changes. We first explore the impact of partial expensing by looking at both the theoretical and the empirical work on the subject. We then discuss the new literature on the impact of the dividend tax reductions, again looking at both theoretical and empirical work. In our final section, we discuss the many open questions that remain.

Partial Expensing

The Job Creation and Worker Assistance Act (JCWAA) was enacted in March 2002. The law provided a temporary increase in depreciation allowances in the form of a 30 percent partial expensing provision for business spending on equipment and software. This temporary increase took a form that fit easily into the user cost framework, and thus the theoretical challenge of identifying the likely *ex ante* effect of this policy depended primarily on that framework's assumptions and parameters.

Cohen, Hansen, and Hassett (2002) undertook the task of quantifying the likely impact of the policy. They found that a number of factors influenced conclusions regarding the theoretical effect of this policy. The first was expectations concerning the policy's expiration. If the policy was expected to be permanent, then its impact on investment, they found, would likely be small. This was because previous law already allowed firms to accelerate depreciation deductions, and since inflation and nominal discount rates were relatively low when the law was changed, the effects of the 30 percent expensing were minor. For example, for equipment with a seven-year depreciation lifetime, the effect on the user cost under the authors' baseline assumptions would be a proportional reduction of only 2.5 percent.

Cohen, Hansen, and Hassett also showed that the effect on investment might have been greater if firms expected the measure to expire. This is because of the strong incentive to pull investment forward from next year if the bonus is available only this year. In that case, the user cost reduction associated with the policy was about 15 percent relative to the old law. In 2003, the Jobs and Growth Tax Relief Reconciliation Act (JGTRRA) increased the bonus depreciation to 50 percent and extended its applicability by a few months. This increase raised the predicted user cost impact from the baseline discussed in Cohen, Hansen, and Hassett approximately proportionally, although it would have had offsetting effects in 2002 had it been anticipated then.

The second factor that influenced the calculated effect on the incentive to invest was the extent to which firms faced significant adjustment costs. In the simple Hall-Jorgenson model with no adjustment costs, investment would depend simply on this year's tax parameters (including the expected change in investment incentives from this year to the next). But as Auerbach (1989) showed, in a model with adjustment costs, current investment would not only be more sluggish in responding to changes in incentives, but it would also depend on both current tax policy and expected future tax policy. When adjustment costs are significant, then a relatively insignificant current user cost effect would be predicted, as the future period wherein the policy expires has an important impact on the target capital stock, and acts as an anchor weighing down the possible impact of the policy.

A third factor was cited by Edge and Rudd (2005), who explored the impact of temporary partial expensing in a general equilibrium model. They found that general equilibrium effects could lead to reversals of the ranking of partial equilibrium results. For example, they found that a temporary policy could have a smaller effect than a permanent one, depending on the endogeneity of saving.

Thus it was not possible to predict whether the policy of bonus depreciation would be effective in stimulating investment; the outcome depended on factors that were not fully known at the time of the policy. It is not at all certain that investors expected the policy to expire, as there were at the time many rumblings from congressional Republicans about the desirability of moving to full expensing. Economists themselves, moreover, showed a great deal of uncertainty regarding the exact nature and significance of adjustment costs.[3] Ultimately, then, it was necessary to turn to empirical work to establish the impact of the policy, not simply to test the predictions of the model, but also to draw inferences about the previously unknown factors.

In their research on the effects of bonus depreciation, House and Shapiro (2008) take a novel approach. They assume that firms expected the expiration of the partial expensing provision and explore the implications of this assumption for investment and asset prices before the expiration occurred. They find that investment increased the most for equipment with a longer recovery period, and that "bonus depreciation had a powerful effect on the composition of investment. . . . In spite of the sizeable effects on investment, the policy had only modest effects on aggregate employment and output" (35).

As part of their investigation, House and Shapiro study the impact that temporarily higher investment demand should have on capital goods prices. Goolsbee (1998) argues that investment subsidies drive up the price of capital goods because these goods are inelastically supplied. House and Shapiro show that theoretically, in a closed economy and under a very short-lived provision, the price of very durable capital goods should fully reflect the tax subsidy irrespective of the elasticity of supply. They find, however, that this effect is not visible in the data; indeed, capital goods prices barely budged, while demand was surging because of the credits.

It is not clear how one reconciles the predictions of theory with these results showing a large investment response and a small price effect. One possibility is the presence of other factors influencing investment. House and Shapiro (2006) explore the impact of the personal income tax cuts that were originally scheduled to be phased in between 2001 and 2006, but were ultimately made law immediately in 2003. They identify a likely large growth effect beginning in the second half of 2003, an effect which might help explain investment responses that were larger than the conventional models might have predicted.

To date, there are few other papers that have explored the same ground as House and Shapiro (2008). Desai and Goolsbee (2004), whose paper will be discussed in more detail in the next section, perform an analysis of Compustat data and conclude that partial expensing provided little stimulus to investment. This conclusion, however, is not based on analysis of the investment response by firms after the tax changes were enacted, but is an inference based on their regression results and a user cost analysis. They assert that the user cost effect of the expensing provisions was small, based on the assumption that firms were surprised by its expiration. But given the parameter estimates from their investment equation, if firms knew that the tax cut would expire, then the effects would be much larger; indeed, their model predicts almost a 20 percent increase in equipment investment in the expiration year under the most aggressive assumptions. Since their sample period was almost exclusively before the changes, they can offer little new empirical evidence regarding the impact of the policy.

Looking beyond the United States, Djankov et al. (2008) find a large impact of the effective tax rate on investment in a large cross-country sample for 2004, providing further support for the view that the higher elasticity estimates derived from the experience in the 1990s are consistent with the experience of the 2000s as well.

Cohen and Cummins (2006) explore the impact of partial expensing using monthly capital goods shipments data collected and compiled by the Bureau of the Census. They cite macroeconomic evidence suggesting that the policy could have had a significant effect on investment. Specifically, National Income and Product Accounts (NIPA) expenditures on equipment and software excluding high-tech equipment and transportation goods experienced an increased growth rate, from 2 percent in 2002 to 6 percent in 2003 to 11 percent in 2004; the growth rate dropped to only 2 percent at the beginning of 2005. However, the data below the surface are less consistent with the predictions of the model, which suggested that the user cost reduction associated with the tax change was larger for long-lived equipment than for short-lived equipment. Accordingly, strong confirmation of the model's predictions would have occurred if the aggregate number had increased more for long-lived equipment than it did for short-lived equipment. The authors perform a difference-in-difference analysis and conclude that the opposite occurred, a pattern that is not consistent with the predictions of the theory. House and Shapiro (2008), however, argue that Cohen and Cummins exclude the longest-lived capital assets (which do not qualify for bonus depreciation) from their analysis, and hence perform a test with little power. House and Shapiro demonstrate that the difference between these two sets of results can be explained by this omission.

However, Cohen and Cummins (2006) also provide other evidence that is consistent with the view that the policy had minor effects. First, they cite a Treasury study that found only minor changes in the 2003 take-up rate, that is, in the fraction of eligible investment dollars that was claimed for the purposes of receiving bonus depreciation.[4] According to those data, about a third of relevant investment was undertaken by firms that were not taxable and hence could not benefit from the measure; and among firms that did claim bonus depreciation, only about two-thirds of investment qualified. Thus applying these fractions to an already small user cost effect, Cohen and Cummins conclude that their failure to find a large effect is understandable. Cohen and Cummins also cite a survey undertaken by the Institute for Supply Management. Nearly two-thirds of respondents indicated that the partial expensing had no effect on the timing of their capital spending.

Auerbach, Chaney, and Hassett (2008) use Compustat data to explore whether the partial expensing measure created shifts in investment consistent with the predictions of the user cost model. Following Auerbach and Hassett (1991), and Cummins, Hassett, and Hubbard (1994), they explore the cross-sectional relationship between investment and the user cost of capital. In particular, they consider whether the investment "surprises"— components of investment that could not have been predicted based on past information—in the years during which the policy changed were larger for assets that had the bigger "surprises" in user cost, with the cross-sectional variation coming from differences in capital stock composition among firms. The authors find evidence that the two sets of surprises were related, and obtain point estimates of the response quite similar to those in the earlier studies.

In sum, there is evidence that investment surged prior to the expiration of the partial expensing provision, and after it as well. There is some evidence that the pattern of investment across assets differed from the predictions of the model, but not enough to cast serious doubt on the a priori view that the partial expensing provision would have a small and positive effect on investment.

Dividend Taxes

We focus here on the findings that are most relevant for understanding the impact of dividend tax changes on investment. There is inevitably some overlap with findings in other areas, as the impact on the effective tax rate is intertwined with the financial policies of the firm. The latter topic is extensively addressed in the chapter by Dharmapala in this volume.

Unlike partial expensing, the original Bush proposal to reduce the dividend tax was not easily characterized in terms of predictions based on the canonical user cost model. The president's plan did not require shareholders to pay tax on a dividend if the corporation paying the dividend had already exposed the income to taxation. If the corporate income had been sheltered from tax, then the distribution was subject to personal income tax. Because of this provision, the incentive effects of lower dividend taxes were potentially muted, depending on the firm's tax status. Accordingly, alternative plans that provided for a tax rate reduction at the individual level that was smaller but not dependent on the firm's tax status could have had incentive effects similar to that of the president's proposal.

The complexity of the original Bush proposal led the authors to have an unusual role in the legislative process. Early in January 2003, one of us (Hassett) was invited by the House Ways and Means Committee to explain the economic effects of the Bush proposal to staff. During the meeting, the special condition attached to the zero tax on dividends that bound the lower rate to an earned dividend account (EDA) was discussed, and it became apparent that the effects of the Bush proposal could not be characterized using the standard model. We therefore proceeded to develop a revised model that included the EDA, and wrote up notes that explored the impact of the EDA on user cost calculations.

Our analysis revealed that the impact of the proposal depended on several factors. In particular, the limitations imposed by the EDA could significantly undermine the marginal impact of the Bush proposal. Consider a simple example. Suppose that a company has $110 in income and has a deduction (perhaps for depreciation) worth $10. If the company claims the $10 deduction, then it has $100 in taxable income and pays a corporate tax of $35. If the company then pays the $65 remaining from the $100 of taxable income as a dividend to its shareholder, then the shareholder pays no additional tax. Suppose that the firm also decides to distribute the $10 it has in cash that was sheltered. At that point, the shareholder will have to pay tax on the income, since it never faced the first level of taxation at the corporate level. Suppose the shareholder has a tax rate of 35 percent. In that case, when he receives the $10, he will have to pay $3.50 tax, leaving him with $6.50 after tax. His total after-tax benefit from both dividends is $65 + $6.50 = $71.50. Notice that this is the same after-tax income he would have received if the company had not claimed the deduction. In that case, the company would have paid 35 percent tax on $110 ($38.50), but then it could distribute the remaining $71.50 tax free. Thus there is no tax benefit for the incremental dividend; put another way, the deduction has completely lost its economic value.[5] Its only effect is to move a $3.50 tax from the corporate level to the individual level.

Our analysis of the incentive effects of the Bush proposal, based on estimates of the impacts on different types of firms, suggested that a simplified proposal that omitted the EDA could have a similar marginal effect with a much smaller reduction (to about 15 percent) in the dividend tax rate. Interestingly, this rate reduction without the EDA was estimated by the Joint Committee on Taxation to cost significantly less in terms of lost tax revenue than the Bush proposal, perhaps because of differences in the timing of tax collections, differences in the interpretation of provisions, or differences between marginal and average effects. Bill Thomas, chairman of the House Ways and Means Committee, seized on this observation to hatch a legislative strategy that "compromised" with dividend tax skeptics by reducing the rate less but also scratching the EDA.[6]

The dividend tax reduction, as passed, is simpler to analyze than the original proposal, but the analysis still hinges on a critical assumption regarding the source of marginal equity finance. Under the traditional view, a firm's marginal source of funds is new equity issues, and investment is responsive to dividend taxes. According to the new view, however, a firm's marginal source of funds is retained earnings. Firms issue new equity only after retained earnings are exhausted, and thus the investment levels of mature firms not dependent on the new equity market are unresponsive to changes in dividend taxes. Under the new view, time-invariant dividend taxes are capitalized into the value of the firm but do not affect investment.

Prior to the dividend tax proposal, research on this topic provided mixed evidence on the relative importance of the two views, with the latest evidence suggesting that firm-level heterogeneity is important, and that some firms are better understood under the new view and some better understood under the old.

Carroll, Hassett, and Mackie (2003) established the *ex ante* prediction of the user cost model. They estimated that under the traditional view, the tax changes reduced the marginal effective total tax rate by about four percentage points under their baseline assumptions, from 33.5 percent to 29.4 percent. Under the new view (and also accounting for the capital gains tax changes, which affect the user cost under both views), the reduction in the user cost was smaller, decreasing from 29.6 percent to 27.7 percent.

In work relying on a sample that predates the dividend change, Auerbach and Hassett (2003) directly examined investment financing to determine the relevance of the different views. They found considerable heterogeneity in their sample of firms, with capital market access an important factor in determining how likely a firm was to issue new shares. Under the new view, the dividend is a residual and, they showed, should be negatively correlated with investment and positively correlated with cash flow once one controls for investment prospects and profitability via Tobin's Q. They utilized this observation to test the validity of the two views and showed that the responsiveness of dividends to cash flow and investment varies significantly across publicly traded U.S. firms. They concluded that about half of firms that had paid dividends, and to whom the new view could thus potentially apply, seemed to display dividend payout behavior consistent with the new view, while half seemed to engage in behavior more consistent with the traditional view. This suggested at the time that perhaps half of this subset of "mature" firms would have relatively large investment responses to the change because they were governed by the old view, whereas the other half would have a relatively small response. Desai and Goolsbee (2004), who looked at the effect of the dividend tax cuts on investment, also found support for the new view. In their analysis of the 2003 dividend tax cuts, Desai and Goolsbee used firm-level investment data to distinguish between the traditional and new views of dividend taxation. They reestimated a variation of the model developed by Poterba and Summers (1985), and found strong confirmation that the new view best describes the data.[7]

As was the case with partial expensing, the investment literature would lead us to expect this user cost reduction to have a modest positive effect on investment. In this case, however, we would also expect the change to influence the marginal incentive to pay a dividend; a large literature has emerged to explore this further implication. That literature is a rich one, and has shed significant new light on a number of key issues in corporate finance.

The Investment Effect of Dividend Tax Changes. Indirect evidence concerning the likely impact of the dividend change on the user cost of capital is provided by Auerbach and Hassett (2007), who examined the dividend response debate directly with an event study of the stock price response to news about the probability of dividend tax changes. They found that firms with higher dividend yields benefited more than other dividend-paying firms, a result which could support either the new or the traditional view, depending on whether firms believed the tax cut was temporary. Additional evidence, contradicting the traditional view, came from the fact that non-dividend–paying firms and firms likely to issue new shares received a larger boost than other firms. Under the traditional view, such firms should not have experienced a larger reduction in the cost of capital, which would be related to the firm's dividend payout rate, a variable already controlled for in the regressions.

Why was such a pattern observed? A tax cut increases the future after-tax value of dividends, which increases the value of the firm today if the firm is expected to pay dividends in the future and the tax cut is expected to last into the future. Furthermore, if a firm is expected to issue new shares in the future, the present value of any future dividends is greater, and thus so is the increase in the value of the firm today.

Auerbach and Hassett (2007) also explored whether similar effects could be observed during the 2004 presidential race. In 2004, Senator Kerry vowed that he would let the dividend tax cut expire, whereas President Bush was committed to its extension. Accordingly, one might expect that the market would correlate the probability of a Kerry victory with the probability of a more temporary dividend tax reduction. To explore whether results consistent with the event study were also observable during the election, the authors related stock market performance to presidential futures. Their results confirmed the earlier event-study results, but also shed additional light on the dividend tax mechanism. In particular, under the new view, firms with high dividend yields should have outperformed other firms when the probability of repeal increased, because they disgorge a higher percentage of their dividends in the low tax years. Under the traditional view, the lower dividend tax should reduce the cost of capital disproportionately for high-dividend firms, giving them a value bonus that should increase with the permanence of the dividend tax cuts. The presidential-futures results suggest that the bonus to paying high dividends *declined* when the dividend taxes were more likely to be permanently low (that is, when the probability of Kerry being elected declined), which is consistent with the new view.

Amromin, Harrison, and Sharpe (2005) interpreted these results differently. They argued that the evidence supports the view that dividend taxes are irrelevant, and specifically that share prices for non-dividend-paying firms and for firms likely to issue new shares outperformed shares of other firms over the entire period, not just during the event days analyzed by Auerbach and Hassett (2007). In addition, Amromin et al. argued that the U.S. stock market did not outperform foreign markets during that period.

Partly in response to Amromin, Harrison, and Sharpe (2005), Auerbach and Hassett (2006) extended their earlier work and analyzed options data around the 2004 election. When President Bush was elected, it likely conveyed a significant amount of information about the probability that dividend taxes would remain low in the future. Prior to the election, uncertainty about the outcome should have led to a high level of volatility, especially for the firms most influenced by dividend taxes. This uncertainty, the authors argued, would be visible in options prices, which are especially sensitive to volatility. Consistent with this theory, they found that President Bush's reelection, and thus the resolution of some of the uncertainty about the tax cuts' extension, caused a greater decline in volatility for the firms most affected by dividend taxes in their earlier study. They also noted in their study large standard errors for the aggregate runs reported in Amromin, Harrison, and Sharpe (2005)—so large that they would be unable to detect the full theoretical effect of the dividend tax reductions even under the most optimistic assumptions of the tax cut's impact, and even assuming that the entire effect occurred in one day.

In the only study to date that has directly estimated the impact on investment of the dividend tax changes, Auerbach, Chaney, and Hassett (2008) divided their user cost regressions according to sample splits that were based on Auerbach and Hassett's (2007) classification of firms. As mentioned previously, the authors found that the user cost effect of partial expensing was significant. When investigating dividend tax policy, the authors found that the user cost effect was biggest for immature firms (that is, firms that had never paid a dividend), which saw the largest market capitalization response to the dividend changes. This suggests that the dividend tax cut may have stimulated investment significantly through this channel. However, the authors also found that firms that were not taxable in this period had little response to the user cost. As there were many such firms, this finding suggests that the aggregate effect of the dividend tax cut on investment was smaller than would have been predicted if one ignored the fact that many firms left the recession with a healthy tax loss carry-forward position. This observation is magnified by Altshuler et al. (2008), who documented a dramatic increase in the proportion of firms that had tax losses during this period.

Thus the literature is somewhat mixed on this issue. The data seem to favor the new view of the user cost effect, which suggests that the impact of the dividend tax change should be small for most mature firms. However, there is evidence that immature firms responded quite a bit. As was the case with earlier studies of the new and old views, firm heterogeneity seems to be quite important in evaluating the investment response to the dividend tax reduction.

Recent findings by Gilchrist and Zakrajsek (2007) are consistent with the view that the dividend tax cut had a significant, if not enormous, effect. They use bond price data to calculate firm-specific interest rates and user costs (assuming the marginal source of finance is debt). They find that a one percentage point increase in the user cost of capital implies a reduction in the investment rate of fifty to seventy-five basis points, a number which rises to a 1 percent reduction in the long run. As their data span the period in question in this section, they thus establish for this period a user cost elasticity consistent with that observed in earlier episodes. Given that the user cost changed under every view of the marginal source of finance, there is reason to believe that investment did respond to policy during this time period.

Dividend Payout Changes. A large literature has emerged that addresses the impact of the dividend change on firm financial policy. That literature was anticipated by Poterba (2004), who prospectively calculated that JGTRRA would gradually increase the long-run level of dividends by 31 percent, or $111 billion, a result that is consistent with the traditional view of dividend taxation. A similar increase under the new view might also be possible if firms considered the tax reduction temporary, since firms would choose to disgorge dividends during the low-tax period.

Chetty and Saez (2005) document that after declining for over twenty years, the fraction of firms paying dividends began to increase after the 2003 tax cut. The tax cut also encouraged dividend-paying firms to increase their payments, and as a result of these changes, total regular dividend payouts increased by 20 percent within six quarters. They estimate an elasticity of regular dividend payments with respect to the marginal tax rate on dividend income of –0.5, a finding that is robust to controls for a variety of firm characteristics. Julio and Ikenberry (2004) find that the increase in dividend-paying firms began in late 2000, that is, before the passage of JGTRRA; but Chetty and Saez (2005) argue that controlling for changes in sample composition confirms their result of an increase beginning in 2003. Chetty and Saez find that the increase in dividends was largest in firms that had strong principals whose tax incentives changed (those with taxable institutional owners, for example), and in firms whose executives owned many shares. They conclude that principal-agent issues play an important role in dividend payout decisions.

This observation is consistent with other work in a large emerging finance literature. Dahlquist, Robertsson, and Rydqvist (2006) document that significant tax clienteles exist, with low-tax investors tending to weigh high-dividend–paying firms more heavily in their portfolios, and high-tax investors moving in the opposite direction. The results are quite striking, with dividend yields for tax-neutral investors a full fifty basis points higher on average than yields for taxable investors. Similarly, Hotchkiss and Lawrence (2007) find that fund managers tend to increase portfolio weights for firms that increase their dividends when their primary shareholders are not taxable, and reduce portfolio weights for firms whose shareholders are taxable.

Blouin, Raedy, and Shackelford (2004) find, for a small sample of firms, a statistically significant increase in both regular and special dividend payments following the tax cut. They argue, however, that the tax cut may not be the cause of the increase. The economy was improving at this time, and investors were increasingly evaluating firms based on dividends, not earnings. Furthermore, they find that firms in which a greater share of stock was held by individuals—the beneficiaries of the tax cut—were not more likely to increase dividends.

Brown, Liang, and Weisbenner (2004) argue that the increase in dividend payouts may have failed to increase total cash flows from firms to shareholders. They show that for many firms, share repurchases tended to decline at the same time that dividend payouts were increasing. Chetty and Saez (2006) take issue with this interpretation, arguing that the comparison of dividend-paying firms before and after the reform is prone to selection bias. The pre-reform firms are an endogenously selected group that chose to pay dividends even before the tax change. Comparing the repurchasing behavior of the two groups of firms is further problematic because there is an upward trend in share repurchases among all firms over time. Controlling for the time trend, Chetty and Saez find that firms that initiated dividends after the tax change were actually less likely to have repurchased shares in the previous year, thus reversing the finding by Brown, Liang, and Weisbenner. Chetty and Saez conclude that further research on share repurchases is necessary to determine the effect of the tax cuts on total payouts to shareholders following the dividend tax cut. Perhaps in response, Blouin, Raedy and Shackelford (2007) investigate whether share repurchases were reduced as firms increased dividends. They find that they were, and that the effect was markedly higher for firms with a higher percentage of individual (and presumably taxable) shareholders.

Desai and Dharmapala (2007) find another interesting portfolio effect of the change. A little-known feature of the dividend tax change is that it applied to dividends from firms headquartered in countries that have a tax treaty with the United States. If a U.S. portfolio investor owned shares of a firm from a tax treaty country, then the low dividend tax rate applied to the dividends received. Dividends from firms domiciled in a country without a tax treaty with the United States would be subject to the older and higher rate. Desai and Dharmapala find that this less well-known provision had a large and significant effect on portfolios; U.S. holdings of lightly taxed assets increased significantly, with an implied tax elasticity larger than unity.

There is also a rich literature exploring the response of share prices on ex-dividend days, and the dividend tax reduction provided researchers with an opportunity to shed new light on this subject. The stylized fact in this literature is that the price of a firm drops by less than a dollar when a dollar of dividend is paid. One explanation for this is that the dividend tax has generally exceeded the capital gains tax for taxable investors, so that the net after-tax cost of forgoing a dollar of dividends is less than 1.

But others have challenged this account. For example, Michaely (1991) finds no significant change in the ex-dividend-day premium to have resulted from the Tax Reform Act of 1986, which eliminated the dividend–capital gains tax rate differential. For the 2003 tax change, which again eliminated this differential, Zhang, Farrell, and Brown (2008) find an increase in the ex-dividend-day share price drop, consistent with the tax rate change. Chetty, Rosenberg, and Saez (2007) find this result as well, but they question the robustness of their finding for a longer period of time; they show that there were periods of important tax changes (such as 1986) when the ex-dividend-day premium did not respond as predicted, and periods without important tax changes when the ex-dividend-day premium changed considerably. Chetty, Rosenberg, and Saez also look at the impact of tax reforms on the excess stock returns on dividend *announcement* dates. According to the signaling theory of dividends, which provides one explanation for why dividends are paid, an increase in the tax cost of paying dividends should increase their signaling value and hence raise the market response per dollar of announced dividends. This result is confirmed for the Tax Reform Act of 1986 (Bernheim and Wantz 1995). But just as they did with respect to ex-dividend-day price movements, Chetty, Rosenberg, and Saez show that this finding is not stable over time.

To sum up: the dividend tax reduction led to both a surge in share prices for firms, which was a function of their dividend-paying and share-issuance behavior, and to an increase in dividend payouts. The underlying pattern of the former change favors the new view, suggesting that the effects of the tax cut on capital spending may be small, unless a surge in investment occurred for immature firms. The jump in dividend payouts would favor the traditional view if the dividend tax reduction were expected to be permanent. If the tax reduction were expected to be temporary, new-view firms would also be expected to accelerate their dividends. While other evidence (for example, from the portfolio responses in the holdings of foreign shares) points to the impact of the 2003 tax changes, investigation of ex-dividend-day and announcement-day price movements has revealed some limitations as to what we can learn from the 2003 experience. That the dividend responses to the 2003 tax changes depended on the tax status of principals and important shareholders suggests the relevance of agency in determining firm behavior, and has led some recent theoretical studies (e.g., Chetty and Saez 2007, Gordon and Dietz 2006) to move beyond existing views of how taxes affect dividend policy and to make use of agency theory, an approach that may tell us much about the welfare implications of dividend tax rate changes.

Conclusion

The various potential effects of the recently enacted tax changes on dividends and investment expensing have been studied to varying degrees. There is strong evidence that the dividend tax changes had an impact on payout behavior, and weaker evidence that it had an impact on investment.

The currently available data are consistent with the view that the partial expensing measure led to an increase in investment. But the partial expensing episode has been studied much less than the dividend tax reduction, and there is accordingly much still to be learned in that area.

Notes

1. See, for example, Clark (1979) and Bernanke, Bohn, and Reiss (1988).

2. See, for example, Hassett and Hubbard (2002), Kaplan and Zingales (2000), Hennessy, Levy, and Whited (2007), and Cummins, Hassett, and Oliner (2006).

3. See, for example, Barnett and Sakellaris (1998) and Abel and Eberly (1999).

4. The study is Knittel (2005).

5. Even in this case, there might be some net tax benefit associated with reductions in future capital gains taxes, but this benefit would likely have been small.

6. Chairman Thomas subsequently arranged for one of us (Hassett) to present these results to House Republicans, perhaps with the intent of garnering support for his compromise.

7. Other studies have also implied that there are significantly more new-view firms than might have been suggested by Poterba and Summers (1985). Gentry, Kemsley, and Mayer (2003) exploit the unique tax characteristics of real estate investment trusts and find that dividend taxes are capitalized into share prices, lending support to the new view. Sialm (2005) uses time-series data from 1917 to 2004 and also finds evidence of tax capitalization, as predicted by the new view.

References

Abel, Andrew B., and Janice C. Eberly. 1999. Investment and q with fixed costs: An empirical analysis. Working Paper. http://www.kellogg.northwestern.edu/faculty/eberly/htm/research/invest13.pdf.

Altshuler, Roseanne, Alan J. Auerbach, Michael Cooper, and Matthew Knittel. 2008. Understanding the recent patterns of net operating losses. NBER Working Paper No. 14405, Cambridge, MA.

Amromin, Gene, Paul Harrison, and Steven Sharpe. 2005. How did the 2003 dividend tax cut affect stock prices? Finance and Economics Discussion Paper Series No. 2005-61. Board of Governors of the Federal Reserve System, Washington, DC.

Auerbach, Alan J. 1989. Tax reform and adjustment costs: The impact on investment and market value. *International Economic Review* 30: 939–62.

———, Eric Chaney, and Kevin A. Hassett. 2008. Dividend taxes, partial expensing and business fixed investment: The case of the Bush tax cuts. Paper presented at Forum for Analysis of Corporate Taxation/American Enterprise Institute conference on effects of corporate taxation, Washington, DC.

.Auerbach, Alan J., and Kevin A. Hassett. 1991. Recent U.S. investment behavior and the tax reform act of 1986: A disaggregate view. *Carnegie-Rochester Conference Series on Public Policy* 35:185–215.

———. 2003. On the marginal source of investment funds. *Journal of Public Economics* 87 (1): 205–32.

———. 2006. Dividend taxes and firm valuation: New evidence. *American Economic Review* 96 (2): 119–23.

———. 2007. The 2003 dividend tax cuts and the value of the firm: An event study. In *Taxing corporate income in the 21st century.* ed. A. Auerbach, J. Hines, and J. Slemrod, 1–33. Cambridge: Cambridge University Press.

Barnett, Steven A., and Plutarchos Sakellaris. 1998. Non-linear response of firm investment to Q: Testing a model of convex and non-convex adjustment. *Journal of Monetary Economics* 42 (2): 261–88.

Bernanke, Benjamin, Henning Bohn, and Peter Reiss. 1988. Alternative nonnested specification tests of time-series investment models. *Journal of Econometrics* 37: 293–326.

Bernheim, B. Douglas, and Adam Wantz. 1995. A tax-based test of the dividend signaling hypothesis. *American Economic Review* 85: 532–51.

Blouin, Jennifer L., Jana Smith Raedy, and Douglas A. Shackelford. 2004. Did dividends increase immediately after the 2003 reduction in tax rates? NBER Working Paper No. 10301, Cambridge, MA.

———. 2007. Did firms substitute dividends for share repurchases after the 2003 reductions in shareholder tax rates? NBER Working Paper No. 13601, Cambridge, MA.

Brown, Jeffrey R., Nellie Liang, and Scott Weisbenner. 2004. Executive financial incentives and payout policy: Firm responses to the 2003 dividend tax cut. NBER Working Paper No. 11002, Cambridge, MA.

Carroll, Robert, Kevin A. Hassett, and James B. Mackie III. 2003. The effect of dividend tax relief on investment incentives. *National Tax Journal* 56 (3): 629–51.

Chetty, Raj, Joseph Rosenberg, and Emmanuel Saez. 2007. The effects of taxes on market responses to dividend announcements and payments: What can we learn from the 2003 dividend tax cut? In *Taxing corporate income in the 21st century*, ed. A. Auerbach, J. Hines, and J. Slemrod, 1–33. Cambridge: Cambridge University Press.

Chetty, Raj, and Emmanuel Saez. 2005. Dividend taxes and corporate behavior: Evidence from the 2003 dividend tax cut. *Quarterly Journal of Economics* 120 (3): 791–833.

———. 2006. The effects of the 2003 dividend tax cut on corporate behavior: Interpreting the evidence. *American Economic Review* 96 (2): 124–29.

———. 2007. An agency theory of dividend taxation. NBER Working Paper No. 13538, Cambridge, MA.

Clark, Peter K. 1979. Investment in the 1970s: Theory, performance, and prediction. *Brookings Papers on Economic Activity* 1: 73–113.

Cohen, Darrel, and Jason Cummins. 2006. A retrospective evaluation of the effects of temporary partial expensing. Finance and Economics Discussion Series, 2006-19. Board of Governors of the Federal Reserve System, Washington, DC.

Cohen, Darrel S., Dorthe-Pernille Hansen, and Kevin A. Hassett. 2002. The effects of temporary partial expensing on investment incentives in the United States. *National Tax Journal* 55 (3): 457–66.

Cummins, Jason G., Kevin A. Hassett, and R. Glenn Hubbard. 1994. A reconsideration of investment behavior using tax reforms as natural experiments. *Brookings Papers on Economic Activity* 2: 1–74.

Cummins, Jason G., Kevin A. Hassett, and Stephen D. Oliner. 2006. Investment behavior, observable expectations, and internal funds. *American Economic Review* 96 (3): 796–810.

Dahlquist, Magnus, Goran Robertsson, and Kristian Rydqvist. 2006. Direct evidence of dividend tax clienteles. CEPR Discussion Paper No. 6005, London.

Desai, Mihir A., and Dhammika Dharmapala. 2007. Taxes and portfolio choice: Evidence from JGTRRA's treatment of international dividends. NBER Working Paper No. 13281, Cambridge, MA.

Desai, Mihir A., and Austan D. Goolsbee. 2004. Investment, overhang, and tax policy. *Brookings Papers on Economic Activity* 2: 285–338.

Djankov, Simeon, Tim Ganser, Caralee McLiesh, Rita Ramalho, and Andrei Shleifer. 2008. The effect of corporate taxes on investment and entrepreneurship. NBER Working Paper No. 13756, Cambridge, MA.

Edge, Rochelle, and Jeremy Rudd. 2005. Temporary partial expensing in a general-equilibrium model. Finance and Economics Discussion Series, 2005-19. Board of Governors of the Federal Reserve System, Washington, DC.

Gentry, William M., Deen Kemsley, and Christopher J. Mayer. 2003. Dividend taxes and share prices: Evidence from real estate investment trusts. *Journal of Finance* 58 (1): 261–82.

Gilchrist, Simon, and Egon Zakrajsek. 2007. Investment and the cost of capital: New evidence from the corporate bond market. NBER Working Paper No. 13174, Cambridge, MA.

Goolsbee, Austan. 1998. Investment tax incentives and the price of capital goods. *Quarterly Journal of Economics* 113 (1): 121–48.

Gordon, Roger, and Martin Dietz., 2006. Dividends and taxes. NBER Working Paper No. 12292, Cambridge, MA.

Hassett, Kevin A., and R. Glenn Hubbard. 2002. Tax policy and business investment. In *Handbook of public economics*. Vol. 3, ed. Alan J. Auerbach and Martin Feldstein, 1293–1343. Amsterdam: Elsevier Science.

Hassett, Kevin A., and Kathryn Newmark. 2008. Taxation and business behavior: A review of the recent literature. In *Fundamental tax reform: Issues, choices and implications*, ed. John W. Diamond and George R. Zodrow, 191–213. Cambridge, MA: MIT Press.

Hennessy, Christopher, Amnon Levy, and Toni Whited. 2007. Testing Q theory with financing frictions. *Journal of Financial Economics* 83: 691–717.

Hotchkiss, Edith S., and Stephen Lawrence. 2007. Empirical evidence on the existence of dividend clienteles. Working Paper, Department of Finance, Boston College.

House, Christopher L., and Matthew D. Shapiro. 2006. Phased-in tax cuts and economic activity. *American Economic Review* 96 (5): 1835–49.

———. 2008. Temporary investment tax incentives: Theory with evidence from bonus depreciation. *American Economic Review* 98: 737–68.

Julio, Brandon, and David Ikenberry. 2004. Reappearing dividends. *Journal of Applied Corporate Finance* 16 (2): 89–100.

Kaplan, Steven N., and Luigi Zingales. 2000. Investment–cash flow sensitivities are not valid measures of financing constraints. *Quarterly Journal of Economics* 115 (2): 707–12.

Knittel, Matthew. 2005. Taxpayer response to partial expensing: Do investment incentives work as intended? Department of Treasury Working Paper.

Michaely, Roni. 1991. Ex-dividend day stock price behavior: The case of the 1986 tax reform act. *Journal of Finance* 46 (3): 845–60.

Poterba, James. 2004. Taxation and corporate payout policy. *American Economic Review* 94 (2): 171–75.

———, and Lawrence H. Summers. 1985. The economic effects of dividend taxation. In *Recent advances in corporate finance*, ed. Edward I. Altman and Marti G. Subrahmanyan, 227–84. Homewood, IL: R.D. Irwin.

Sialm, Clemens. 2005. Tax changes and asset pricing: Time-series evidence. NBER Working Paper No. 11756, Cambridge MA.

Zhang, Yi, Kathleen A. Farrell, and Todd A. Brown. 2008. Ex-dividend day price and volume: The case of 2003 dividend tax cut. *National Tax Journal* 61 (1): 105–27.

12

A Response to Alan J. Auerbach and Kevin A. Hassett

Matthew D. Shapiro

Several changes in tax laws beginning in 2001 potentially have significant implications for firms' decisions to invest in fixed capital. Bonus depreciation, the temporary partial expensing of certain fixed investment, had significant and differential effects on the costs of capital. The reduction in the dividend and capital gains tax rates significantly reduced the taxation of the returns to capital income. These tax changes, because of their magnitude and timing, are important vehicles for testing theories of business fixed investment and of corporate finance. Alan Auerbach and Kevin Hassett are major contributors to the literature on both these topics. Their chapter in this volume provides a very valuable analytical review of a substantial literature on the recent changes in tax law affecting business.

The tax changes discussed in their chapter are also very much on the current agenda for policymakers. Like most of the major tax changes enacted during the Bush administration, the dividend and capital gains tax rate reductions have expiration dates. Together with the income tax rate reductions originally enacted in 2001, the reduction in capital gains and dividend tax rates were important topics for debate during the 2008 election and will be important topics for policy action early in President Obama's administration. The research on these tax changes will be available to inform this debate. The chapter by Auerbach and Hassett will be a central reference for those who want to understand the behavioral response to these tax changes and the consequences of alternative proposals for dealing with their expiration.

The bonus depreciation provisions are also on the immediate policy agenda. The 2008 economic stimulus bill provided 50 percent bonus depreciation during calendar year 2008. This business incentive was targeted identically to the 50 percent bonus depreciation provision of 2003 and 2004. The bonus depreciation, although it represented roughly one-third of the approximately $150 billion economic stimulus package, was passed with much less debate and attention than the economic stimulus payments ("rebates") targeted to households. I will return to the 2008 stimulus at the end of this discussion.

Auerbach and Hassett's chapter examines both the change in dividend tax rates and the bonus depreciation provisions. I will focus my attention on the bonus depreciation provisions. The specific features of the policy have sharp implications for predicting its effect on the economy and for testing theories of business fixed investment. Under the bonus depreciation provision of the Job Creation and Worker Assistance Act of 2002 (JCWAA), 30 percent of qualified investment could be expensed in the year of the investment. The remaining 70 percent of the investment would then be depreciated using the existing modified accelerated cost recovery schedule (MACRS). To be eligible for bonus depreciation, the asset purchased had to have a tax recovery period of twenty years or less and an acquisition date after September 11, 2001. The Jobs and Growth Tax Relief Reconciliation Act of 2003 (JGTRRA) increased the bonus rate to 50 percent, with the remaining 50 percent depreciated according to MACRS. The 2003 bill fine-tuned the expiration date of the bonus depreciation. Most equipment needed to be both acquired and installed prior to January 1, 2005, to be eligible for the bonus. For certain large projects, firms could complete the installation of the project during calendar year 2005. Figure 11-1 above provides a timeline for the introduction and passage of these provisions.

The bonus depreciation policy provides a valuable experiment for testing theories of business fixed investment and for estimating parameters determining how investment responds to the cost of capital. Several features of the policy are salient for these purposes. First, the policy was explicitly temporary. Though there was some uncertainty on the part of businesses, the policy was scheduled to expire after the end of 2004 (and indeed did expire then). The onset and expiration of the investment subsidy implied by bonus depreciation provide a valuable lever for studying the effects of investment incentives. Second, the value of bonus depreciation differed by the tax lifetime of assets. The bonus had modest value for most equipment because depreciation allowances are already substantially accelerated. On the other hand, the bonus was more valuable for long-lived equipment (mainly quasi-structures). Third, there was no bonus for capital goods with tax lifetimes of more than twenty years (structures). This discontinuity at the twenty-year lifetime—between quasi-structures that benefited substantially from the bonus and structures that received no subsidy—can yield sharp estimates of the effects of the policy.

Table 12-1 shows how bonus depreciation subsidized various types of investment. Assets that constitute the majority of investment received little subsidy since they have short tax lifetimes, and they therefore received little incremental benefit from expensing relative to their tax treatment under MACRS. Five-year capital (e.g., computers, office equipment, and cars and trucks) received a subsidy of between 0.8 percent and 1.3 percent (depending on assumptions about the nominal rate of interest). Seven-year capital (e.g., machine tools, office furniture, agricultural equipment) received a subsidy of between 1.1 percent and 1.8 percent. Together, these two asset classes account for almost 8 percent of GDP, and make up a substantial majority of business fixed investment.

Assets with ten- to twenty-year tax lifetimes received bigger subsidies under bonus depreciation—ranging as high as almost 5 percent of the purchase price. For assets depreciated over many years, there is indeed a noticeable tax subsidy relative to MACRS of expensing half of investment in the first year. These assets include water transportation equipment, utilities' transmission equipment, and farm equipment and structures. Many of these long-lived assets are specialized structures or quasi-structures, e.g., cell phone towers or pipelines. The technology for installing them is closer to that of commercial structures, which get no subsidy, than to that of short-lived equipment such as computers, cars, and machine tools. The similarity of the quasi-structures that received a substantial subsidy and the commercial structures that received no subsidy makes commercial structures an effective control group for studying the effects of bonus depreciation.

Table 12-1 shows how narrowly targeted the investment subsidies are for the bonus depreciation. The heavily subsidized ten- to twenty-year assets account for just over one-half of 1 percent of GDP.

Though its varying treatment of different types of investment and its known expiration date make bonus depreciation a relatively clean experiment

TABLE 12-1

SUBSIDY FROM 50 PERCENT BONUS DEPRECIATION

Tax Life (years)	Subsidy	Share in GDP	Examples
5	0.8–1.3%	5.1%	Computers, office equipment, autos and trucks
7	1.1–1.8%	2.7%	Machine tools, office furniture, agricultural equipment
10	1.6–2.8%	0.0%	Water transportation equipment, single purpose agricultural structures
15	2.6–3.9%	0.3%	Radio towers, cable lines, pipelines, electricity generation and distribution systems, drainage systems, docks, bridges, engines and turbines.
20	3.3–4.8%	0.3%	Farm buildings, railroad structures, telephone communications, electric utilities, water utilities structures including dams, and canals
39	0%	1.7%	Commercial structures.

SOURCES: House and Shapiro 2008 and author's calculations.

for studying the effects of changes in investment tax subsidies, there are complications. First, there was some uncertainty about whether the provision would expire at the end of 2004. The uncertainty about expiration does not remove the incentive to invest in advance of the legislated expiration. If there is some probability of expiration, it is optimal to take advantage of the subsidy while it remains in effect. Other complexities are more significant. The long gestation lags of the quasi-structures receiving the bulk of the subsidy pushed much of the effect of the bonus into quarters well before the expiration. These gestation lags obscure the effects of the policy's expiration.

Section 179 expensing also clouds the expiration of bonus depreciation. The 2003 bill substantially increased the amount that small businesses could expense. Unlike bonus depreciation, this provision did not expire at the end of 2004.

Despite these complications, the 2002–2004 bonus depreciation provides powerful variation across time and type of asset for testing investment theories and estimating parameters. House and Shapiro (2008) derive the implications of the standard model of capital accumulation for temporary investment incentives targeted to long-lived capital. An important but over-looked implication of the standard model of the demand for capital is that the price of long-lived capital goods moves by exactly the amount of a temporary investment tax subsidy. This implication follows from arbitrage alone. Consider a firm contemplating acquiring a long-lived capital good. Since the service flow of a long-lived capital good comes over many years, the firm should be indifferent between installing in the period when it is subsidized and the period after the subsidy expires. Consequently, demand for invest-ment will shift into the subsidized period just to the point that equalizes the net-of-subsidy purchase price of the asset. Thus the pretax purchase price must move by the amount of the subsidy. House and Shapiro show that this argument remains a good approximation for temporary subsidies that last several years. If adjustment costs are internal, the argument applies to the shadow price of investment goods rather than the market price.

Since the change in the price (shadow price) of investment goods should move one-for-one with the subsidy, the elasticity of investment good supply (internal adjustment costs) can be inferred from quantity data alone. House and Shapiro (2008) examine bonus depreciation econometrically, taking into account the time series and cross-asset variation in the subsidy. A simple cal-culation, however, is illustrative. Long-lived investment increased by up to 40 percent relative to baseline. The subsidy was roughly 4 percent of the pur-chase price. Hence the elasticity of investment supply is approximately 10.

There was no discernible effect on the price of investment goods from the bonus depreciation. Any effect would be quite hard to detect, because the magnitude of the subsidy was small relative to the volatility of observed prices. Moreover, because internal adjustment costs are likely an important part of the price of investment, the effects of the subsidy need not appear in market prices.

Cohen and Cummins (2006) also examine the effect of bonus deprecia-tion using the differential subsidy across assets. They report that the policy had little effect. Why do they get this result? Cohen and Cummins compare investment in two groups: capital with service lives of five years or less, versus capital with service lives of seven years or more. The two groups function as a treatment group and a control group. Because of the relative abundance of five- and seven-year capital in total investment, this aggrega-tion implies that Cohen and Cummins are effectively comparing five-year capital to seven-year capital, neither of which gets much benefit from bonus depreciation. Moreover, Cohen and Cummins date the onset of the policy from its enactment. In fact, the policy was retroactive, and firms appear to have anticipated its enactment in their investment behavior.

The bonus depreciation episode has other interesting features. There was concern that its expiration would create a "pothole" for the economy when it expired. There was no such pothole. As discussed earlier, the expiration effects were smoothed out because of the gestation lags for installing the types of assets that benefited most from the bonus. Moreover, as a matter of theory, investment should not fall below steady state when the incentive expires. Instead, it simply returns to normal. Since the subsidy affects long-lived capital, the incremental investment during the period of the subsidy brings forward investment that would have occurred over a long period in the future.

A puzzling feature of bonus depreciation is that many firms that were eligible for it did not elect to use it. This finding is reported by Knittel (2006, 2007). There needs to be more research to account for this surprising finding.

Finally, it is important to bear in mind that bonus depreciation has substantial inframarginal effects. Firms that would have purchased capital absent the bonus still get the tax advantage of bonus depreciation. The effect on corporate cash flow is significant. According to tabulations by Knittel (2007), bonus depreciation deductions reduced corporate income taxes by $58.8 billion dollars in 2004, that is, by over one-quarter of corporate taxes after credits.[1] This extra cash flow during the period of the bonus is offset by reduced cash flow in later years when depreciation deductions are correspondingly reduced. While the magnitudes of the effect on the timing of cash flow are significant, it is not clear what implications they have for the behavior of corporations. Corporations with positive profits are unlikely to be liquidity-constrained, so the extra cash flow should not affect their behavior.

What implications does this research on the episode of bonus depreciation have for the 2008 stimulus? First, the bonus depreciation enacted in 2008 should have provided a substantial boost to a narrow range of investment in the second half of 2008. As emphasized in this discussion, only long-lived assets benefited much from the policy, and they are a small fraction of investment. For these assets, the subsidy was substantial. The maximum effect likely occured in the second half of 2008 because of the gestation lags for investment in these assets. The 2008 policy was not anticipated far in advance, so it likely took time to implement investment projects that took advantage of the bonus. The overall impact of the policy was probably small because the policy is so narrowly targeted. Second, there was a significant decline in corporate tax receipts in 2008, mainly offset by higher receipts over the next nineteen years. The Joint Committee on Taxation scored the bonus depreciation provisions at $43.9 billion in FY2008 (U.S. Congress 2008). Again, these changes in corporate cash flow seem unlikely to have affected behavior since they accrued only to profitable corporations. Hence, the bonus depreciation provisions of the 2008 economic stimulus provided at best only a modest boost to aggregate demand in the second half of 2008.

Moreover, the economy has been hit with enormous shocks since the stimulus was enacted in early 2008. The credit crisis caused a sharp decline in economic activity and corporate profits. It is likely that the effects of the credit crisis swamped the effects of bonus depreciation in late 2008. Hence, it will be very difficult to disentangle in the data the effects of the 2008 bonus depreciation policy from the huge disturbances hitting the economy.

Note

1. See Knittel (2007, table 4). He reports bonus depreciation deductions of $168 billion and corporate taxes after credits of $220 billion for all corporations in tax year 2004. My calculations are based on a 35 percent corporate tax rate.

References

Cohen, Darrel S., and Jason Cummins. 2006. A retrospective evaluation of the effects of temporary partial expensing. Finance and Economics Discussion Series, 2006-19. Board of Governors of the Federal Reserve System, Washington, DC.

House, Christopher L., and Matthew D. Shapiro. 2008. Temporary investment tax incentives: Theory with evidence from bonus depreciation. *American Economic Review* 98: 737–68.

Knittel, Matthew. 2006. Small business utilization of accelerated tax depreciation: Section 179 expensing and bonus depreciation. In *Proceedings of the ninety-eighth annual conference on taxation*, 273–86. Washington, DC: National Tax Association.

———. 2007. Corporate response to accelerated tax depreciation: Bonus depreciation for tax years 2002–2004. U.S. Department of Treasury, OTA Working Paper 98. May.

U.S. Congress. Joint Committee on Taxation. 2008. Estimated budget effects of the revenue provisions contained in H.R. 5140, the "Recovery Rebates and Economic Stimulus for the American People Act of 2008." JCX-6-08. January 28.

Index

About the Authors

Alan J. Auerbach is Robert D. Burch Professor of Economics and Law, director of the Burch Center for Tax Policy and Public Finance, and former chairman of the Economics Department at the University of California, Berkeley. He is also a research associate of the National Bureau of Economic Research in Cambridge, Massachusetts. Previously, he taught at Harvard University and the University of Pennsylvania and was deputy chief of staff of the Joint Committee on Taxation of the U.S. Congress. Professor Auerbach has been a consultant to several government agencies and institutions in the United States and abroad. He has served as a member of the Executive Committee and as vice president of the American Economic Association and currently is editor of that organization's *American Economic Journal: Economic Policy*. He is a fellow of the Econometric Society and of the American Academy of Arts and Sciences.

Steven J. Davis is a visiting scholar at AEI, the William H. Abbott professor of International Business and Economics at the University of Chicago Booth School of Business, and a senior consultant with CRA International. He has published on employment and wage behavior, worker mobility, job loss, the effects of labor market institutions, business dynamics, industrial organization, economic fluctuations, public policy, and other topics. His research appears in the *American Economic Review*, the *Journal of Political Economy*, the *Quarterly Journal of Economics* and other leading scholarly journals. Mr. Davis is the recipient of numerous research grants, including several from the U.S. National Science Foundation. He coedits the *American Economic Journal: Macroeconomics*, published by the American Economic Association, and he was an economic adviser to the presidential campaign of Senator John McCain.

Dhammika Dharmapala is an associate professor of economics at the University of Connecticut. His dissertation, on the political economy of congressional budgeting, received the National Tax Association's Outstanding Doctoral Dissertation Award. He has been a visiting assistant professor at the University of Michigan, a postdoctoral fellow at Harvard University, and a John M. Olin Visiting Fellow at Georgetown University Law Center. His research focuses on tax and fiscal policy, with particular emphasis on the effects of corporate and international taxation on the behavior of firms.

John W. Diamond is the Edward A. and Hermena Hancock Kelly Fellow in Tax Policy at the James A. Baker III Institute for Public Policy of Rice University and CEO of Tax Policy Advisers, LLC. He was the principal investigator on a sponsored research project for the U.S. Treasury Department's Office of Tax Analysis, which examined the economic effects of the tax reform options recommended by the President's Advisory Panel on Federal Tax Reform. Mr. Diamond served on the staff of the Joint Committee on Taxation from 2000 to 2004, where he was responsible for modeling the macroeconomic effects of major tax policy changes.

Nada Eissa is an associate professor of public policy and economics at the Georgetown Public Policy Institute and a research associate at the National Bureau of Economic Research (NBER). From 2005 to 2007, she was deputy assistant secretary of the treasury for economic policy. Previously, she was on the economics faculty at the University of California, Berkeley, a national fellow at NBER, a visiting economist at the International Monetary Fund, and a visiting scholar at AEI. Ms. Eissa's research evaluates the design of tax and transfer policy and its impact on work activity and family formation and the impact of school choice on student performance and public schools. In addition to publications in academic journals, her work has been widely cited in major newspapers and magazines. Ms. Eissa also appears as an economics commentator on *Nightly Business Report*. She is a member of the National Academy of Social Insurance and a consultant to the Urban-Brookings Tax Policy Center. Ms. Eissa has also been a consultant to the World Bank, the Congressional Budget Office, and the U.S. Treasury Department.

Daniel Feenberg is a research associate of the National Bureau of Economic Research, where he has been a member of the public economics program since its inception in 1978. He has taught at Princeton University, held staff positions at the U.S. Treasury, and been a member of the IRS Statistics of Income Division Advisory Panel since 1982. His research interests focus on behavioral effects of the personal income tax system, and he maintains the NBER TAXSIM model of the U.S. income tax system.

Seth H. Giertz is an assistant professor of economics at the University of Nebraska–Lincoln. He worked for the Congressional Budget Office's tax division in Washington, D.C. from 2001 to 2008. His work at CBO examined the effects of taxation on various parts of the economy. He has worked on tax issues relating to higher education finance, charitable giving, executive compensation, financing for Social Security and possible reforms to the U.S. markets for healthcare and health insurance. In 2005, while on leave from CBO, Mr. Giertz served as a staff economist for the President's Advisory Panel on Federal Tax Reform. From 2005 to 2008, he served on the board of the Society of Government Economists. Mr. Giertz received his PhD in economics from Syracuse University in 2001.

Kevin A. Hassett is the director of economic policy studies and a resident scholar at AEI. He is also a weekly columnist for Bloomberg. Before joining AEI, Mr. Hassett was a senior economist at the Board of Governors of the Federal Reserve System and an associate professor of economics and finance at Columbia Business School. He was an economic adviser to the George W. Bush campaign in the 2004 presidential election and was the chief economic adviser to Senator John McCain during the 2000 presidential primaries. He has also served as a policy consultant to the U.S. Department of the Treasury during both the former Bush and Clinton administrations. Mr. Hassett is a member of the Joint Committee on Taxation's Dynamic Scoring Advisory Panel. He is the author, coauthor, or editor of six books on economics and economic policy, including Toward Fundamental Tax Reform (AEI Press, 2005). He has published scholarly articles in the *American Economic Review*, *Economic Journal*, the *Quarterly Journal of Economics*, the *Review of Economics and Statistics*, the *Journal of Public Economics*, and many other professional journals. Mr. Hassett's popular writings have been published in the *Wall Street*

Journal, The Atlantic Monthly, USA Today, the *Washington Post*, and numerous other outlets. His economic commentaries are regularly aired on radio and television, including recent appearances on the *Today Show*, CBS's *Morning Show*, *The NewsHour with Jim Lehrer, Hardball, Moneyline*, and *Power Lunch*.

Laurence J. Kotlikoff is a professor of economics at Boston University, a research associate at the National Bureau of Economic Research, a fellow of the American Academy of Arts and Sciences, a fellow of the Econometric Society, and president of Economic Security Planning, Inc., a company specializing in financial planning software. From 1977 to 1983 he served on the faculties of economics of the University of California, Los Angeles, and Yale University. In 1981–82, he was a senior economist with the President's Council of Economic Advisers. Mr. Kotlikoff has been a consultant to several financial and governmental institutions and corporations. He has provided expert testimony on numerous occasions to committees of Congress, including the Senate Finance Committee, the House Ways and Means Committee, and the Joint Economic Committee. Mr. Kotlikoff is the author or coauthor of thirteen books and hundreds of professional journal articles. His most recent books are *Spend 'Til the End: The Revolutionary Guide to Raising Your Living Standard Today and When You Retire* (with Scott Burns; Simon & Schuster, 2008) and *The Healthcare Fix* (MIT Press, 2007). Mr. Kotlikoff publishes extensively in newspapers and magazines on issues of deficits, generational accounting, the tax structure, social security, Medicare, health reform, pensions, saving, insurance, financial markets, and personal finance.

Gilbert E. Metcalf is a professor of economics at Tufts University and a research associate at the National Bureau of Economic Research. He is also a research associate at the Joint Program on the Science and Policy of Global Change at the Massachusetts Institute of Technology. Mr. Metcalf has taught at Princeton University and the Kennedy School of Government at Harvard University and has been a visiting scholar at MIT. He has served as a consultant to numerous organizations including the U.S. Department of the Treasury, the U.S. Department of Energy, and Argonne National Laboratory. Mr. Metcalf currently serves as a member of the National Academy of Sciences Committee on Health, Environmental, and Other External Costs and Benefits of Energy Production and Consumption. He serves or has served on the editorial boards of *The Journal of Economic Perspectives*, *The American Economic Review*, and the *Berkeley Electronic Journals in Economic Analysis and Policy*. Mr. Metcalf's primary research area is applied public finance with particular interests in taxation, energy, and environmental economics. His current research focuses on policy evaluation and design in the area of energy and climate change. He has published papers in numerous academic journals, edited two books, and contributed chapters to several books on tax policy. Mr. Metcalf received a BA in Mathematics from Amherst College, an MS in Agricultural and Resource Economics from the University of Massachusetts Amherst, and a PhD in Economics from Harvard University.

Douglas A. Shackelford is the Meade H. Willis Distinguished Professor of Taxation at the University of North Carolina at Chapel Hill's Kenan-Flagler Business School. He created and directs the UNC Tax Center and is a research associate at the National Bureau of Economic Research and an international research fellow at the Oxford University Centre for Business Taxation. His research and teaching address taxes, accounting, and business strategy. He has published widely in accounting, economics, and finance journals.

Matthew D. Shapiro is the Lawrence R. Klein Collegiate Professor of Economics and a research professor at the University of Michigan. He is also a research associate at the National Bureau of Economic Research. Mr. Shapiro's general area of research is macroeconomics. He has carried out research on investment and capital utilization, business-cycle fluctuations, consumption and saving, financial markets, fiscal policy, monetary policy, time-series econometrics, and survey methodology. During 1993–94, Mr. Shapiro was a senior economist at the President's Council of Economic Advisers. He was also a junior staff economist at the council during 1979–80. Prior to joining the faculty of the University of Michigan in 1989, he was an assistant professor of economics at Yale and a member of the Cowles Foundation for Research in Economics. Mr. Shapiro coedited the American Economic Review from 1997 to 2000. He was chair of the Michigan economics department from 2003 to 2007. Mr. Shapiro is currently chair of the Federal Economic Statistics Advisory Committee and a member of the Academic Advisory Panel of the Federal Reserve Bank of Chicago.

Alan D. Viard is a resident scholar at AEI. Prior to joining AEI, he was a senior economist at the Federal Reserve Bank of Dallas and an assistant professor of economics at Ohio State University. He has also worked for the Treasury Department's Office of Tax Analysis, the President's Council of Economic Advisers, and the Joint Committee on Taxation. Mr. Viard has written on a wide variety of tax and budget issues.

Roberton C. Williams III is a tenured associate professor of economics at the University of Texas at Austin and a research associate at the National Bureau of Economic Research, and he has held visiting research positions at the Brookings Institution and Stanford University. His research focuses on taxation and environmental regulation and has examined a range of specific issues, including gasoline taxation and climate change policy.

Research Staff

Gerard Alexander
Visiting Scholar

Ali Alfoneh
Visiting Research Fellow

Joseph Antos
Wilson H. Taylor Scholar in Health
Care and Retirement Policy

Leon Aron
Resident Scholar

Michael Auslin
Resident Scholar

Jeffrey Azarva
Research Fellow

Claude Barfield
Resident Scholar

Michael Barone
Resident Fellow

Roger Bate
Resident Fellow

Walter Berns
Resident Scholar

Douglas J. Besharov
Joseph J. and Violet Jacobs
Scholar in Social Welfare Studies

Andrew G. Biggs
Resident Scholar

Edward Blum
Visiting Fellow

Dan Blumenthal
Resident Fellow

John R. Bolton
Senior Fellow

Karlyn Bowman
Senior Fellow

Alex Brill
Research Fellow

Richard Burkhauser
Visiting Scholar

John E. Calfee
Resident Scholar

Charles W. Calomiris
Visiting Scholar

Lynne V. Cheney
Senior Fellow

Steven J. Davis
Visiting Scholar

Mauro De Lorenzo
Resident Fellow

Christopher DeMuth
D. C. Searle Senior Fellow

Thomas Donnelly
Resident Fellow

Nicholas Eberstadt
Henry Wendt Scholar in Political
Economy

Mark Falcoff
Resident Scholar Emeritus

John C. Fortier
Research Fellow

Ted Frank
Resident Fellow; Director, AEI Legal
Center for the Public Interest

David Frum
Resident Fellow

David Gelernter
National Fellow

Newt Gingrich
Senior Fellow

Robert A. Goldwin
Resident Scholar Emeritus

Scott Gottlieb, M.D.
Resident Fellow

Kenneth P. Green
Resident Scholar

Michael S. Greve
John G. Searle Scholar

Robert W. Hahn
Senior Fellow; Executive Director,
AEI Center for Regulatory and
Market Studies

Kevin A. Hassett
Senior Fellow; Director,
Economic Policy Studies

Steven F. Hayward
F. K. Weyerhaeuser Fellow

Robert B. Helms
Resident Scholar

Frederick M. Hess
Resident Scholar; Director,
Education Policy Studies

Ayaan Hirsi Ali
Resident Fellow

R. Glenn Hubbard
Visiting Scholar

Frederick W. Kagan
Resident Scholar

Leon R. Kass, M.D.
Hertog Fellow

Herbert G. Klein
National Fellow

Marvin H. Kosters
Resident Scholar Emeritus

Irving Kristol
Senior Fellow Emeritus

Desmond Lachman
Resident Fellow

Lee Lane
Resident Fellow

Adam Lerrick
Visiting Scholar

Philip I. Levy
Resident Scholar

James R. Lilley
Senior Fellow

Lawrence B. Lindsey
Visiting Scholar

John H. Makin
Visiting Scholar

N. Gregory Mankiw
Visiting Scholar

Aparna Mathur
Research Fellow

Lawrence M. Mead
Visiting Scholar

Allan H. Meltzer
Visiting Scholar

Thomas P. Miller
Resident Fellow

Hassan Mneimneh
Visiting Fellow

Charles Murray
W. H. Brady Scholar

Roger F. Noriega
Visiting Fellow

Michael Novak
George Frederick Jewett Scholar
in Religion, Philosophy, and
Public Policy

Norman J. Ornstein
Resident Scholar

Richard Perle
Resident Fellow

Tomas J. Philipson
Visiting Scholar

Alex J. Pollock
Resident Fellow

Vincent R. Reinhart
Resident Scholar

Michael Rubin
Resident Scholar

Sally Satel, M.D.
Resident Scholar

Gary J. Schmitt
Resident Scholar; Director,
Program on Advanced
Strategic Studies

David Schoenbrod
Visiting Scholar

Nick Schulz
DeWitt Wallace Fellow; Editor-in-Chief,
The American magazine

Joel M. Schwartz
Visiting Fellow

Kent Smetters
Visiting Scholar

Christina Hoff Sommers
Resident Scholar; Director,
W. H. Brady Program

Samuel Thernstrom
Resident Fellow; Director, AEI Press

Bill Thomas
Visiting Fellow

Richard Vedder
Visiting Scholar

Alan D. Viard
Resident Scholar

Peter J. Wallison
Arthur F. Burns Fellow in
Financial Policy Studies

David A. Weisbach
Visiting Scholar

Paul Wolfowitz
Visiting Scholar

John Yoo
Visiting Scholar